Religion in the Roman Empire

Blackwell Ancient Religions

Ancient religious practice and belief are at once fascinating and alien for twenty-first century readers. There was no Bible, no creed, no fixed set of beliefs. Rather, ancient religion was characterized by extraordinary diversity in belief and ritual.

This distance means that modern readers need a guide to ancient religious experience. Written by experts, the books in this series provide accessible introductions to this central aspect of the ancient world.

Published

Religion in the Roman Empire
James B. Rives

Ancient Greek Religion
Jon D. Mikalson

Forthcoming

Religion of the Roman Republic
Christopher McDonough

Death, Burial and the Afterlife in Ancient Egypt
Steven Snape

Magic in the Ancient Greek World
Derek Collins

Religion in the Roman Empire

James B. Rives

Blackwell Publishing

BLACKWELL PUBLISHING
350 Main Street, Malden, MA 02148-5020, USA
9600 Garsington Road, Oxford OX4 2DQ, UK
550 Swanston Street, Carlton, Victoria 3053, Australia

The right of James B. Rives to be identified as the Author of this Work has been
asserted in accordance with the UK Copyright, Designs, and Patents Act 1988.

First published 2007 by Blackwell Publishing Ltd

1   2007

Library of Congress Cataloging-in-Publication Data

Rives, J. B.
    Religion in the Roman Empire / James B. Rives.
        p.   cm. – (Blackwell ancient religions)
    Includes bibliographical references and index.
    ISBN-13: 978-1-4051-0655-9 (hardcover : alk. paper)
    ISBN-10: 1-4051-0655-7 (hardcover : alk. paper)
    ISBN-13: 978-1-4051-0656-6 (pbk. : alk. paper)
    ISBN-10: 1-4051-0656-5 (pbk. : alk. paper)
        1. Rome–Religion.   2. Rome–Religious life and customs.
    3. Rome–Civilization.   I. Title.   II. Series.
    BL803.R58 2006
    200.937–dc22
                                                    2005030973

A catalogue record for this title is available from the British Library.

Set in 9.75/12.5pt Utopia
by Graphicraft Limited, Hong Kong
Printed and bound in Singapore
by Fabulous Printers Pte Ltd

The publisher's policy is to use permanent paper from mills that operate a sustainable
forestry policy, and which has been manufactured from pulp processed using acid-free
and elementary chlorine-free practices. Furthermore, the publisher ensures that the text
paper and cover board used have met acceptable environmental accreditation
standards.

For further information on
Blackwell Publishing, visit our website:
www.blackwellpublishing.com

Contents

Illustrations

Maps

Text Boxes

Acknowledgments

This book is necessarily an experiment: after thinking about this topic for some 20 years, I still find it almost impossible to pin down. My goal has thus been not to present a definitive account of religion in the Roman Empire, but merely to sketch out a possible framework for thinking about the subject further, and to illustrate the incredibly wide range of material that needs to be considered. In connection with the latter, all translations of ancient texts are my own unless noted otherwise; further information about the published translations that I have quoted can be found either in the Glossary of Authors and Texts or in the list of References.

I am deeply indebted to the Faculty of Arts at York University for awarding me a research fellowship for the academic year 2004–5, without which I could not have completed this book as quickly as I did. I also owe thanks to C. Robert Phillips III and Harold Remus for their generous support of this project at a crucial juncture. Jonathan Edmondson shared with me his expertise on Roman Spain and provided valuable feedback on a number of points; Steve Mason read a draft of the entire book and by his learning and astuteness greatly improved it; to both I offer my thanks. I am also very grateful to the anonymous readers for the press, both those who commented on the initial proposal and especially the one who gave me detailed feedback on the final draft; their input was invaluable, both in helping me clarify my ideas and in pointing out errors. None of these generous colleagues should be held responsible for the imperfections and idiosyncrasies that remain. My partner John Johnston has helped me from the start, discussing my ideas and approaches, reading chapters as I wrote them, and commenting on the final draft of the entire book; his good sense and support have been invaluable. At a later stage, he spent many hours helping me work out the details of the maps. For this, and for much else, I owe him as always more than I can say. I am also grateful to everyone at Blackwell Publishing, especially Al Bertrand, who prodded me into taking on this project, Sophie Gibson, who helped me shape the book into its final form, and Angela Cohen, who managed all the complexities of its production. I am particularly grateful to my desk-editor, Louise Spencely, for seeing the book through its copy-editing and proofing stages. It was a pleasure working with them all.

Lastly, I dedicate this book to my sister Carol and my brother John. When I was growing up, they always inspired me with their enthusiasm for learning and their range of interests; I hope that in return they will find something of interest in this book.

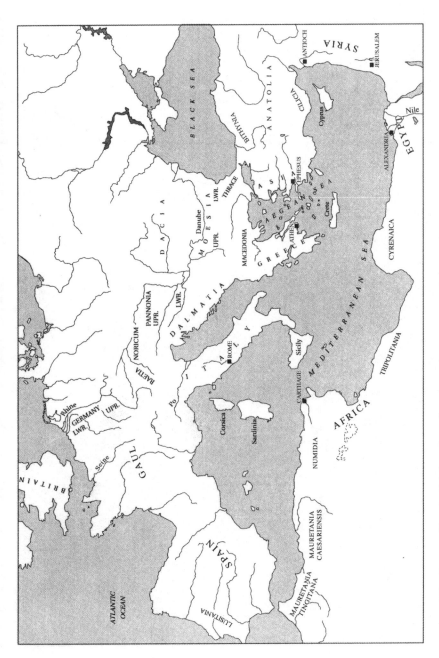

Map 1 The Roman Empire in the second century CE

Map 2 Greece and eastern Europe

Map 3 Asia Minor, Syria, and Egypt

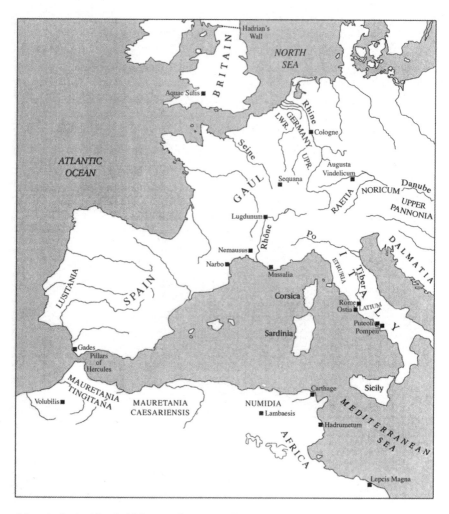

Map 4   Italy, North Africa, and western Europe

Introduction

╒╗╒╗╒╗╒╗

Trying to sketch an overview of religion in the Roman Empire is in some ways like putting together a jigsaw puzzle: although we can glimpse intriguing colors and shapes in the individual pieces, we cannot appreciate the overall pattern until we have put them all together. But this particular puzzle is more confusing than most, because a large number of pieces are certainly missing, and those that do exist can fit together not just in one way to form a single image, but in many different ways to produce a range of possible patterns. In order to make any progress at all, we must not only examine the available pieces, but also clarify what sort of pattern we expect to create. In the second part of this introduction I discuss the pieces, that is, the different sorts of evidence available to us, but it is important first to consider the overall pattern that I have in mind, the assumptions that shape my survey. The most basic of these assumptions are implicit in the title, and the best way to bring them out is to examine its elements more closely.

1 The Roman Empire

The phrase "the Roman Empire" refers simultaneously to a territory, a form of government, and a period of history. In this book the geographical and chronological senses will be key, although in the book itself the political sense will also be important. Moreover, since all three aspects of the term are interconnected, it is useful to consider them as a group.

In geographical terms, "the Roman Empire" was the territory ruled by the city of Rome, at least originally: starting in the third century CE Rome became increasingly less important as the seat of government, although it never lost its symbolic significance. In origin, Rome was simply one town among many in the western coastal plains of central Italy. In the late fifth century BCE, however, the Romans began to conquer neighboring towns and in various ways incorporate them into their own territory; by the early third century BCE, the Romans controlled the entire Italian peninsula. This expansion made Rome a major power in the Mediterranean world and eventually brought it into conflict with the other powers of the time: the North African city of Carthage and the Greek states of the eastern Mediterranean. By the middle of the second century BCE the Romans had wiped out the former and either conquered or cowed the latter; a century later the Mediterranean Sea was almost entirely surrounded by Roman territory. The Romans also extended their rule further north. The acquisition of southern Spain from Carthage in the early second century BCE made it useful to pacify the Mediterranean coast of Gaul (roughly modern France) as well, and in the mid-first century BCE Julius Caesar conquered the rest of Gaul. The emperor Augustus (31 BCE–14 CE) pushed back the boundaries of Roman rule to the Rhine and the Danube, and his successor Claudius (41–54 CE) added Britain. In the early second century CE the emperor Trajan (98–117 CE) conquered Dacia (roughly modern Romania) and briefly Mesopotamia; although the latter was soon abandoned, Roman power continued to extend to the Euphrates and in some cases beyond. By the mid-second century CE the Roman Empire was an immense territory stretching from Scotland to Sudan and from Portugal to Iraq.

As long as expansion was limited to the Italian peninsula, Roman authorities did not impose direct rule on the peoples they conquered. In most cases local political institutions continued with little change, and their subject status (or "allied" status, as the Romans often preferred to call it) consisted largely in obligations to support Rome militarily. Many communities even obtained partial or full Roman citizenship, thus in a political sense becoming Roman themselves. Roman expansion overseas resulted in some new policies: instead of military support, these more distant conquests were required to contribute financially in the form of taxes. And although the Romans continued to allow or even encourage local political institutions at the municipal level, they also appointed one of their own officials as a governor of an entire region to ensure peace and order, and to ensure the smooth collection of taxes. The region for which a governor was responsible was known as a province: Sicily and Sardinia were the first provinces, followed by two in Spain, one in North Africa, and so forth. By the end of the first century CE there were 35 or more provinces. Although the Romans ruled these provinces directly, they did so for centuries with relatively little investment of manpower: the governor, one or two chief financial officers, and a fairly small staff might constitute the entire Roman bureaucracy in a region the size of many modern

European countries. Only in areas liable to internal or external military threats was the Roman presence significantly greater, because of the legions that would be stationed there. The Romans' ability to manage their empire with so little bureaucracy was largely due to the fact that they left much of the day-to-day governance to local elites and local municipal institutions. These local elites, whose cooperation with the central power was so crucial to the smooth functioning of the empire, tended to adopt many Roman ways themselves. Roman citizenship eventually began to spread overseas as it had in Italy, and in 212 CE the emperor Caracalla issued a decree making all free inhabitants of the empire Roman citizens. Thus the empire was gradually transformed from an empire ruled by Rome into an empire of Romans, although this development did not prevent local allegiances from continuing to be strong.

The expansion of Roman power began when Rome itself was governed by a group of annually elected magistrates (consuls, praetors, and the like) who were advised and assisted by the Senate, an assembly of all magistrates and ex-magistrates that functioned in effect as the chief policy-making body. This system, conventionally known as the Republic, functioned in one form or another for almost 500 years, but in the first century BCE gradually began to collapse, in part because of the pressures created by Roman territorial expansion. A series of individual leaders began amassing more and more political and military power in their own hands, climaxing in the foundation of a monarchy by Augustus, the first "emperor" of Rome. Augustus was an extremely savvy politician, however, and realized that earlier leaders, including his adoptive father, Julius Caesar, had alienated other elite Romans by making too obvious changes in the traditional political system. He himself, therefore, made as few concrete changes as possible, and did not even create any new specific office for himself; the Senate and the traditional magistracies continued, in name at least, as before. Augustus instead made great use of propaganda and what would nowadays be called a cult of personality. The position that he established for himself and that we now call that of the "Roman emperor" was one that gradually became more fixed and defined as successor followed successor, and one whose powers gradually became more extensive and more established. The cult of personality that Augustus began also continued and even spread, but soon became attached more to the office itself than to individual emperors. This was the Roman Empire in the political sense.

It is worth keeping in mind that geographically Rome ruled an empire long before there was a Roman emperor. But "the Roman Empire" in its chronological sense refers only to the period in which the imperial system of government was in effect. Historians generally regard this as beginning in 31 BCE, when Augustus defeated his last rival and became sole ruler of the Roman world. When the Roman Empire ends is a much more problematic question. The last emperor in the western part of the Roman world was deposed in 476 CE, but in the eastern part a virtually unbroken succession of emperors continued until 1453, when Constantinople fell to the Ottoman Turks. The reigns of Diocletian (284–305 CE) and Constantine (306–37 CE), however, saw a number of substantial changes to the organization of the Roman world, not the least being Constantine's decision to favor Christianity over all other religious traditions. It is thus conventional to describe the subsequent period as "the later Roman Empire" or "late antiquity" in distinction with the earlier Roman Empire or simply "the imperial period." In terms of religion, Constantine's recognition of Christianity naturally signals a major shift, which in a brief survey it would be impossible to treat adequately. For the purposes of this book, therefore, "the Roman Empire" refers primarily to the period from Augustus to Constantine, although I draw on earlier or later material whenever that seems useful.

2 Religion and Religions

As we move to the other term in the title, we immediately enter treacherous waters. "Religion" is an extremely difficult term to pin down, as the countless attempts to do so attest. Although there is fortunately no need here to propose a rigorous and comprehensive definition, it is nevertheless important to reflect on what assumptions the term may invoke, and how useful these are in studying the Roman Empire. Most people probably use the term "religion" in everyday speech to mean something like the following: "a conception of, reverence for, and desire to please or live in harmony with some superhuman force, as expressed through specific beliefs, principles, and actions." If we understand the term in this general sense, we can readily apply it to the culture of the Roman Empire. Evidence for a conception of and a desire to please or live in harmony with some superhuman force is both abundant and varied, and implies an equally varied array of religious beliefs, principles, and actions. To this extent it is easy enough to identify the topic of this book.

It is in the attempt to come to grips with the very variety of religion in the Roman Empire that the problems begin. These problems lie not simply in the variety itself, but more importantly in the way we think about it, in the overall pattern that we use to guide our interpretation of the evidence. Variety in religion is in itself nothing unfamiliar to most people today, given the constantly increasing interconnections between different cultures and traditions. Indeed, the academic study of religion normally always includes an introductory survey of "the world's great religions," Judaism, Christianity, Islam, Hinduism, Buddhism, Taoism, Shinto, and so forth. Such surveys might seem to provide a suitable model for discussing the variety of religion in the Roman world, and there is indeed a well-established tradition of studying "the religions of the Roman Empire." But the plural noun "religions" tends to bring with it assumptions that the singular "religion" does not, and it is important to consider whether these also fit the culture of the Roman Empire.

The plural "religions" tends to imply different and distinct conceptions of a superhuman force, or at least conceptions that are expressed in different sets of beliefs, principles, and actions. For example, people might disagree whether or not Judaism, Christianity, and Islam involve fundamentally different conceptions of God, but almost everyone would agree that these three traditions involve different sets of specific beliefs, principles, and actions. Moreover, notwithstanding their very considerable internal variety, most people would probably regard each of them as in some way a system and a unity, that is, as "a religion," and their individual varieties merely as sects or denominations or the like. "A religion," therefore, usually implies a distinct and broadly coherent system of beliefs and principles. In addition, many people would probably assume that a religion would have several if not all of the following features: a set of sacred scriptures; some sort of professional or full-time authorities; specific places and times for worship; a moral code; and a number of associated practices and customs. Again, these elements are generally regarded as peculiar to each different religion, and somehow as expressions of its distinctive beliefs and principles. The study of different "religions," then, implies the study of the different sets of core beliefs and principles together with all the other features that accompany them.

Although this may be a convenient model for studying religion across the many cultures of the world, I would argue that it is fundamentally misleading for studying religion in the Roman Empire. The diversity of religion in the Roman world was not that of separate and distinct "religions," each with its own set of core beliefs and principles and its particular scriptures, clergy, shrines, rituals, and customs. Two points are of crucial importance. First, it is almost impossible, apart from a few exceptions such as Judaism and Christianity, to identify any coherent or unified systems of religion at all (and even Judaism in this period may fit the model less well than many people would suppose). Instead, the coexistence of religious conceptions and practices that would seem incompatible to people used to the idea of "a religion" was apparently taken for granted in the Roman Empire. Furthermore, some things that many people would regard as normal elements of a religion, such as a set of scriptures, a distinct clergy, or an associated moral code, are often largely or entirely lacking. In chapter 1 I discuss in more detail the nature of religion in the Roman Empire, or at least in its dominant cultural tradition.

This brings us to the second crucial point. As my brief discussion of the geographical extent of the empire should make clear, the Roman world encompassed a tremendous range of ethnic groups and cultural traditions. Most of these had their own local customs with respect to the divine, and in chapter 2 I briefly survey them. The two most important cultural traditions of the empire, those of the Greeks and the Romans, shared so many religious practices and beliefs that we can reasonably talk about a single Graeco-Roman religious tradition. There were of course differences between the two, and both Greeks and Romans were aware and even proud of them. But their common ground constituted a sort of implicit religious standard, a set of practices and beliefs that the social and cultural elite of the empire regarded as normal; it is this normative tradition of the Graeco-Roman elite that I examine in chapter 1. As I discuss in chapter 7, the elite often sneered at religious customs that differed from this normative tradition, and at times even restricted or banned them outright. Yet we must be careful not to make too much of this intermittent concern with difference. The fact remains that on a fundamental level the various religious traditions of the empire had more similarities than differences. As a result, when people from one tradition were confronted with another, they often found much that was familiar and immediately understandable, and tended to treat what was unfamiliar simply as a local peculiarity. In short, the impression we get from the sources is that people thought not so much in terms of "different religions," as we might today, but simply of varying local customs with regard to the gods.

This book is thus a study not of "the religions of the Roman Empire," but of "religion in the Roman Empire," the commonalities and differences in religious life as it existed throughout the Roman world. My goal is to provide a clear and systematic overview of what I regard as the most important phenomena and to locate them in the social and conceptual world of the people of the time. It is important to keep in mind that this world was not the same as ours; although we cannot simply set aside our own assumptions about the way the world works, we can at least be aware that in many cases they are different from those current in the Roman Empire. Most of the traditions that I discuss effectively ended centuries ago, although there have in modern times been various movements to revive some of them. In these cases, the challenge is to interpret sympathetically the fragments of evidence that have come down to us. With Judaism and Christianity the situation is of course very different: these traditions are very much alive and play an important role in our own world. For that reason, it is tempting to interpret them in terms of contemporary experience and to assign to them more importance than they perhaps had at the time. It is thus all the more necessary to stress that my approach here is to treat them strictly as historical phenomena, part of the complex pattern of religious life in the Roman Empire.

After establishing some of the fundamental features of the Graeco-Roman tradition in the first chapter and surveying the main regional traditions in the second, in the following chapters I explore religion in practice. Chapter 3, "The Presence of the Gods," looks at people's experience of the divine world and its role in their lives. In chapter 4, "Religion and Community," I discuss the role of shared cult practices and beliefs in the formation of communities at various levels, from the household to the city. Chapter 5, "Religion and Empire," explores the various mechanisms that functioned to link together the different regions of the empire. In chapter 6, "Religious Options," I examine the various possibilities for connections with the divine that went beyond those available to the average person, and in chapter 7, "Roman Religious Policy," I consider the role of the ruling authorities in defining and policing the limits of acceptable religious behavior. For the sake of simplicity, my approach is for the most part a synchronic one, with only occasional discussion of change over time. For that reason it is all the more important to stress here that religion in the Roman Empire was a dynamic rather than a static phenomenon, constantly moving and developing. Indeed, it was this dynamic quality that allowed for the effective religious integration of the empire, as I suggest in chapter 2 and discuss more fully in chapter 5. In the epilogue I return to this problem, and consider more explicitly the nature of religious change in the Roman imperial period.

3 The Sources

In studying a particular religious tradition, the usual place to begin is with its sacred scriptures. This is not a practical option for studying religion in the Roman Empire, however, because by and large sacred scriptures played only a marginal role. In the normative Graeco-Roman tradition, there were no writings at all that were regarded as "the Word of God" and that functioned as the tradition's center or foundation. This is not to say that texts were not important; on the contrary, there was a wide range of texts dealing in one way or another with religion. Some, such as hymns, served to praise the gods by describing their distinctive qualities and powers, and by recounting their great deeds and benefits. Other writings recorded ritual lore and prescriptions for different sorts of rites, festivals, and ceremonies, and still others, like the Sibylline books in Rome, collected the utterances attributed to various oracles or seers. Yet none of them in any way constituted the core of the Graeco-Roman religious tradition, but simply filled specific and limited functions within it. Moreover, the vast majority of these texts have not survived, and for many of them our knowledge is limited to references and citations in other writers.

Outside the mainstream of the normative Graeco-Roman tradition, texts were if anything even more important. A wide variety of prophetic and oracular texts was in circulation, and there was apparently an equally large number of texts purporting to record secret lore, many of which would now be classed as magical or astrological. Last but not least, there were divine revelations, texts that provided privileged insight into the nature of the cosmos and the relationship between the divine and the human: what we might regard as sacred scriptures in the usual sense of the term. In some traditions sacred scriptures of this sort played a central and foundational role, most notably in Judaism and its offshoot Christianity, but they existed even on the margins of the Greek tradition. I discuss this material more fully in chapter 6; here it is important to note not only that it lay largely on the fringes of the mainstream Graeco-Roman tradition, but that again the vast bulk of it has not survived.

If it is not possible or even desirable to base the study of religion in the Roman Empire on a set of sacred scriptures, what sort of evidence can we use? First of all, despite the general lack of sacred scriptures, there is an extensive and varied body of Greek and Latin literature that has come down through the manuscript tradition, copied and recopied over the centuries. Virtually all of this contains some information about conceptions of the divine or human interactions with it. Poetry, particularly epic and tragedy, is rich in descriptions of the gods and accounts of their deeds; history and oratory provides considerable information about the worship of various deities and the ways they were imagined to affect people's lives; philosophical texts often include speculation about the nature of the divine and its relationship with the physical and human spheres. Special mention should be made of what we may broadly describe as antiquarian texts, the works of scholars who gathered together information and speculation about a wide range of customs and traditions: for example, M. Terentius Varro, who in the mid-first century BCE wrote a 16-volume work on the religious traditions of the Romans, or M. Verrius Flaccus, who under Augustus compiled a detailed commentary on the Roman religious calendar. Although these works too are lost, some of their material was preserved by later writers. But a few important texts of this sort do survive, such as Pausanias' *Description of Greece*, a guidebook to the ancient sites of the Greek mainland that provides considerable information about local shrines and rituals.

The literary evidence is thus wide-ranging and extensive; although invaluable, however, it is also limited in some very important ways. For one thing, although we occasionally find information about religious traditions in other parts of the empire, particularly in historical works, by and large these works concern only the Graeco-Roman tradition; the chief exceptions are Jewish and Christian writings. Moreover, the Graeco-Roman texts are largely limited to the most elite aspects of that tradition: we learn a fair amount about philosophical debates on the nature of the divine, but not much about what ordinary people thought; we have numerous reports about the urban shrines and festivals patronized by the socio-economic elite, but few about the practices of the masses and people in rural areas; we have access to the myths enshrined in classic works of high literature, but not to the stories that may have circulated only orally. I do not want to suggest that there was a sharp dichotomy between the religion of the elite and that of the masses, but simply to stress that the literary evidence is by and large very one-sided and that any account of religion in the Roman Empire based solely on it is necessarily a very partial one.

There are, however, several other types of evidence that allow for a much broader approach to the topic. Of crucial importance are texts written on stone or metal or papyrus that have survived by chance and been rediscovered only in the last century and a half. The papyri that have been found in large numbers in Egypt and other parts of the Middle East include such spectacular discoveries as the Jewish sectarian writings found at Qumran on the shores of the Dead Sea and the library of gnostic texts found at Nag Hammadi in upper Egypt, as well as the collections of spells collectively known as the "Greek Magical Papyri." The chance preservation of texts like these has provided access to entire religious literatures that would have otherwise been largely or entirely unknown. The epigraphic evidence (inscriptions on stone and metal) is in some ways even more important. Unlike the papyrological material, however, its importance lies not in individual large-scale texts or collections of texts, but instead in the vast numbers of brief inscriptions that document offerings to the gods. Although individually these are normally too short and stereotyped to provide much information, collectively they give us an idea of the variety of religious life in the empire that would otherwise be completely hidden.

Because I make frequent reference to these sorts of inscriptions throughout the book, it is useful at this point to consider some representative examples in more detail (see Text Box 0.1). The first thing to note is

Text Box 0.1

1 Latin inscription from Africa (*ILS* 4461)

In accordance with a command; sacred to the Greek Ceres; Marcus Lartidius Ambugaeus, the son of Aulus, first priest, dedicated an altar with stairs on his own property.

2 Greek inscription on a marble column found
in Phrygia (*MAMA* 10.49)

To Zeus Bennios, on behalf of the Guild of the Gardeners of Mother Steunene, Neikophanes and Agathenor the son of Menis made [this] dedication.

3 Latin inscription on a small altar from a fort near
Hadrian's Wall in Britain (*RIB* 1.1778)

To Fortuna Augusta, on behalf of the well being of Lucius Aelius Caesar [adopted son of the emperor Antoninus Pius], in accordance with a vision; Titus Flavius Secundus, prefect of the First Cohort of Hamian Archers, discharged his vow willingly and deservedly.

4 Greek inscription on a plaque from Odessus, on the coast of
Lower Moesia; probably third century CE (*IGBulg* 1^2 86 bis)

To Asklepios, the savior of the world; Marcus Aurelius Caecilius Junior, son of Caecilius, [made a] thank-offering for his recovery.

5 Latin inscription on a marble plinth from
the vicinity of Rome (*ILS* 3526)

To holy Silvanus; a votive offering in accordance with a vision, on account of his freedom [from slavery]; Sextus Attius Dionysius erected a statue with its base as a gift.

6 Greek inscription on a limestone relief depicting the Thracian
Rider God from Augusta Traiana in northern Thrace; probably
third century CE (*IGBulg* 3.1597)

Good fortune! To the God Who Listens, greatest Aularchenos; Aurelius Valens, soldier of the Eleventh Claudian Legion, made [this] dedication because of his vow. With good fortune!

7 Latin inscription on a small altar from
Upper Germany (*ILS* 4553)

To Jupiter Optimus Maximus and Mars Caturix, *genius* of the place; Gaius Julius Quietus, *beneficiarius consularis*, discharged his vow joyfully, willingly, and deservedly.

8 Greek inscription on a statue base from Ephesus,
mid-second century CE (*IEph* 1266)

To Artemis of Ephesus; Cominia Iunia [discharged] her vow; after dedicating at her own expense a statue with all its associated adornment, she also dedicated an altar.

that these inscriptions accompanied offerings to the gods. Since most offerings consisted of perishable goods, they have left no trace. At times, however, people chose to commemorate them with permanent inscriptions. Sometimes these are found on simple plaques, but more often they adorn objects that themselves constituted part or even all of the actual gift: altars, either functional or symbolic (as in nos. 1, 3, and 8), more rarely statues (as in nos. 5 and 8) or reliefs (as in no. 6; see Figures 3.1 and 5.1 for examples). The information provided in these inscriptions is always highly select. The one item they always include is the name of the deity to whom the offering was dedicated, which is usually the first thing in the inscription. They normally, although not invariably, also include the name of the dedicator as well, and sometimes an indication of his or her social status or position as well (as in nos. 1, 3, 6, and 7; a *beneficiarius consularis* is a soldier assigned to a governor for specific duties). Other information is less standard. Occasionally they record the specific reason for the offering (for example, recovery from a health problem in no. 4, freedom from slavery in no. 5) or connect it with some manifestation of the deity (as with the divine command in no. 1 and the visions in nos. 3 and 5). In many cases they indicate that the offering was the result of a vow (Latin *votum*, Greek *euchê*). A vow was a prayer in which a person asked a deity for some blessing and promised a specific offering in return; if the deity granted the request, the person then "discharged the vow" by making the specified offering. These offerings are conventionally described as "votive." It is through inscriptions like these that we get some sense of the incredible range of deities worshipped in the Roman Empire and of the frequency with which people turned to them for blessings.

Another category of evidence is not textual at all, although it sometimes includes texts as a subordinate element. This is what might broadly be classed as material evidence, and takes a wide range of forms. Images of the gods constitute one obviously important type; these exist in every medium and every size, from larger-than-life marble statues and reliefs to small terracotta figurines, from costly and elaborate mosaics to crude engravings; I discuss these further in chapter 1. Coins also provide valuable evidence, particularly about which deities were honored in different cities and in different periods. Lastly, there are the remains of buildings and shrines, both the buildings themselves and their contents, which can include statues and votive dedications of all sorts. In the absence of inscriptions, it is often impossible to identify the deity for whom a shrine was built, and sometimes difficult to determine whether a given structure was in fact a shrine or not. Yet even so we can learn much from these remains about the integration of worship into a particular area and the cultural forms that worship might assume in different times and places.

It is important to draw on as many types of evidence as possible in order to build up an overview of religion in the Roman Empire, but to do so is far from easy: the interpretation of each type of evidence requires specialized knowledge and training. The student of religion in the Roman Empire must therefore rely on the work of philologists and literary critics, papyrologists and epigraphers, art historians and archaeologists, whose interests are often quite removed from his or her own. Nevertheless, it is with these pieces that he or she must work, and we must remember that any larger picture is made up from them. Although this is not a sourcebook, I have tried so far as possible to incorporate specific pieces of evidence into the discussion, at times including images or more extensive quotations in sidebars, as with the inscriptions discussed above. It is only through the integration of these individual pieces into the overall pattern that a general overview of religion in the Roman Empire is possible.

FURTHER READING

Many overviews of the Roman Empire are available: recommended are Wells 1992 (very brief) and Goodman 1997 (more detailed), although neither goes beyond the second century CE. Huskinson 2000 takes a thematic approach to some key issues; Potter (forthcoming) provides a very recent and more comprehensive survey. The bibliography on the study of religion is enormous; good starting points are J. Z. Smith 1998, short yet provocative, and the more thorough discussion of W. C. Smith 1963. Other studies of religion in the Roman Empire do things that the present book does not, and therefore serve as useful complements. Koester 1995 and Klauck 2003 are excellent examples of the "survey of religions" approach; they contain much information, systematically and intelligently presented. MacMullen 1981 and Lane Fox 1986 are impressionistic rather than systematic, but abound with interesting material and striking observations; Kraemer 1992 surveys the role of women. Useful sourcebooks, all of which extend beyond the period considered here, include Grant 1953, MacMullen and Lane 1992, and Kraemer 2004 (largely Jewish and Christian material).

CHAPTER 1

Identifying "Religion" in the Graeco-Roman World

〓〓〓〓

In the introduction, I asserted that in the normative Graeco-Roman tradition it is difficult to identify any coherent and unified system of beliefs, practices, and institutions that we could label "a religion" in the usual sense of the term. Even the concept of "a religion" does not seem to have been part of traditional Graeco-Roman culture, although it perhaps began to develop in the second century CE. Although it is impossible to know how people really view the world, especially the people of a now-lost civilization, the words they used can give us some important insights into the way they thought.

It is thus significant that in neither Greek nor Latin was there a word that really corresponds to the English term "a religion." In both languages there were words for "sacred" or "holy," such as *hieros* and *hagios* in Greek and *sacer* in Latin, and words for the proper reverence that a person should have towards the divine, such as *eusebeia* in Greek and *pietas* in Latin. Both languages also had words to describe what people did to demonstrate that reverence. Greek terms included *latreia*, literally "service," and *thrêskeia*, "worship" or "ritual." In Latin, the verb *colere* meant literally "to tend, look after" someone or something and thus, with specific reference to the gods, "to make the object of religious devotion"; the related noun *cultus* often meant "worship." We can even find terms that approximate the English word "religion" in its more general sense of "a conception of, reverence for, and desire to please some superhuman force." In Greek the phrase *nomizein theous* meant something like "to acknowledge the gods by engaging in customary practices." In Latin there was the noun *religio*, which as the source of the English word "religion" requires somewhat more detailed discussion.

The original meaning of *religio* is rather hard to pin down. Its primary connotation seems broadly to have been "an obligation with respect to the divine," often with the negative force of "prohibition or scruple," but sometimes with the positive sense of "prescribed ritual or customary practice"; the historian Livy, for example, relates how two young men violated the secret rites of Demeter at Eleusis, unaware of the *religio* that prohibited participation by non-initiates (*History of Rome* 31.14.7). Writers of the second century CE and later come increasingly to use *religio* to mean the worship of a particular deity, stressing belief and commitment to a way of life. So for example Lucius, the hero of Apuleius' novel *The Golden Ass*, having become a devotee of the goddess Isis in Greece, joins her worship in Rome as a stranger to her local temple but a native of her *religio* (*The Golden Ass* 11.26). Christian writers took this tendency further, and used the word to contrast their own beliefs and practices with those of non-Christians; so for example Tertullian, writing around 200 CE, can describe Christianity as "the true *religio* of the true god" (*Apology* 24.2). For Tertullian, then, and the Christian writers who came after him, the word *religio* had come to mean something similar to what we mean by "a religion," that is, "a distinct and broadly coherent system of beliefs and practices"; this shift in meaning reflects the significant changes that came with the development of Christianity, as I argue in the epilogue. But before that time, the linguistic evidence suggests that most people would have found the modern concept of "a religion" rather alien.

But if most people of Graeco-Roman culture did not think about their religious practices and beliefs in terms of "a religion," how did they think about them? That is the question I attempt to answer in this chapter. In the first section I examine Graeco-Roman conceptions of the divine, a category that was much more fluid and less sharply defined than it has usually been in cultures dominated by monotheistic religious traditions. In the second section I argue that in Graeco-Roman culture there were several different approaches to the divine, approaches that were not simply alternative or complementary to one another, but existed in a sense on different levels. I discuss in some detail the four most important of these: cult, myth, art, and philosophy. Lastly, in the third section I treat three particularly problematic issues: authority, belief, and morality. It is important to keep in mind that what I am sketching here are the chief characteristics of the mainstream Graeco-Roman tradition, the features of religious practice and belief that most members of the social and cultural elite would have regarded as normal. There were numerous traditions within the Roman Empire that did not share all these characteristics, as we will see in chapter 2; nor did even all members of the Graeco-Roman elite agree on all points, for reasons that will become clear. Far from being a definitive account of the nature of Graeco-Roman religion, this is simply a point of departure for further investigation.

1 The Nature of the Divine

When most people think about the way that the ancient Greeks and Romans envisioned the divine world, the first thing likely to occur to them is the pantheon of great deities whose roles and personalities are familiar from myth and art: the Greek Zeus and his Roman counterpart Jupiter as king of the gods and master of the sky and weather, Hera/Juno as queen, Athena/Minerva as the goddess of wisdom, Aphrodite/Venus as the goddess of sexual desire, and so forth. These deities were indeed important, and a quick glance at any collection of inscriptions is enough to show how frequently they were invoked in worship. But the situation was much more complex than the standard lists of gods would suggest.

To begin with, the number of Greek and Roman gods greatly exceeds the 12 or 15 major deities familiar from art and myth. Although many of these lesser deities had limited appeal, some were extremely popular. The rural god Silvanus, for example, appears in over 1,100 inscriptions from the western empire (for one example, see Text Box 0.1, no. 5). Moreover, there were often multiple versions, so to speak, of a single deity. Although a poet like Vergil could write in the *Aeneid* about the goddess Juno as one individual deity, he would have been well aware that several different Junos were worshipped in Rome and the neighboring regions of Italy: Juno Lucina, the goddess of childbirth, was quite different from the martial Juno Sospita, with her goatskin cloak and her spear and shield. The purpose of the supplementary names "Lucina" and "Sospita" was to specify which version of Juno a worshipper had in mind. Supplementary names of this sort, usually called "epithets," are very common in dedications, as with the Greek Ceres (see Text Box 0.1, no. 1), Fortuna Augusta (no. 3), Jupiter Optimus Maximus (no. 7), and Artemis of Ephesus (no. 8). In some cases, as with Zeus Bennios (no. 2) and Mars Caturix (no. 7), the epithets indicate that a native deity has been identified with a Greek or Roman one, a phenomenon that I discuss more fully in chapter 5.

We must also keep in mind that there were various types of deities, not all of which had the distinct personalities that characterize the gods of myth. We can get some idea of this variety from the classification of gods that Artemidorus of Ephesus included in his handbook on the interpretation of dreams (see Text Box 1.1). The major deities whom we expect to find are indeed here, but interspersed among them are others that are more surprising. For one thing, there are numerous deities who are simply aspects of the physical world. The idea that different deities had different spheres of power is a familiar one, and it is customary to say, for example, that Poseidon was "the god of the sea." But Artemidorus includes in his list not

Text Box 1.1

Artemidorus, *The Interpretation of Dreams* 2.34 (selections)

Of the gods, some are perceptible by the intellect, others by the senses; there are more of the former, few of the latter. The following discussion will make this clearer. Of the gods, we say that some belong to Olympus (or similarly to the aether), some to the heavens, some to the earth, some to the sea and the rivers, and some to the underworld. Zeus, Hera, Aphrodite Ourania [of the Heavens], Artemis, Apollo, Aetherial Fire, and Athena are reasonably said to belong to the aether. Helios [Sun], Selene [Moon], the Stars, the Clouds, the Winds, . . . and Iris [Rainbow] belong to the heavens; all these are perceptible by the senses. Of the gods who belong to the earth, those perceptible by the senses are Hekate, Pan, Ephialtes, and Asklepios (who at the same time is also said to be perceptible by the intellect); those perceptible by the intellect are the Dioskouroi, Herakles, Dionysos, Hermes, Nemesis, Aphrodite Pandemos [of the People], Tyche [Fortune], Peitho [Persuasion], the Graces, the Hours, the Nymphs, and Hestia. The sea gods perceptible by the intellect are Poseidon, Amphitrite, Nereus, the Nereids, Leukothea, and Phorkys; those perceptible by the senses are Thalassa [the Sea] itself, the Waves, the Seashores, the Rivers, the Marshes, the Nymphs, and Acheloös [the longest river in Greece]. The underworld gods are Pluto, Persephone, Demeter, Kore, Iakkhos, Sarapis, Isis, Anubis, Harpokrates, underworld Hekate, the Furies, the *daimones* who attend them, and Phobos [Fear] and Deimos [Panic], whom some call the sons of Ares.

only Poseidon but also "the Sea itself": Poseidon falls into the category of gods perceptible by the intellect, and the Sea into that of gods perceptible by the senses. In other words, he treats the Sea, the actual sea that people can see and feel and taste, as just as much a god as Poseidon, "the god of the sea." And not only the Sea, but the Sun, the Moon, the Winds, the Rivers, and so on.

That aspects of the physical world could count as gods was not something dreamt up by Artemidorus; on the contrary, it can be traced back to the earliest stages of the Graeco-Roman tradition. Nor was it simply a figure of speech, a metaphor that could be literalized in myths about the chariot of the Sun or river gods who seduced young maidens. Votive dedications to the Sun and the Moon, to Heaven and Earth, and to Storms and Winds indicate that people actually invoked these deities in prayer and believed that they responded. Bodies of water were especially popular. The poet Horace wrote a short lyric describing his gratitude to a spring on his country estate, promising to sacrifice to it a young goat (*Odes* 3.13). Although for Horace the impulse to honor the spring was perhaps largely a pretext for the exploration of literary concerns, the same impulse could strike non-poets, such as man named Lucius Postumius Satullus who dedicated an altar to a "divine spring" in a town in southern Spain (*ILS* 3885). Rivers were also popular objects of devotion, and we must assume that most people would have found nothing surprising in a dedication like this one on a small altar from Aquincum (modern Budapest): "to the downstream-flowing Danube; Tiberius Aterius Callinicus discharged his vow" (*ILS* 3911).

If Artemidorus' list shows that the category "god" could shade off into aspects of the physical world, it also shows that it could encompass abstractions. We notice, for example, that he includes among the earthly gods not only Herakles, Dionysos, and Hermes, but also Fortune and Persuasion, and similarly includes Fear and Panic among the underworld gods. Again, this tendency to regard abstract concepts as divinities was by no means peculiar to Artemidorus. The worship of such abstractions goes back to an early period in Greek history, and was by the imperial period very well established. In the second century CE, the travel writer Pausanias reported that the Athenians had public altars dedicated to Eleos (Mercy), Aidos (Respectfulness), Pheme (Rumor), and Horme (Impulse) (*Description of Greece* 1.17.1). Similarly, in the city of Rome, there were public temples to Spes (Hope), Pietas (Piety), Concordia (Concord), Victoria (Victory), and Fides (Good Faith), among others. Although it might seem that cults like these were sheer propaganda, attempts to promote virtues conducive to the public good, all these deities and others like them were also the recipients of votive dedications.

One of the most popular abstractions was Fortune or Chance (Tyche in Greek, Fortuna in Latin). The elder Pliny, writing in the 70s CE, complained that "in the entire world, and in all places and at all times, Fortuna alone is invoked and named by the voices of all. . . . We are so subservient to chance, that chance itself takes the place of god, whereby god is proved unreliable" (*Natural History* 2.22). The numerous temples, statues, and dedications to this goddess lend support to Pliny's observation. In art she was often depicted holding a rudder, to show that she guided people's lives, or holding a cornucopia, to indicate that wealth and prosperity were hers to give. The depiction of Fortuna in art is a reminder that deified abstractions were not always merely abstract; some people actually had visions of Fortuna, such as the military officer Titus Flavius Secundus who dedicated an altar "in accordance with a vision" (see Text Box 0.1, no. 3). In the eastern part of the empire, Tyche often functioned as the divine embodiment or the guardian spirit of particular cities, and was often depicted wearing a headdress in the shape of towers and ramparts.

The words that we usually translate as "god" or "goddess" were the Greek *theos/thea* and the Latin *deus/dea*. These words normally occur in the plural (*theoi* and *di*, respectively), as we would expect in a religious tradition that was polytheistic (from Greek *poly-*, "many"). They also often appear in the singular, not only in reference to a particular god or goddess, but more surprisingly to denote "the divine" in a very general sense; it was not uncommon for an ancient writer to use both "the gods" and "god" in the same passage as almost interchangeable terms. In addition to *theos* and *deus*, there were other words that denoted entities with superhuman power: *daimôn* and *hêrôs* in Greek, *numen* and *genius* in Latin. Each of these requires further discussion.

The word *daimôn* was originally almost a synonym for *theos*, although it tended to be used of less clearly defined superhuman forces. Under the influence of the philosopher Plato it came to be used in particular of entities that were intermediate between the human and divine spheres. The second-century writer Apuleius, in a lecture on the subject, defines *daimones* as beings of an animate nature and rational mind (like both gods and humans), emotional temperament (like humans but not gods), eternal existence (like gods but not humans), and aerial body (unique to them); their main function is to act as intermediaries between gods and mortals. Despite his pat definition, however, Apuleius clearly struggles to accommodate all the various ways in which the word was used in his day: he thus allows that guardian spirits, the souls of the dead, and even the souls of the living can also be considered *daimones* (*On the God of Socrates* 13–16). Christians, who reserved the word *theos* or *deus* for what they regarded as the one true God, used the word *daimôn* (or *daemon* in its Latinized form) for the traditional Graeco-Roman deities, whom they viewed as malevolent spirits; it was thus that the English word "demon" came to acquire its negative connotations. The word *hêrôs*, in contrast, had a more or less clearly defined meaning. Although poets applied it to the great figures of the past whose deeds they celebrated (hence the meaning of the English word "hero"), in worship it denoted a human being who continued to exert power after death and so had to be propitiated through prayer and offerings. Traditional heroes included the legendary founders of cities as well as figures from myth; the Greek satirist Lucian, for example, writing in the second half of the second century CE, implies that people still made offerings to Hektor and Protesilaos, two heroes of the Trojan War (*The Assembly of the Gods* 12). In the historical period, it became common to treat notable benefactors as heroes after their death; the people of Tarsus in Cilicia, for example, honored their fellow-citizen Athenadoros as a hero because he had won tax relief for them from the emperor Augustus (Lucian, *Long-Lived Men* 21). Starting in the fourth century BCE, there was a growing tendency to refer even to the ordinary dead as "heroes."

The Latin word *numen* meant "divine power" or "divine will." Some writers used it almost as a synonym for *deus*, especially when referring to a deity whose existence was perceived but whose specific identity remained uncertain. In the imperial period, the word was also applied to the godlike aspect of the Roman emperor; in some places, as we will see in chapter 5, people made regular offerings to the emperor's *numen*. *Genius* originally designated the divine alter-ego or guardian spirit of an individual person (usually male: the *genius* of a woman was often distinguished as a *iuno*). Over time, people began to use the word more widely, and attribute a *genius* to virtually any locality or institution. We thus find dedications to the *genii* of particular buildings (markets, granaries, theaters) and places (mountains, woods); most common of all is the simple *genius loci*, the "guardian spirit of the place" (see for example Text Box 0.1, no. 7). There are also dedications to the *genii* of a wide range of corporations: military units (legions, detachments), civic and administrative bodies (cities, provinces), and various clubs and associations. These can sometimes be difficult for modern observers to take seriously: when we read the dedication erected by a certain Claudius Myron in Lugdunum (modern Lyon) to "the *genius* of the Most Splendid Corporation of Carpenters and Plasterers" (*ILS* 7263), we may wonder whether Myron genuinely believed that his guild had a specific divinity attached to it. But it is perhaps more helpful to think that concepts like that of the *genius* allowed people to feel that every aspect of their day-to-day lives was in some way represented on the divine plane.

With terms like *daimôn* and *hêrôs*, *numen* and *genius*, we see how the notion of superhuman force in the Graeco-Roman tradition could sometimes come very close to the human sphere. This is also apparent in the widespread tendency to honor the dead. As we will see in chapter 4, it was customary to make offerings to the dead, especially the dead of one's own family, who were widely if vaguely thought to have power to help or harm the living; the Greek worship of heroes is in some respects a special expression of this general tendency. Although the Romans apparently lacked a concept analogous to that of the Greek *hêrôs*, they seem to have gone further than the Greeks in emphasizing the quasi-divinity of the dead in general. The Romans actually referred to the dead as gods, the *di manes*; the etymology of the name *manes* remains uncertain, although it may have been a euphemistic title derived from the archaic adjective *manus*, meaning "good." Tombstones in Latin-speaking parts of the empire, thousands of which survive, were inscribed with the formula *dis manibus sacrum* (frequently abbreviated "D. M. S."), "sacred to the *di manes*," using the same sort of phrase employed in dedications to the gods. This formula suggests that the tomb was an offering dedicated to the spirits of the dead, and indeed Roman law classed tombs as *res religiosae*, "religious property," a category analogous to that of *res sacrae*, "sacred property," which included offerings to the gods.

But it was not only the dead who were thought to wield superhuman power; in certain circumstances the living could as well. Starting in the third century BCE, with a few earlier foreshadowings, some Greek rulers began to be honored in the same ways as the traditional gods, with sacrifices, shrines, priests, images, and hymns. These practices are conventionally called "ruler cult" or, with specific reference to the Roman emperor, "imperial cult"; I discuss this topic in more detail in chapter 5, but mention it here only as another example of the fluidity in the Graeco-Roman concept of the divine. Early Christian writers, who drew a sharp distinction between God and the rest of the world, mocked these practices as the ultimate absurdity: who could genuinely believe a man to be God? Until recently, most modern scholars took more or less the same view, and interpreted ruler cult simply as a debased form of political flattery. In the past 25 years or so, however, there has been a growing movement to take ruler cult seriously and interpret it as a way for people to incorporate the figure of the ruler into their religious world-view. Moreover, some scholars now stress that although rulers were treated like gods, there was usually something to distinguish them from the traditional gods. A Roman emperor who was officially deified after his death, for example, was described not as *deus* but as *divus*; although the two words are closely related and were originally synonyms, in the imperial period they were sharply distinguished. This is simply one indication that while Roman emperors and other rulers were often regarded as gods, they were gods of a particular sort.

Lastly, we should note that in the philosophical tradition it had long been customary to apply the language of divinity to what we would describe as fundamental physical or metaphysical principles. In the Platonic tradition, for example, especially in the dogmatic form that flourished in the second century CE and is conventionally known as "Middle Platonism," the divine was understood to be the absolute and transcendent first principle. Here, for example, is how Alcinous, the author of a second-century textbook on Platonism, describes this transcendent deity: "The primary god, then, is eternal, ineffable, 'self-perfect' (that is, deficient in no respect), 'ever-perfect' (that is, always perfect), and 'all-perfect' (that is, perfect in all respects); divinity, essentiality, truth, commensurability, beauty, good" (*Handbook of Platonism* 10.3, trans. J. Dillon). In contrast, those who followed the Stoic school of philosophy had what we might call a pantheistic understanding of the divine, seeing the divine as in a sense the "soul" of the universe. For example, the poet Manilius, who composed a heavily

Stoic-influenced verse treatise on astronomy and astrology, introduces his discussion of the zodiac in the following way: "I shall sing of god, silent-minded monarch of nature, who, permeating sky and land and sea, controls with uniform compact the mighty structure; how the entire universe is alive in the mutual concord of its elements and is driven by the pulse of reason, since a single spirit dwells in all its parts and, speeding through all things, nourishes the world and shapes it like a living creature" (*Astronomica* 2.60–6, trans. G. P. Goold).

The point of this brief survey is to give some sense of the varied conceptions of superhuman force that were current in the Graeco-Roman tradition. For the sake of convenience, I use the general term "the divine" to refer very broadly to the entire range of gods, *daimones*, heroes, *genii*, and so forth, although it is important to keep in mind that this term glosses over a great deal of variety. Yet we must also be careful not to be overwhelmed by this variety and conclude that the Graeco-Roman conception of the divine was simply chaotic. For one thing, I have deliberately brought together here as wide a range of material as possible; it is unlikely that any single individual would have given equal weight to all these ideas or even have associated them all with one another. On the contrary, it seems clear that people invoked the idea of the divine in very different contexts for very different purposes. For example, some scholars see votive dedications as evidence that people truly regarded a particular being as divine, since they sought and acknowledged its aid in day-to-day life; because virtually no votive dedications to emperors have been found, these scholars conclude that people did not really consider the emperors divine. But it would be better to conclude that emperors were simply not divinities of the sort invoked in vows. After all, philosophically-minded writers speak with great reverence of the Platonic One or the Stoic World-Soul, but no one concludes from the lack of dedications to these entities that their devotion was not real; it is simply that the Platonic One was not the sort of divinity to whom one made a votive dedication. To a certain extent, this conceptual flexibility reflects the variety of approaches to the divine that were current in the Graeco-Roman tradition, an issue that I discuss in the next section.

2 Approaches to the Divine

In the first book of his survey of Roman religious traditions, the scholar Varro discussed an analysis of the different ways people might think about the gods; this analysis, first developed by Greek philosophers, is conventionally known as the "tripartite theology." According to this analysis, there were three different ways to think about the gods (in Greek, *theo-logiai*), propagated by three different types of people: "the mythical, which poets in particular employ; the physical, which philosophers employ; and the civil, which peoples employ." The first of these is what we would call Greek and Roman myth, and the second is philosophical speculation about the nature of the divine; Varro describes it as "physical," because *physis* is the Greek word for "nature." This second category includes all the sorts of questions that philosophers discuss: "who the gods are, where, what kind, and of what nature; whether the gods have existed only since a certain time or always; whether they are made of fire, as Heraclitus thinks, or numbers, as Pythagoras thinks, or atoms, as Epicurus says." The third theology is "what citizens, especially priests, ought to know and put into practice; it concerns what gods should be worshipped publicly and what rites and sacrifices it is proper to offer to each." Varro concluded that "the first theology is especially suited to the theater, the second to the world, the third to the city" (quoted by Augustine, *The City of God* 6.5).

There are several interesting things about this passage. First, Varro suggests that each of the three theologies he describes has its own sphere, within which it is appropriate, but outside of which it can be problematic. Varro himself seems to have favored the philosophical approach: he harshly criticizes the myths of the poets as containing much that is "contrary to the dignity and nature of the immortal gods," and elsewhere points out that civic institutions are likewise not in keeping with nature (cited by Augustine, *The City of God* 4.31). Yet even so he considers myth as suitable for literature and popular entertainment, upholds the traditional religious institutions of Rome, and says that the speculations of philosophers are better within the walls of schools than in public squares. In other words, Varro was evidently not worried about consistency: although myths and civic religious institutions might be "wrong" from a philosophical point of view, they were not to be rejected for that reason, but remained appropriate enough within their own spheres.

As I have noted, Varro took this scheme of the tripartite theology from earlier Greek philosophers, and it was in fact something of a commonplace. References to it crop up in some half dozen writers, and its indirect influence can be traced even more widely. Some thinkers even felt free to adapt it. The Greek orator and popular philosopher Dio Chrysostom, addressing a large crowd at the Olympic games in the late first century CE, took advantage of his proximity to the splendid statue of Zeus at Olympia, one of the seven wonders of the ancient world, to suggest that to the theologies of the poets, philosophers, and statesmen should be added that of artists, who fashion likenesses of the gods in a whole array of media. As Dio points out, although these artists follow the lead of the poets in many respects, they also add their own touches, by interpreting the attributes of the gods visually in a way that speaks directly even to the uneducated masses (Dio Chrysostom, *Orations* 12.39–47). Dio's lack of hesitation in introducing the tripartite theology into a popular lecture or in modifying it to add a fourth suggests that this analysis was perhaps familiar and certainly understandable to a fairly broad audience.

For the purposes of understanding religion in the Roman Empire, it is important to note not only that the notion of three theologies was apparently quite widespread, but that Varro's assumptions about their separate spheres were equally commonplace. That is to say, in almost direct opposition to modern assumptions about "a religion" as a broadly unified and coherent system, most people in the Graeco-Roman world, if they bothered to reflect on such things at all, would have regarded it as perfectly normal for there to be three or four separate and even inconsistent theologies, or approaches to the divine. In this section I sketch out the most important of these approaches, the chief modes of thought or discourses about the gods, that existed in the Graeco-Roman tradition. I take as my framework Dio's four-fold expansion of the more usual three-fold scheme, with one significant modification. Rather than discussing the civic theology, the institutions of public cult, I talk more basically about cult practices in general. These practices were for the most part common to all forms of worship, whether carried out individually or in groups, and it seems best to consider them in themselves, before exploring their use in particular contexts.

2.1 Cult

In contemporary English, the word "cult" generally has negative overtones, calling to mind a religious group characterized by exclusivity, secrecy, and obsessiveness. The Latin word *cultus*, however, had none of these connotations, but as we have seen meant simply "worship." In discussions of Graeco-Roman religion, therefore, "cult" normally refers to worship, and specifically the various practices and rituals employed in worship. Although there was an enormous range of such practices in the Roman Empire, for the sake of an overall analysis we can divide them into three or four main types: requests for benefits from the gods, that is, prayers; sacrifices and other offerings to the gods; divination, or the interpretation of messages from the gods; and lastly, rituals such as purifications and initiations that in various ways transformed a person's situation with respect to the divine. In what follows I discuss each of these briefly.

Because prayers were oral and often improvised to fit the specific occasion, our best sources are literary, either narrative works that depict a character praying or lyric poems written in the form of prayers. Although there were some traditional prayers with set wording, especially in public cults, the records that contained these are almost entirely lost and so contribute relatively little to our knowledge. The evidence that we have indicates that most prayers followed the same basic format. They began with an invocation that detailed the god's name, functions, and qualities. Then came a central section listing reasons why the deity ought to grant the request: for example, evidence of the petitioner's piety and devotion, appeals to the god's beneficence, or reminders of the god's past blessings. In the specific type of prayer known as the vow, discussed in the introduction to this book, this middle section contained the promise of an offering. The last part was the petition, which could range from a specific request (for example, "please help my child recover from illness") to a very general appeal for goodwill (for example, "please look upon us with favor"). In some cases, the focus was not so much on the final request as on the first two parts, which were elaborated to include detailed descriptions of the god's distinctive characteristics and sometimes quite lengthy accounts of the god's past deeds. Such compositions are generally known as hymns, from the Greek word *hymnos*, and were intended more to praise than to petition the deity in question.

In this respect, hymns belong also to the second category of cult practices, that of offerings or gifts to the gods. In a vow, the offering was part of a *quid pro quo* arrangement: the worshipper promised a gift to the god if the god granted his or her petition. It is tempting to think of this as a mere exchange, lacking in the sense of awe and devotion appropriate to a religious act. But we must keep in mind two points. First, since the formal exchange of benefits was something that characterized a wide range of social relationships in the Graeco-Roman world, it is not surprising that it also helped structure relationships between mortals and immortals. Secondly, the external form of a religious act is not in itself evidence for the worshipper's state of mind; we may reasonably expect that people who made vows did so with varying levels of emotional involvement and intellectual commitment. We must also note that offerings to the gods were by no means limited to the fulfillment of vows. In many cults sacrifices were organized on a regular schedule; people also made offerings in thanksgiving for particular benefits, even when these were not the subject of a previous vow.

Offerings could take a wide range of forms, from simple and inexpensive gifts of flowers, cakes, or incense to elaborate statues, reliefs, and altars (for examples, see Text Box 0.1 and Figures 3.1 and 5.1). Liquids constituted an entire sub-group called libations: wine was the most common, but in particular contexts worshippers might also use milk, oil, honey, or even water. But the type of offering most closely associated with Graeco-Roman religion is blood sacrifice, the ritual slaughter of an animal (specifically a domesticated animal, most often a sheep, pig, or cow). This was indeed very common, and was in some ways the most culturally significant: in art, for example, representations of animal sacrifice frequently served as symbols of piety. Emperors in particular were often shown in the act of sacrificing, as in this relief from a now-lost arch in Rome honoring the emperor Marcus Aurelius (161–80 CE) (see Figure 1.1). It depicts a preliminary rite in the performance of a sacrifice, which was an elaborate ritual with several distinct stages. It began with a procession in which the participants led the victim (the technical term for the animal to be sacrificed) to the altar; as we see here, the altar was normally outside, in front of the temple, and virtually never inside the building itself. There they symbolically purified the space around them and called for ritual silence; the Romans, as shown here, had a musician play the pipes in order to drown out unwanted noises. The officiant then made a preliminary offering of grain (in the Greek tradition) or incense (in the Roman); here, Marcus Aurelius is depicted throwing grains of incense from a box held by an attendant onto a small portable brazier set up near the main altar. The actual killing came next, typically performed by a professional (shown here on the right, stripped to the waist and carrying an ax). The latter also carved up the carcass, and the officiant burned or otherwise offered a portion to the deity. Lastly, in most cases the remaining meat was cooked on the spot, and all the participants joined together in a feast. Many variations on this general scheme were possible, and there were some notable differences between the Greek and the Roman traditions; in the Roman tradition, for example, the officiant always covered his head with a fold of his toga, as we see here, whereas in the Greek tradition he was bareheaded. The essential elements, however, were fairly constant.

Prayers and offerings were the two main components of actual worship, the two ways in which people communicated with the gods. But it was also widely accepted that the gods for their part could communicate with people: the interpretation of these divine communications is known as divination. An extremely wide range of divinatory techniques existed in the Graeco-Roman tradition; among the most common were oracles, the interpretation of dreams, the observation of birds, the "reading" of the entrails of a sacrificial victim, and the interpretation of omens (chance or unusual events regarded as significant). Since divination has been rigorously excluded from the dominant religious traditions of Europe and the Middle East ever since the conversion of Constantine, many people are now apt to think of it as mere fortune-telling, a way of looking into the future. This was of course important, but there was generally more to it

Figure 1.1 Relief panel from a triumphal arch of Marcus Aurelius. Rome, Musei Capitolini (Palazzo dei Conservatori), inv. no. 807. Alinari Archives, Florence

than that. Divination was thought to give people insight into the will and the mood of the gods, and to indicate in particular whether they supported or opposed a given initiative. Although philosophers argued whether the things revealed through divination were irrevocably destined or were simply possible, most people in practice operated on the latter assumption and responded to divine messages by either changing their plans or attempting to win divine favor. Divination was thus an essential complement to prayer and sacrifice, completing the circle of communication between gods and mortals.

These three types of cult practice were common to almost every religious tradition within the Roman Empire. There were in addition many less widespread types of rituals and customs, which it would not be practical to survey. But it is important to mention at least two others: purifications and initiations. The former were rituals intended to remove pollution and render people pure. A sort of general purification was often a necessary preliminary to other religious acts, such as entering a sanctuary or performing a sacrifice; other purificatory rituals were required to cleanse people from specific sources of pollution, such as childbirth or contact with a corpse. The role of purification varied significantly in the Greek and Roman traditions. Initiations were secret rituals that put the participant into a privileged relationship with the deity, often through the revelation of some arcane doctrine. Although they were a defining feature of what are conventionally called "mystery cults," they were by no means limited to private associations of a few devotees. Some of the most famous initiations, such as those in the cult of Demeter at Eleusis near Athens, were publicly organized and held on a large scale.

We may note in conclusion two final points. Firstly, cult activities were not restricted to certain set times, such as weekly religious services, or defined places, like churches or mosques. Although civic communities and other groups typically observed a calendar of set festivals, people regularly incorporated prayers, offerings, and divination into a wide range of day-to-day activities. Temples were public buildings intended as honors for the gods rather than homes to congregations of worshippers; private individuals often made offerings at a temple, but were free to do so wherever they pleased. In short, cult practices were a pervasive part of everyday life. Secondly, cult represented a conception of the divine world that was enacted in a set of practices, not codified in a set of beliefs. It is easy enough to formulate the basic beliefs that these practices implied: for example, that there existed a range of superhuman forces concerned with human behavior that responded to human interventions and communicated with the human sphere. In their details, rituals could even embody quite specific ideas about the relationship between gods and humans. But it is crucial to keep in mind that the cult acts themselves constituted these ideas and beliefs. Cult practices were not the expression of a formalized doctrinal system, but were instead a self-sufficient approach to the divine. At the same time, cult did not constitute the whole of religion as I defined it above, but was simply one of several approaches to the divine that coexisted in Graeco-Roman tradition. We must now consider the others.

2.2 Myth

For most people, the most familiar aspect of Graeco-Roman religion is probably myth, traditional tales about the deeds of gods and heroes. Many people might even identify myth as its core, playing the same role that scripture plays in Judaism or Christianity, and conclude that it was an article of faith among Greeks and Romans that the gods had human form and human emotions, and that they quarreled and fought, seduced and raped, and engaged in incest and murder. All these things, to be sure, are found in myths, but it is a mistake to think of myth as the core of Graeco-Roman religion. The scholarly tendency has if anything been the opposite, to treat cult as the core of Graeco-Roman religion in the imperial period and to regard myth as an essentially literary and artistic phenomenon. Yet it is just as much a mistake to deny the religious significance of myth as it is to overrate it. In this section I consider the problems with both extremes, and suggest a more balanced approach.

As I noted in the introduction, there is a certain tendency in western culture to assume that every "religion" has at its center a set of scriptures that embody its key assumptions. When people look for scripture in the Graeco-Roman religious tradition, the closest thing that they can find is myth. Yet Graeco-Roman myth differs from the usual idea of scripture in a number of important respects. For one thing, there was no fixed canon of texts or even stories. Myth was in origin a fluid oral tradition, and there was never any move to establish a particular set of myths as distinctively authoritative or true. Although poets at times claimed divine inspiration, people never regarded their works as "the word of God" in the way that Jews traditionally regard the Torah and Christians the Bible. The centrality of the Homeric epics to Greek culture has sometimes led people to compare their role with that of the Bible in later European culture, but the analogy is only partially apt: not even the poems of Homer were sanctified as "the word of God." Instead, myth remained a fluid tradition, reworked and adapted to new contexts by successive generations of writers, artists, and political leaders.

Another major difference between myth in the Graeco-Roman tradition and scripture in the monotheistic traditions is that myth played a relatively marginal role in actual worship. There was of course some interaction between myth and cult. As I noted in the previous section, prayers might include references to the mythic exploits of the deity being petitioned, and hymns often contained detailed accounts. Public festivals in honor of a deity typically involved the performance of hymns and sometimes also the enactment of myths on stage. In these ways myths could intersect with cult. In some cases, myths also provided aetiologies, stories that explained the origin of a particular rite by connecting it with some deed of the deity in question. Yet these aetiologies were rarely integral to the performance of the rituals, as for example the story of the Last Supper is to the celebration of the Christian Eucharist; the myth was not so much a part of the ritual as a gloss on it. In short, although cult practices might incorporate myths and myths might comment on cult practices, myth and cult remained in essence two separate things. In many important respects, myth was much more integral to literature and art than it was to cult. For all these reasons it is highly misleading to regard myth as the core of Graeco-Roman religion in the same way that people regard the Torah as the core of Judaism or the Qur'an as the core of Islam.

Indeed, as I noted above, many scholars have assumed that, in the imperial period at least, myth had lost all genuine religious significance and survived only as an element of high culture. Two lines of argument seem to support this proposition. First, the dominant mode for the transmission of myth apparently did gradually shift from popular oral tradition to elite literary and artistic culture. The great Greek and Latin literary classics were steeped in myth, and an intimate familiarity with these classics was the main goal of secondary education. There was consequently a market, then as now, for "dummy guides" that allowed a quick and painless acquisition of the essentials. The existence of these "dummy guides to myth," conventionally known as mythographies, seems to suggest that traditional myths were no longer familiar to the masses and could consequently have played no role in their religious lives. Secondly, it is certainly true that some members of the educated elite voiced strong objections to traditional myths: Varro's criticism of "the theology of the poets," which I mentioned above, had a long pedigree. As early as the sixth century BCE, the philosopher Xenophanes insisted that "Homer and Hesiod have attributed to the gods everything that among people is shameful and a reproach: theft and adultery and the deception of one another" (fragment 166 in Kirk, Raven, and Schofield 1983), and Plato famously proposed banning poets from his ideal state because of their wicked lies about the gods (*Republic* 2, 377b–383c). Other writers did not so much criticize traditional myths as poke fun at them. The second-century satirist Lucian, for example, wrote a number of works in which his tongue-in-cheek treatment of myth served to underline its absurdity, and we find similarly ironic material in the writings of Ovid and Seneca and Apuleius. It may thus appear that if traditional myths had become alien to the lower classes, the upper classes regarded them with contempt. Yet neither proposition is really true.

To begin with, although a knowledge of myth was indeed closely tied to higher education, it was by no means restricted to the elite. For one thing, the very popularity of mythographies suggests that people with any leisure for study were often keen to learn more of the traditional myths: they were clearly regarded as something worth knowing. More importantly, myth also flourished in more public contexts. The prayers and hymns of public festivals provided a forum for the literati to pass on their learning to a wider audience. Temples and other public buildings were often adorned with frescos or bas-reliefs depicting the deeds of the gods; the pediments of the Parthenon in Athens, for example, were decorated with scenes of Athena's birth from the head of Zeus and of Athena's and Poseidon's contest for the land of Attica. Such visual narratives functioned like the stained-glass windows of medieval cathedrals to communicate these stories to the illiterate.

Lastly, but surely not least in popular significance, myths often provided plots for the mass entertainments presented in the theaters and amphitheaters of the empire: as Varro noted, "the theology of the poets" was especially suited to the theater. Apuleius describes the staging of what sounds like a soft-porn version of the Judgment of Paris in a theater in Corinth, in which the girl who portrayed Venus, naked except for a single gauzy garment, performed an erotic dance (*The Golden Ass* 10.30–4). It is no surprise that early Christian writers denounced popular performances like this with such vehemence: "the literature of the stage sketches out all the foulness of the gods: for your enjoyment the Sun mourns his son [Phaethon] thrown down from the heavens, and without a blush from you Cybele pants for her haughty shepherd [Attis]; you allow the indictments of Jupiter to be sung aloud, and Juno, Venus, Minerva to be judged by a shepherd [Paris]." Even the punishments of criminals could be staged as myths: "we have seen at various times Attis, the god from Pessinus, being castrated, and a man who was being burned alive dressed up as Hercules" (Tertullian, *Apology* 15.2 and 5). At least in urban areas, then, it seems likely that some knowledge of traditional Graeco-Roman myth was fairly widespread.

Likewise, the fact that the educated classes criticized and satirized traditional myths does not mean that they regarded them as unimportant. Christian intellectuals, for example, would hardly have bothered to attack something that their opponents did not themselves take seriously. And indeed, it is clear that many of them did. The travel-writer Pausanias provides an interesting insight into the way that one educated person viewed traditional myth: "when I began this work I used to look upon these Greek stories as markedly on the foolish side; but when I had got as far as Arcadia my opinion about them became this: I guessed that the Greeks who were accounted wise spoke of old in riddles and not straight out, and that this story about Kronos [and his castration of his father Ouranos] is a bit of Greek wisdom" (*Description of Greece* 8.8.3). In other words, the more Pausanias thought about traditional myths, the more weight he was willing to attach to them.

The views that Pausanias came to espouse seem to have been popular among the intellectuals of the imperial period: again and again in our evidence we come across writers treating traditional myths as a sort of code whose true significance had to be unlocked by means of a particular interpretive key. Some people used a historical key, arguing that the gods of myth were in origin early kings and heroes, whose deeds were exaggerated as they were retold over the centuries; this strategy is known as Euhemerism, after the fourth-century BCE writer Euhemerus, who first applied it systematically. Others suggested that myths were not stories about the true gods, whom they regarded as above human emotions and incapable of wickedness, but about *daimones*, who were thought to have superhuman powers but human failings. But the most common strategy was to treat myths as allegories, in which the gods and their deeds were symbolic representations of philosophical truths; I discuss this approach further in the section on philosophy below. The key point about all these strategies is that their very existence shows that, while intellectuals of the imperial period may have had trouble in accepting myths at face value, they were nevertheless unwilling to dismiss them entirely.

Myth, then, was an old and well-established way of thinking about the divine world, and remained an integral part of Graeco-Roman culture. Traditional myths continued to be familiar to a broad range of people, at least where there were temples and public festivals, and remained of great significance to the educated classes in particular. It is true that myth did not constitute an authoritative account of the divine world; on the contrary, from a philosophical viewpoint there was much about it that was objectionable, and the literal meaning of many traditional myths was typically rejected in favor of historicizing or allegorical interpretations. It is also true that myth played only a minor and superficial role in the actual worship of the gods, and that myth and cult instead constituted largely separate approaches to the divine. But neither fact means that myth in the imperial period lacked religious significance, because there is no reason to regard either philosophy or cult as more genuinely "religious" than myth. Myth remained a vital and pervasive way of envisioning the divine world, and as such constituted a crucial element of the Graeco-Roman religious tradition.

2.3 Art

Much of what I have said about myth can be applied to the depiction of the gods in art as well: as Dio Chrysostom points out in his speech on the statue of Zeus at Olympia, the two go hand in hand. Just as myth described the gods as having human characteristics and engaging in human activities, so too in art: with a very few exceptions, such as the Romans' double-faced god Janus, gods in the Graeco-Roman tradition were never depicted in anything other than ordinary human form. The small cameo shown here, for example, depicts the god Jupiter (see Figure 1.2). But what indicates that this is a god at all, and not simply a man? To a certain extent, the idealization of the face and form alone suggests that this is not meant to represent an ordinary person, much less a particular individual; similarly, the figure's partial nudity implies that he is someone apart from day-to-day life. But the only unmistakable indication that this is meant to be Jupiter is the presence of his usual attributes, objects that evoked the distinctive powers of a god: the scepter in his left hand, symbolizing his rule over gods and mortals; the stylized lightning bolt in his right hand, indicating his power over the heavens; and the eagle at his feet, a bird associated with imperial power. Most of the important Graeco-Roman deities are similarly identifiable through attributes of this sort: Apollo with his lyre (see for example Figure 4.4), Demeter/Ceres with ears of grain, and so forth. In particular contexts, other conventions might also indicate that a certain figure represents a god. When gods and worshippers are depicted in the same scene, for example, the former are shown in a larger scale than the latter (see for an example the top register of the relief in Figure 4.4, with the deities on the right and the humans on the left); this was a literal representation of the gods' great-ness. But because the gods were normally depicted in ordinary human form, some such conventions were necessary to distinguish particular figures as divine.

Like the stories about the gods found in myth, these visual conventions in the representation of the gods are among the most familiar aspects of Graeco-Roman religion. And as with myth, the challenge is to attach neither too much nor too little importance to the role of divine images. Too much importance is suggested by the widespread conception of traditional Graeco-Roman religion as idolatry (from Greek *eidôlolatria*, literally "idol-worship"). "Idolatry" naturally implies that images of the gods

Figure 1.2   Sardonyx cameo depicting Jupiter, set in a frame of the fourteenth century. Paris, Cabinet des Médailles 1. Reproduced by permission of akg-images/Erich Lessing

were the all-important and essential focus of worship. But this was far from the case. There were certainly various ceremonies that centered on cult statues. The poet Ovid, for example, describes an annual festival of Venus in Rome in which women removed the jewelry from a statue of the goddess, washed and dried it, restored the ornaments, and presented it with flowers (*Fasti* 4.133–8). Similarly, Artemidorus' discussion of what it means to dream about cleaning and anointing statues of the gods or wreathing them with flowers (*The Interpretation of Dreams* 2.33) suggests that these were perfectly normal activities. In many cities there were religious festivals in which statues of the gods were carried in procession. Another widespread practice was the celebration of divine banquets, in which divine images were placed on couches and presented with food and drink. Despite the importance of such rituals, however, Graeco-Roman religion can hardly be characterized as idol-worship. None of the key practices that I outlined in the section on cult required the presence of divine images, and although they did at times focus on images, most normally took place without them. Animal sacrifice required an altar, not an idol, and as I noted above most sacrificial altars were placed in front of temples, not inside with the statues of the gods. Images of the gods were in fact largely incidental to the essentials of Graeco-Roman cult.

The characterization of Graeco-Roman worship as idolatry is in origin a Jewish and Christian construct, derived ultimately from the second of the Ten Commandments: "You shall not make a carved image for yourself. . . . You shall not bow down to them or worship them" (*Exodus* 20.4–5, New English Bible translation). The Israelite prophets developed this idea by arguing that it was an insult to the true God to worship the products of human manufacture (for example, *Isaiah* 44.9–20 and *Jeremiah* 10.1–16). Criticisms of this sort may have had some point in their original context, since idols apparently did play an important role in the cult practices of the early Israelites' Near Eastern neighbors. But the authority of scripture led later Jewish and Christian writers to characterize Graeco-Roman worship in the same way (for example, *Wisdom of Solomon* 13–15; Paul, *Letter to the Romans* 1.18–30); their influence is still felt today, despite the fact that "idolatry" does not accurately describe the Graeco-Roman tradition.

The opposite mistake is to regard images of the gods simply as decoration with no real religious significance. This is easy to do, because from the Renaissance onwards that is precisely what images of the Graeco-Roman gods have been in European art: although widely familiar, there has never been any question of their having any religious meaning. By the time of the Renaissance, of course, the Graeco-Roman religious tradition had effectively been dead for a thousand years; there was simply no potential for images of its gods to have any religious significance. The situation was far different in antiquity, however, when the gods depicted in art were actually objects of worship. How then should we assess the role of divine images in Graeco-Roman religion?

We must begin with the fact that in the Roman Empire representations of the gods were omnipresent, occurring in virtually all media and all contexts. Although we associate them primarily with temples, such as the famous statue of Athena in the Parthenon, they could be found in many other public buildings as well: council-houses, basilicas, libraries, even establishments like markets and baths that we would not necessarily associate with religion. Statues of the gods were also erected in the open air; Pausanias' account of the market-place of Corinth, for example, indicates that it contained single statues of Poseidon, Apollo, Aphrodite, and Athena, two of Hermes, and three of Zeus (*Description of Greece* 2.2.8–3.1). It was equally common for people to have images of the gods in their homes. Cicero, when decorating his new villa in a suburb of Rome, commissioned his friend Atticus in Greece to find some ornaments suitable for a lecture hall and was quite delighted when the latter came up with a bust of Minerva (*Letters to Atticus* 1.6.2 and 1.4.3). Smaller scale depictions of the gods were also common. Some were finely crafted out of expensive materials, like the exquisite cameo of Jupiter (see Figure 1.2). At the other end of the scale, cheaply manufactured clay figurines of gods have been found in great numbers all over the territory of the Roman Empire. In addition to works that had no function beyond that of representing the gods, divine images occur on an incredibly wide range of utilitarian objects: signet rings, hairpins, mirrors, tableware, lamps, and coins. Some are bound to seem either shocking or laughable to modern viewers: what, for example, are we to make of the steelyard weights from Britain cast in the forms of Bacchus and Isis (Henig 1984: 179)?

The depiction of gods in what appear to be such secular contexts has led many people to distinguish images that had genuine religious significance from those that were merely decorative. Yet here too we must be careful. This distinction originates with Jewish rabbis of the Roman period. The Mishnah preserves an anecdote in which a gentile asked Rabban Gamaliel II (active c.80–110 CE) why he bathed in a bath-house of Aphrodite when the Torah forbade all contact with idolatry. Gamaliel replied that the behavior of the gentiles themselves proved that the image of Aphrodite in the baths was simply an ornament, since they would never appear naked or urinate before an actual cult statue of the goddess (Mishnah, *Abodah Zarah* 3.4). This careful distinction between cultic and decorative images of the gods allowed the rabbis to function in a world where images of the gods were everywhere. As a way of understanding the role of divine images in the Graeco-Roman religious tradition, however, it is seriously deficient. Two points must be kept in mind.

First, any image of a deity was potentially, if not actually, an object of devotion. We know, for example, that statuettes of gods were sometimes cult objects and not simply objets d'art. When Apuleius was tried on a charge of magic, one of the allegations made by the prosecution was that he had commissioned a woodworker to carve a ghoulish statuette to which he paid cult. Apuleius countered that it was in fact a charming figure of Mercury, and explained that "it is my custom, wherever I go, to carry an image of some deity tucked away among my books and on holidays to make offerings to it of incense and wine and occasionally a sacrifice" (*Apology* 63). Similarly, Suetonius reports that the emperor Nero had a statuette of a girl, presumably some divinity, to which he made offerings three times a day (Suetonius, *Nero* 56). In view of such stories, we should be very cautious in assuming a clear-cut distinction between "religious" and "decorative" images of gods. Instead, the cultic potential of a divine image was always present and perceived as a kind of subtext. It is striking that Cicero, who merely wanted a nice ornament for his lecture hall, nevertheless thanks Atticus by writing that "your bust of Minerva pleases me a great deal; it is so elegantly placed that the entire lecture-hall looks like an offering to it" (*Letters to Atticus* 1.1.5). There is no suggestion that Cicero ever thought of making an actual offering to the image, yet even so he naturally thought of it in those terms. The devotional significance of a divine image was thus a potential that might at any time be actualized.

Even more important was the fact that these omnipresent images provided an important way to think about the divine. In my discussion of myth I suggested that visual representations of myth functioned like the stained glass windows of medieval cathedrals. The same was true on a more fundamental level of divine images in general. In a society where illiteracy rates were by modern standards unimaginably high, images of the gods played a crucial part in shaping people's understanding of the divine world. We can make some guesses about the ideas that they propagated: that the divine was in some sense understandable and approachable because it was so similar to the human, yet also involved a degree of perfection and power beyond that of ordinary mortals. We can also trace some of its implications: in this context, for example, it is not surprising that the line between divine and human was much less sharp than in Judaism and Islam, which reject absolutely any representation of the deity. But it is difficult to get at the experience of the ordinary person, because virtually all our evidence for reactions to divine images comes from the educated elite, who, just as with myth, seem often to have been uncomfortable with anthropomorphic representations of the gods.

This discomfort stemmed from long-standing philosophical objections. Xenophanes mocked the practice of depicting gods in human form by suggesting that if horses and cows could draw, "horses would draw the forms of the gods like horses and cows like cows"; he himself urged the existence of "one god, greatest among gods and humans, completely unlike mortals in both body and thought" (fragments 169 and 170 in Kirk, Raven, and Schofield 1983). The Roman scholar Varro believed that the Romans originally worshipped the gods without images, and thought that those who first set up divine images had decreased religious awe and increased error (cited by Augustine, *The City of God* 4.31). Yet few intellectuals actually proposed doing away with images of the gods, and most seem to have found ways to accommodate that tradition, just as they did myth. Dio Chrysostom, for example, argued that because artists cannot visually represent mind and thought, essential qualities of the divine, they instead employ the form in which those qualities are embodied, that is, human form (*Orations* 12.59); moreover, just as people express the beneficence of Zeus by calling him "Father" and "God of Friendship" and "Protector of Suppliants," so too the artist tries to capture these aspects by depicting him as an adult male, powerful and just, yet gentle (*Orations* 12.75–7). Even so, they were careful to insist that the image of a deity was not the deity itself. The Greek scholar Plutarch, writing around 100 CE, admitted that there was a widespread tendency to make this identification, but argued that it was simply a mistake of language: just as someone who buys the books of Plato might say that he is "buying Plato," so too the unthinking will refer to a statue of Athena simply as "Athena" (*On Isis and Osiris* 70–1, 379a–d).

Like myth, then, the tradition of representing the gods in human form was firmly established in Graeco-Roman culture and was if anything even more widely spread. Although divine images were sometimes the focus of cult activities and were always potential objects of devotion, their real importance lay in shaping people's ideas about the divine world. Cicero, in his dialogue about the nature of the divine, has one of his characters admit that "from childhood we are familiar with Jupiter, Juno, Minerva, Neptune, Vulcan, Apollo, and the other gods in the form that painters and sculptors have wanted to present them, not only in appearance but also in adornment, age, and dress" (*On the Nature of the Gods* 1.81). No philosophical critique was going to alter the hold that this tradition had over people's ideas about the gods. Yet it is clear from what I have already said that philosophy itself provided another way to think about the divine world. We must now consider this in more detail.

2.4 Philosophy

Greek philosophy, as a distinct type of intellectual activity, had its origins in the sixth century BCE, and by the imperial period was a crucial if sometimes contentious element of elite culture. From the start, philosophy involved speculations about the divine as part of its wider concern with the nature of the world in general. Not surprisingly, philosophers were in no more agreement about the nature of the divine than they were about anything else. Each of the major philosophical schools developed its distinctive theories, so that in the mid-first century BCE Cicero could frame his treatise *On the Nature of the Gods* as a debate between representatives of the three leading schools of his day (Stoics, Epicureans, and Academics, the followers of Plato). Nevertheless, there emerged in the imperial period a set of somewhat generic ideas about the divine with which most philosophically-minded people would probably have agreed: that the divine was by definition perfect and morally good, the source of all blessings and virtues, remote from the corruption of the everyday world yet linked to it by intermediary levels of being. It is obvious that this philosophical conception of the divine differed from that found in myth and art and even from that implicit in cult. As we have already seen, those interested in philosophy tended either to criticize these traditional approaches or to accommodate them within their own beliefs. At the same time, philosophy offered something much closer to the western conception of "a religion" than could be found in traditional cult and myth and art: that is, a distinctive way of life based on an integrated understanding of the cosmos.

In the preceding sections I have already mentioned the philosophical critique of the traditional depiction of the gods in myth and art. The key objections are easily summarized: that the gods did not actually resemble humans in either appearance or behavior, and that they certainly did not engage in the sorts of immoral activities so commonly ascribed to them in myths. The fact that these ideas occur in a range of texts suggests that they were widespread among the educated classes, although we should be cautious in assuming that everyone accepted them without reservation. Somewhat less common, although by no means unknown, are philosophical criticisms of traditional cult practices. A few radicals, for example, rejected offerings altogether, on the principle that the gods, being perfect, did not require anything from people, who were imperfect. Others, following a strain of Greek thought associated with the early philosopher Pythagoras, regarded all animal products as impure and hence viewed the practice of blood sacrifice as impious. A letter attributed to the Pythagorean philosopher and holy man Apollonius of Tyana expresses this position very succinctly: "Priests defile altars with blood. Then some people wonder why their cities, whenever they are in great trouble, are suffering misfortunes. Oh folly!" (*Letters* 27). Similarly, some people expressed doubts about the reality of divination. One of our best sources for such criticisms is Cicero's treatise *On Divination*, written as a debate between Cicero and his brother, of which the first book presents his brother's arguments in support of divination and the second book Cicero's own arguments against it.

But although we find a few philosophical rigorists who categorically rejected traditional cult, myth, and art, they were clearly exceptions. Most people were perfectly willing to accept these traditions even if they clashed with their philosophical beliefs. For those interested, there were ways to make them fit within a philosophical framework. One of the most effective was allegory, whereby one could interpret a traditional myth or artistic convention or even cult practice as symbolic of a philosophical truth. There were several different types of allegory. The writer Sallustius, writing in the 360s CE but drawing on earlier traditions, illustrates their variety by referring to the myth of Kronos devouring his children: on a "theological" reading, the story indicates that the essence of the god is intellect, since the intellect always turns back to itself; on a "physical" reading, Kronos is Time (Greek *chronos*), which consumes what it produces; on a "psychical" reading, the myth shows that our thoughts, even when they are externally expressed, continue to remain in our souls (*On the Gods and the Universe* 4). Some Jewish and Christian thinkers were similarly keen to apply the techniques of allegory to their sacred scriptures; in this way, for example, the philosopher Philo of Alexandria was able to reconcile the Jewish scriptures with Platonic philosophy.

Despite its variety, all allegorical interpretation served to make other modes of thinking about the divine subordinate to philosophy; the underlying assumption was that only philosophy revealed the true significance of traditional myth, art, and cult. Plutarch, in his long treatise on the myth and cult of Isis and Osiris, makes this point several times: "if you understand matters concerning the gods in [the way I have discussed] and receive them from people who interpret the myth piously and philosophically . . . , you will avoid superstition, which is no less an evil than atheism"; likewise, "it is necessary especially with regard to [cult practices] that we take as our guide the understanding that comes from philosophy, and reflect piously on everything that is said and done" (*On Isis and Osiris* 11, 355c–d, and 68, 378a–b). In other words, although Plutarch by no means rejected traditional approaches to the divine, he believed that philosophical exegesis was required to prevent them from degenerating into superstition.

Other people, however, apparently felt no need to reconcile their philosophical opinions about the divine with traditional cult, myth, and art. Cicero, for example, apparently regarded the cultic institutions of Rome and philosophical inquiry as two separate things. In his dialogue *On the Nature of the Gods*, the character Cotta, who like Cicero himself maintained the skeptical philosophical stance of the Academic school, was challenged by the Stoic Balbus to remember that he was a public priest of Rome. The response that Cicero puts into Cotta's mouth is instructive: "I always will defend and always have defended [traditional beliefs and practices], nor will a lecture by anyone, whether learned or unlearned, move me from the beliefs about the cult of the immortal gods that I have received from our ancestors. . . . Here, Balbus, you have the opinion of Cotta the priest; help me now to understand your opinions, for from you as a philosopher I ought to receive a rational account of religion, just as I ought to give credence to our ancestors even without a rational account" (*On the Nature of the Gods* 3.5–6). For Cicero, it seems, philosophical skepticism and institutional conservatism could coexist without friction. The Stoic philosopher Epictetus, in sharp contrast to the skeptical Cicero, asserted that "the supreme factor in piety towards the gods is to have correct notions about them as beings that exist and administer all things well and justly, and to hold yourself ready to obey them and to yield to everything that happens and to follow it willingly, as something brought to pass by the most perfect judgment; for in this way you will never blame the gods or accuse them of neglecting you." Yet he nevertheless similarly concludes that "it is appropriate on each occasion to offer libations and sacrifices and first fruits, in accordance with ancestral traditions" (*Handbook* 31). Regardless of philosophical position, most people apparently had no desire to reject or subvert traditional beliefs and practices with regard to the divine.

In the Graeco-Roman tradition, then, philosophy constituted another mode of thinking about the divine that sometimes supplemented but never supplanted the older modes of cult, myth, and art. But as the passage from Epictetus suggests, philosophy also offered something that the other modes did not: an integrated way of life in which one's moral values and everyday behavior was grounded in a particular view of the cosmos and of its relationship to human life. In modern western culture, philosophy is often regarded as an abstract intellectual pursuit, remote from and often irrelevant to people's actual lives. In Graeco-Roman antiquity the situation was very different: "philosophy" would for many people have suggested first and foremost a whole way of life, and only secondarily the sorts of academic investigations that the term now ordinarily implies. Philosophers even composed what we might call "missionary tracts," intended to convert people from shallow worldly values to the pursuit of wisdom and virtue. Aristotle wrote one such work, now lost but famous in antiquity, called *Protreptikos* (literally, "Exhortation"), which later inspired Cicero to write a similar work of his own, the dialogue *Hortensius*. The latter in turn was to have a profound effect on the young Augustine, whose comments in his *Confessions* give us some idea how a person might respond to such writings: "The book changed my feelings; it redirected my prayers, Lord, to you yourself and transformed my wishes and desires. Suddenly every empty hope became worthless to me; I longed for the immortality of wisdom with an incredible fervor in my heart, and began to rise up so that I might return to you" (*Confessions* 3.4).

Although earlier philosophers would have found Augustine's Christian beliefs baffling, they would have recognized and approved his reaction here. It was in fact commonly agreed in the imperial period that the ultimate goal of philosophy was to become like the divine, a view that ultimately derived from Plato. This goal was not, however, a sort of mystical union, but rather a recognition that the divine provided a model of the perfection to which humans ought to aspire. Apuleius, in his textbook on Platonic philosophy, put it this way: "It is the goal of wisdom that the wise man should advance to the merit of a god, and that his task will be to approach the conduct of the gods by imitating them in his life; moreover, this will come about for him if he shows himself a perfectly just, pious, and thoughtful man" (*On Plato and his Doctrine* 23). For Apuleius, as for many other philosophers, the model for such behavior was Socrates: "are we ourselves not also elevated by the example and recollection of Socrates, and do we not entrust ourselves to the beneficent pursuit of philosophy with due regard for a like assimilation to the divine?" (*On the God of Socrates* 21). Passages like these give some taste of the Graeco-Roman idea of philosophy as a way of life that grounded the pursuit of virtue and wisdom in a particular understanding of the divine, a way of life that in some respects is much closer to what many people today would regard as "a religion."

Just as philosophy was generally understood more as a way of life than as a narrow academic pursuit, so too philosophers often had more popular appeal than we might expect. Men like Apuleius and Dio Chrysostom were celebrities who could attract large crowds to their lectures and command sizeable fees for their appearances; they were in many ways more akin to the self-help gurus of today than to professional philosophers. Philosophy was thus a culturally significant force in the Graeco-Roman world. It was nevertheless in practice probably the least important of the four approaches to the divine that I have sketched: readily available to those who were interested, but hardly inescapable in the way that cult, art, and even myths were. And although philosophers might insist that only philosophy allowed for the true understanding of the divine world and the correct interpretation of traditional cult and myth, they had no authority to compel others to agree; it is likely that most people neither knew nor cared. One of the key religious developments of the imperial period is that philosophy gradually takes on a more important role and ultimately becomes the center of a new, more integrated conception of religion, as I discuss in the epilogue. But this development takes on widespread importance only with the dominance of Christianity in the fourth century CE; for most of the imperial period, the Graeco-Roman tradition remained largely unchanged.

2.5 Conclusion

Despite the gradual development of a more cohesive conception of religion, it is highly misleading to think of the Graeco-Roman religious tradition in terms of an integrated system with an identifiable core. Attempts to outline such a system by focusing on any one approach to the divine inevitably result in the dismissal of other approaches and consequently a very partial representation of the tradition. Scholars who treat cult or philosophy as the "essence" of real Graeco-Roman religion, for example, tend to downplay the role of art and myth. And yet as I have argued the latter must have had a profound and widespread impact on people's ideas about the divine world. Debates about whether they were really "religious" or not are meaningful only if we are thinking of "a religion" as a coherent system of beliefs, practices, and institutions that reflect and build on one another. Most people in the Graeco-Roman tradition, however, seem to have thought instead in terms of multiple "theologies," in which cult, myth (together with art), and philosophy constituted separate modes of thinking about the divine, modes that interacted in various ways but remained essentially independent. There has been considerable debate in the last two decades over how we may best understand the interrelation of these modes, although the basic structure seems clear enough. As we have seen, myth and art were closely interrelated in their depictions of the divine, despite a few minor differences. Cult constituted a largely separate area, although images and, to a lesser extent, myths could play a part in various cult practices. Philosophy developed a conception of the divine that was in many respects radically opposed to that underlying traditional myth and art and even cult. Although the philosophically inclined sometimes criticized these other approaches to the divine, they very rarely advocated their abolition; much more often they either subordinated them to philosophy through a process of reinterpretation or simply accepted them for the sake of tradition. Yet the fact that none of these modes was necessarily coherent with the others does not mean that any one of them was outside the pale of "real" religion. The Graeco-Roman religious tradition was instead constituted by this entire set of largely separate, sometimes contradictory, yet equally important approaches to the divine.

3 Three Problematic Topics

If we think of the Graeco-Roman religious tradition not as "a religion" but as a set of approaches to the divine, we are in a much better position to understand it. In other respects as well the Graeco-Roman tradition does not conform to the expectations that many people have of "a religion"; I have for example already noted the absence of anything like the "sacred scriptures" that exist in the great monotheistic traditions. In this last section I explore three other particular areas in which it differed: the nature and organization of religious authority, the role of belief in religious life, and the connection between morality and religion. Each of these topics is complex enough to require detailed consideration.

3.1 Authority

As I noted in the introduction, many people would expect to find in any religious tradition some sort of priestly class, a set of people with a privileged role who act as the authoritative representatives of that tradition for the rest of the population. There certainly existed in the Graeco-Roman tradition people with special authority in matters pertaining to the divine, but they did not constitute anything like a priestly class such as existed in medieval Christianity or traditional Hinduism.

Two facts are fundamental to an understanding of religious authority in the Graeco-Roman tradition. The first is that people were to a very large extent in charge of their own religious lives and had no need of religious specialists. We can best understand this fact by contrasting it with the situation in other traditions. In some religious traditions, only members of certain strictly defined groups can perform key rituals, as, for example, in medieval Christianity only priests could baptize or celebrate the Eucharist; these figures are consequently the necessary intermediaries between the human and divine spheres, and without them no one can have a full and correct relationship to the divine. A priestly class of this sort did not exist in the Graeco-Roman tradition. The basic cult practices that I sketched above – prayer, sacrifice, and to some extent divination – were open to all, so that people generally had no need of any third party to mediate between them and the gods. It was only as members of a group that individuals depended on someone else for the performance of basic rituals, since in every group, whether a household or an association or a city, there were people whose role was to represent the group in its dealings with the divine; I explore this topic further in chapter 4. Likewise, in some religious traditions there are people with the authority to determine and even enforce a "correct" understanding of the divine, as the medieval Church identified and condemned beliefs it deemed heretical. Again, in the Graeco-Roman tradition such authorities did not exist. Some people did claim to have a deeper and better understanding of the divine world than others, and consequently criticized and rejected other people's beliefs; I noted a few examples in my discussion of philosophy above. Yet their claims were not widely accepted, and they expressed their opinions through debate and polemic rather than enforceable rulings. What a person believed about the gods was thus very much a matter of personal taste and inclination.

But the fact that there was no priestly class that governed people's religious lives and dictated their religious beliefs does not mean that there were no religious authorities. On the contrary, there was a wide range of figures with different types of authority and concerned with different areas. This is the second fundamental fact that is important to keep in mind. To a certain extent, it simply reflects the general diversity of approaches to the divine that constituted the religious tradition: since cult and myth and philosophy constituted largely separate areas rather than an overarching system, it is not surprising that there was no single priestly class with authority over them all. At the same time, nothing precluded the development of such a class, and as we have seen some philosophers did claim an authoritative understanding of all the other areas. There is in fact a further crucial aspect to the diversity of religious authorities in the Graeco-Roman tradition, and that arises from the central role of the city in Graeco-Roman culture.

The classical city-state (Greek *polis*) was in essence a collectivity of male citizens who, with their women, children, and dependents, constituted an autonomous political community. Although city-states differed considerably in their specific institutions, virtually all of them had a governing council with more or less permanent membership and a set of civic officials who handled day-to-day business. These officials had jurisdiction over everything that affected the welfare of the community, and included both administrative officers, or magistrates, and priests. The term "priest" is in fact slightly misleading in this context, since there was no single word in either Greek or Latin that applied to the whole range of figures whom we lump together under that English word (although Greek *hiereus* and Latin *sacerdos* perhaps come close). It is also important not to think of magistrates and priests as constituting respectively the secular and religious hierarchies of the city-state. For one thing, magistrates, together with the governing council, often made key decisions about the community's interactions with the gods and acted on behalf of the community in prayer, sacrifice, and divination. For another, the same people, members of the local socio-economic elite, served as both magistrates and priests, and an individual might well hold a magistracy and a priesthood simultaneously. It is better to think of these civic priesthoods as a particular type of public office with certain distinguishing characteristics: for example, many priesthoods were held for life, whereas most magistrates served for only a limited period, and some priesthoods could be held only by women, who otherwise had few public roles in the city-state. Broadly speaking, it was the role of priests to carry out specific ritual duties and to act as experts in the city's ritual traditions.

Together, a city's magistrates and priests claimed authority over all interactions between the community and the gods; they were the religious authorities within what Varro describes as "civic theology." Yet it is important to note the limits of their claims. On the one hand, their focus was on the correct performance of rituals: they were concerned with behavior, not belief. Their chief responsibility was to ensure that the prescribed public rituals were performed as they were supposed to be performed, although in some cases they could also be consulted by individual citizens on points of ritual. What they did not do was to determine any community teachings about the gods or monitor people's beliefs. Insofar as they oversaw the correct performance of cult acts, they naturally tended to propagate the beliefs that those acts implied, for example, that there were gods who had power to help or harm and who would respond to human prayers and offerings. But their concern was nevertheless with the cult acts themselves and not with the explication of their meaning. Even though the interpretation of a public ritual in terms of myth or philosophy might have been an important part of someone's religious experience, the interpretation itself was so to speak part of the private sphere. On the other hand, their concern with actions extended only to those that might affect relations between the community as a whole and the gods; the religious behavior of people in their private lives was of no interest unless it threatened to have some negative impact on the wider community. As a result, most people were able to conduct their own religious lives as they saw fit. Obviously, then, a great deal lay outside the scope of these civic religious officials' authority.

In many significant respects, the growth of the Roman Empire did not alter the central place of the city in Graeco-Roman culture or the corresponding role of civic religious officials: there were never any imperial religious officials analogous to those of the traditional city-state. It is sometimes said that the emperor was the head of official Roman religion in the empire, but this is misleading. It is true that every emperor from Augustus on served as *pontifex maximus*, the president of the chief association of civic priests in Rome, and was also a member of all the other major Roman priestly colleges. This undoubtedly contributed to the religious aura that the emperor enjoyed (*pontifex maximus* was a standard element in the emperor's titles), but in practical terms it was significant only in the city of Rome itself; the other cities in the empire all had their own civic priests, who were not subordinate to those in Rome. Of course, both the emperor and lesser Roman officials intervened as they liked in matters concerning the divine, bestowing benefits on favored cults and restricting groups or practices of which they disapproved. But these interventions resulted from their general power, not from any special religious authority, and they tended to be even more limited in scope than those of traditional civic officials.

Alongside the priests and magistrates of the traditional city-state was a wide range of individuals who claimed a more profound and privileged understanding of the divine world or some special expertise in rituals of divination, purification, or initiation. In chapter 6 I discuss these free-lance religious authorities in more detail; here it is important simply to consider their general role in the Graeco-Roman religious tradition. We find such figures in the Greek world from a very early date; in some cases, at least, they seem to have been itinerant professionals working in traditions imported from the ancient Near East. With the development of the classical city-state, civic officials moved either to co-opt or, more often, to marginalize them. The religious officials of the city-state tended to view free-lance ritual specialists with suspicion, since the latter constituted a potential alternative to their own authority over public religion, and they sometimes took action against them. But because public authorities were concerned above all with the community as a whole, they were generally content to let these free-lance specialists operate in peace outside the public sphere.

Here again it is important to recall that civic officials were to a large extent concerned only with public cult (Varro's "civil" theology), and not with myth or philosophy (Varro's "mythical" and "physical" theologies). To be sure, the elite of a city could employ poets and artists to present certain myths in such a way as to promote a particular civic identity, and they occasionally took action against philosophers whom they regarded as spreading subversive ideas (the condemnation of Socrates in Athens in 399 BCE is the most famous example). But by and large myth and philosophy were the concern of poets, artists, and philosophers, not civic officials, and their works constituted an entirely separate source of religious authority in the Graeco-Roman tradition. Indeed, when ancient writers discussed ideas about the nature of the gods, they cited as their authorities not priests and magistrates, but rather "poets and philosophers."

When we talk of religious authorities in the Graeco-Roman tradition, then, it is important to keep in mind this diversity. There was no single priestly order, but rather a range of figures whose roles varied considerably. Magistrates and priests were authorities in the context of public cult, but their concerns did not cover all of what we mean by religion. In addition, there was a variety of free-lance specialists, poets, philosophers, and sages whose lore and specialized knowledge could be regarded as authoritative by those who were so inclined. Provided that they did not appear to threaten public order, all these figures could operate without hindrance from public officials, since their authority lay outside the sphere in which public officials were interested. People could thus choose from a whole range of religious authorities according to their tastes. Most importantly, they were ultimately not dependent on any authorities at all, but were instead in a very important sense responsible for their own religious lives.

3.2 Belief

In the western tradition, there is a strong tendency to identify belief as the real core of religion, so that in English, for example, it is perfectly common to refer to someone's religion as his or her "beliefs" and to describe people without religious affiliation as "non-believers." Idioms like these reveal an underlying assumption that for any given religion one can draw up a list of key propositions or doctrines that constitute its essence. This assumption has had a significant impact on the study of religion in the Roman Empire. Some scholars have rejected certain aspects of the Graeco-Roman tradition as not genuinely religious, either because people did not seem to accept them as true, as for example myth, or because they did not involve any doctrines at all, as with most cult activity. Others have focused on phenomena in which doctrines evidently played a more central role, notably philosophical schools and cult groups that emphasized initiations; this approach characterizes many works that survey "the religions" of the Roman Empire. In recent decades, a number of scholars have rejected these strategies and argued that we should not study Graeco-Roman religion in terms of belief at all, because the whole notion of religious belief is Christian in its origins and implications; for such scholars, to ask about the beliefs of the ancient Greeks and Romans is simply to ask the wrong question.

The role of belief in the Graeco-Roman religious tradition is thus a highly contentious issue. It is undoubtedly true that Christianity has foregrounded belief in a way that few other religions have. Christian leaders have from the beginning emphasized the necessity of belief that is both sincere and correct; the role and specific content of belief has been central to most intra-Christian conflicts from the doctrinal controversies of the early church to the Protestant Reformation. Because scholars of Graeco-Roman religion have generally been Christian by culture if not always by confession, it has been all too easy for them to introduce these specifically Christian connotations of the word "belief" into contexts where they are irrelevant or misleading. There is thus good reason to be cautious in discussing Graeco-Roman religion in terms of belief.

At the same time, we must be careful not to throw out the baby with the bathwater. In everyday language, most people use the word "belief" simply to mean something like "a proposition that a person accepts as true even without proof." If by "religious beliefs" we mean propositions of this sort regarding the nature of the divine world and its interaction with the mortal sphere, then there can be little question that religious beliefs played an important role in the Graeco-Roman tradition; indeed, I will be discussing them throughout this book. On occasion we find explicit statements of belief, such as this remark of the elder Pliny: "it accords with life's experience to believe that the gods exercise an interest in human affairs, and that punishment for misdeeds, though sometimes slow in coming . . . , is all the same never ineffectual, and that humanity was not born closest to god in order to rival beasts in worthlessness" (*Natural History* 2.26). But much more often, as I have already suggested, beliefs about the divine world were left implicit, embedded in cult acts and myth and art. It was only in particular contexts that people bothered to formulate these beliefs explicitly, especially contexts where philosophical influence was strong. What distinguishes the Graeco-Roman religious tradition from Christianity is thus the absence not of religious beliefs, but of pressures to define and scrutinize those beliefs. Three aspects of this situation should be kept in mind.

First of all, belief need not be the only marker of significance. This is true even in the context of Christianity. For example, the number of people in North America over the age of six or so who accept the existence of Santa Claus is presumably miniscule, yet the image of Santa Claus is nevertheless of great cultural significance and plays a major role in the way many people think about one of the most important Christian festivals. Similarly, many people may be active participants in a church and regard it as a central part of their lives, and yet be relatively uncon-cerned about the sincerity of their beliefs. There is of course a strong tradition in Christianity of denying the religious value of participating without truly believing. Christian leaders from St Paul to Martin Luther have insisted that salvation is achieved only by true faith, and have consequently regarded the quality of belief, the intensity of one's inner assent to particular propositions, as the only real marker of religious signi-ficance. But such a tradition never existed in mainstream Graeco-Roman religion, so that there was little impulse to treat sincerity of belief as a central issue. In order to evaluate religion in the Roman Empire on its own terms, then, we must be careful not to think of religious significance solely in terms of belief, but to give equal if not greater weight to social and cultural factors.

Secondly, belief in the strong Christian sense requires there to be a coherent and internally consistent set of propositions or doctrines in which to believe. As we have already seen, however, no such coherent set of doctrines existed in the Graeco-Roman tradition. If we ask about religious beliefs in the Roman Empire, we must first ask whether we are talking about cult or myth or philosophy, since in different contexts a person might well have had different beliefs. The existence of different ways of thinking about the divine meant that most people had little concern for a logical consistency in their beliefs about the gods and no interest in developing a unified set of doctrines. The philosophically inclined were a partial exception, since they tended to give priority to their philosophical doctrines and to interpret traditional cult and myth in conformity with them. But as I have noted, even among this group there were many who were perfectly willing to accept traditional cult practices without reference to their philosophical beliefs. Instead of a coherent set of doctrines, then, what we find in the Graeco-Roman tradition is a number of vaguely formulated and sometimes mutually contradictory beliefs.

Lastly, as I have already mentioned in my discussion of authority, there was no mechanism in the Roman Empire to define or much less to impose "correct" beliefs about the divine world. Civic religious officials generally had no interest in people's beliefs, whereas the people who did, philosophers and other free-lance experts, lacked the social authority and political power to take effective action. Civic officials were instead interested in actions, and the crucial element of any civic cult was the correct performance of the prescribed rituals. One can say more broadly that the marker of piety in the mainstream Graeco-Roman tradition was external behavior rather than internal belief: to be pious meant to honor the gods by offering prayers and sacrifices according to established precedents. If it has become common in a Christian context to talk about orthodoxy (from Greek *orthos*, "straight" or "correct," and *doxa*, "opinion" or "belief"), some scholars now describe the norm in the Graeco-Roman tradition as orthopraxy (from Greek *praxis*, "action"). The emphasis placed on correct practice by those in positions of social and political authority allowed individuals to believe more or less what they liked without interference.

In all these respects, then, belief played a very different and much less central role in Graeco-Roman religion than it has in Christianity. Although religious beliefs abounded, they were not fraught with the same significance or scrutinized with the same intensity; there was no set of doctrines that constituted the core of the religion. Instead, beliefs remained largely implicit and unformulated, a topic for debate among those interested, but largely ignored by those in power.

3.3 Morality

Just as western tradition identifies religion with belief, so too does it closely associate religion with morality. There is certainly good reason to do so. Ethical concerns have a central place in many religious traditions, and in the three great monotheistic traditions the connection is particularly direct. In these traditions God is the source of all moral value as well as all power; the ethical principles enunciated in their sacred scriptures are understood as God's directives to humanity, and the cosmic fate of individuals is bound up with their observance. In all these respects, the mainstream Graeco-Roman tradition was radically different. Insofar as there were no sacred scriptures, there was also no moral code that was regarded as "the word of God." Similarly, because there was no orthodoxy, there was no generally accepted belief in an afterlife in which individuals would be rewarded or punished for their behavior in life. Such a view of the afterlife did exist, but only as one among a number of competing views. Consequently, morality was simply not a part of religion as it is in Judaism, Christianity, and Islam.

This does not mean, however, that moral concerns played no part whatsoever in the Graeco-Roman religious tradition. Many people who encounter traditional Graeco-Roman myths are initially shocked at the immorality of the gods, who are often depicted as deceptive, adulterous, violent, and cruel. This reaction is not at all new: as I have already discussed, Greek philosophers had from an early date criticized such stories as not in keeping with the true nature of the divine and had gradually developed various interpretive techniques in order to explain them away. According to philosophers, the gods were wholly good and incapable of evil, and people who attributed to them any sort of wickedness were simply ignorant and foolish. Thus Plutarch argues that atheists, who deny the existence of the gods, are in fact less impious than the superstitious, who fear the gods and so suppose "the good to be evil" (*On Superstition* 6, 167e). Many philosophers also taught that the gods were likewise concerned with human behavior, and that they blessed the virtuous and punished the wicked. Some went so far as to assert that the offering most desired by the gods was not sacrifice but virtue. In one of his letters on ethical topics, the Roman philosopher Seneca sums up these themes: the gods "neither give nor have evil, but they chastise, they check, they assign penalties and sometimes punish in the form of blessing. Do you want to propitiate the gods? Be good: the person who has imitated them has worshipped them enough" (*Epistles* 95.50).

The idea that the gods were deeply concerned with the moral behavior of mortals was by no means restricted to philosophical circles; the comment of the elder Pliny quoted in the previous section is a good example. Even in traditional myths the gods were regularly if somewhat vaguely treated as the guardians of what is right, so that the wicked were often said to "despise the gods." Such beliefs also show up in cult. Some people took very seriously the notion that the gods would punish criminals, and turned to them for help against those who had wronged them. We see this, for example, in an inscribed potsherd from Egypt: "Claudius Silvanus and his brothers to mistress Athena against Longinus Marcus. Since Longinus – against whom we have often appealed to you because he was after our lives while we did no wrong, poor as we are – while he wins nothing with this, he still continues to be malicious against us, we beg you to do justice. We have already asked Ammon for help as well" (trans. Versnel 1991: 72). Similarly, from Britain, at the other end of the empire, comes this inscribed lead tablet: "Cenacus complains to the god Mercury about Vitalinus and Natalinus his son concerning the draught animal that was stolen. He begs the god Mercury that neither may have health unless they repay me promptly the animal they have stolen and repay to the god the devotion which he himself has demanded from them" (trans. MacMullen and Lane 1992: 14). Although people prayed to the gods for all sorts of benefits, prayers like these seem to suggest a specific conviction that the gods had a particular interest in ensuring that justice was done.

Similarly, the notion that the gods would more willingly accept offerings from the good than from the wicked was fairly widespread, although few people went so far as to substitute virtuous behavior for sacrifices. In a comedy of Terence, for example, when a father advises his son to pray to the gods to grant him the girl he loves, the son replies, "you go, Father, you pray to the gods instead; I am sure they're much more likely to listen to you, since you're so much better a man than I" (*The Brothers* 703–5). This tendency was especially strong in cults that emphasized initiations, some of which required the initiate to observe a strict moral code. The connection could work the other way as well, so that worship of the gods could result in moral reform; the historian Livy, for example, tells the story of a dissolute young Roman noble who, on being made the public priest of Jupiter, was led by the regular performance of his cultic duties to become a model of virtue (*History of Rome* 27.8.4–10).

We find traces, then, of a widespread belief in the gods' concern with moral behavior. Yet outside of philosophical circles this belief remained for the most part vague and ill-defined. Few people would have denied the goodness of the gods, but the normal assumption was that their favor was obtained first and foremost by the performance of the proper rituals. Moral instruction was traditionally the concern of wise men and philosophers, not of priests or public religious authorities, and although philosophers built on commonly accepted principles when they emphasized the connection between morality and cult, the close connection they advocated was not widely enacted. In short, although morality was bound up to a greater or lesser degree with all the various approaches to the divine that I have outlined, it was by no means a part of Graeco-Roman religion in the way that many people would expect.

4 Conclusion

In this chapter I have sketched out some of the key elements of the mainstream Graeco-Roman religious tradition, the tradition of the Roman Empire's social, economic, and political elite. I have tried in particular to illustrate the ways that it did not conform to the expectations that many people would have of "a religion": there was no one unified and coherent set of beliefs and principles, no sacred scriptures, no priestly class, and no associated moral code. Instead of "a religion," we can more usefully think of it as a group of loosely related but largely distinct ways of thinking about and interacting with the divine world. This fluid and open organization allowed people to maintain simultaneous beliefs and practices that we might regard as inconsistent with one another and even mutually contradictory. There were indeed some impulses, particularly among the philosophically inclined, to work out a more coherent system, in which a few philosophical principles would serve as the basis for a correct approach to cult and myth. Yet these impulses were effectively limited to the philosophical sphere, what Varro called "physical" theology, and did not until relatively late have much impact on the religious tradition as a whole. One reason for this is that the economic and political elite, those with the social power actually to effect changes, were simply not interested in doing so; some of them liked to discuss these philosophical ideas in their private lives, but few if any were interested in promoting them in their official capacities. Instead, public authorities continued for the most part to restrict their concerns to public cults, Varro's "civil" theology, and maintain a laissez-faire attitude to other aspects of religious life.

This is not to say that the elite did not have a number of implicit assumptions about what constituted normal religious tradition. My other main goal in this chapter has been precisely to indicate what those were.

We should not suppose that all members of the ruling class would have agreed on all points, since fluidity and openness were what characterized the Graeco-Roman tradition. There would nevertheless have been a number of widely held assumptions about normal religious practice and belief. We should keep this in mind as we survey the various regional traditions within the empire, since understanding the "normative" Graeco-Roman tradition is of crucial importance to understanding religion in the empire as a whole. On the one hand, members of the Graeco-Roman elite encountered some religious traditions that in one or more ways did not conform to their religious norms; in some cases, imperial officials took active and formal measures to restrict or prevent deviant behavior, but they more often exerted informal pressures to promote greater conformity. More importantly, many aspects of the mainstream Graeco-Roman religious tradition were shared by the various regional traditions within the empire, a fact that allowed for their smooth integration. It is these fundamental points of agreement that allow us to consider religion in the Roman Empire as a whole, and it is to that topic that we turn in the next chapter.

FURTHER READING

On the Graeco-Roman tradition in general, see also the suggestions for further reading on Greece and Italy in the following chapter. On Silvanus, see Dorcey 1992; for discussions of deified abstractions, see Stafford 2000 on the Greek tradition and Fears 1981 for the Roman. Versnel 1981 is an interesting study of prayer; Furley and Bremer 2001 provides a valuable collection of Greek hymns, with detailed discussion. For a general introduction to Greek myth, see Buxton 2004; Coleman 1990 is a brilliant discussion of its role in public spectacles, and Feeney 1998: 47–75 is valuable on myth in Rome. On the role of art in conceptions of the divine, see especially Gordon 1979 and Elsner 1996; Schwartz 2001: 165–74 provides insight into the rabbinic distinction between idols and ornaments. Hadot 2002 is an excellent overview of ancient philosophy as a way of life; on the philosophical response to traditional cult practices, see Attridge 1978 and Meijer 1981; Nock 1933, especially pp. 164–86, remains the most evocative discussion of conversion to philosophy.

On civic religious authority, see the papers in Beard and North 1990, and the further reading for civic cult in chapter 4 below. The main lines for the debate over belief can be found in Phillips 1986: 2697–711, Feeney 1998: 12–21, and King 2003. On religion and morality, see the brief discussion of Liebeschuetz 1979: 39–54.

CHAPTER 2

Regional Religious Traditions of the Empire

╔╝╔╝╔╝╔╝

In the year 197 CE, the North African writer Tertullian composed an impassioned attack on the Roman persecution of Christians. Among the many arguments he employed was the observation that it made no sense for imperial authorities to single out Christians, because they were otherwise untroubled by religious variety: "Each province and city has its own god: Syria has Astarte, Arabia Dusares, Noricum Belenus, Africa Caelestis, Mauretania its own princes"; the Egyptians even worship animals (*Apology* 24.7). Some 20 years earlier the Greek writer Athenagoras had made the same point in the defense of Christianity that he addressed to the emperors Marcus Aurelius and Commodus: "Your world, great emperors, employs different customs and laws in its different parts, and none of them is prevented by a law or the fear of a trial from loving its ancestral traditions, even if they are ridiculous"; on the contrary, "people conduct whatever sacrifices and mysteries they wish, according to their nation and district" (*Embassy for Christians* 1). Although these writers were more interested in supporting their arguments than in providing an objective assessment of contemporary conditions, their basic point was quite correct. The Graeco-Roman elite considered it normal for every people to have their own deities and religious traditions. Consequently, imperial authorities not only tolerated variety in local religious traditions, they even expected and, within limits, supported it.

In this chapter I sketch out some key features of the local religious traditions that existed within the Roman Empire, examining in turn the different major regions. Although for the sake of convenience I will talk of "regional religious traditions," there was in reality almost as much variety within these regions as between them. But since it would be impossible, even in a much longer book than this, to render accurately all the variety of local customs, I will instead simply trace some general patterns. My goal is two-fold. On the one hand, I want to emphasize the cultural and religious diversity that existed within the Roman Empire, from Egypt with its millennia-old traditions to the tribal societies of continental Europe, from the long established cities of the Greek world to the semi-nomadic peoples on the edge of the Sahara. On the other hand, I want to draw attention to the ways that regional traditions both differed from and conformed to the Graeco-Roman norm outlined in the previous chapter. Although the differences were at times a source of tension, as we shall see in chapter 7, the various traditions within the empire in fact shared a good deal of common ground, and this uniformity within diversity was one of the things that made possible the integration and stability of the empire.

1 Greece

As I have already suggested, the Greek religious tradition was by no means limited to Greece itself but was instead a dominant strand in the imperial norm. Its importance in the Mediterranean world was due in part to the steady expansion of Greek culture. From their original homeland in the Greek peninsula and the Aegean islands, Greeks had in very early times settled the Aegean coast of Asia Minor (modern Turkey) and had later, in the eighth to sixth centuries BCE, established colonies along the coasts of the northern Aegean, the Black Sea, Cyrenaica (the coast of eastern Libya), Sicily, southwestern Italy, and even southern Gaul. In the wake of Alexander the Great's conquests in the late fourth century BCE, Greek cities were founded in the ancient Near East, including most spectacularly Alexandria on the coast of Egypt. Greek culture, already widespread, thus became the culture of the elite throughout the eastern Mediterranean. Roman conquests helped spread Greek culture still further, since the Roman rulers regarded cities of the Greek type as essential to their govern-ance and so encouraged their foundation. In studying religion in the Roman Empire, it is important to keep in mind that Greek cities existed far beyond the boundaries of modern Greece, and that the influence of Greek traditions was even more pervasive.

We should also keep in mind that in the imperial period mainland Greece was something of a social and economic backwater, apart from Corinth, its commercial and administrative center, and Athens, which served in many ways as the chief "university town" of the empire. Some of the other cities had currency as tourist attractions, as the guidebook of Pausanias suggests, but the really vibrant area of Greek culture was western Asia Minor, where cities like Ephesus, Smyrna, and Pergamum reached a peak of wealth and brilliance in the second century CE. It is on this cultural heartland of the Greek peninsula and the Aegean coast of Asia Minor that I focus here.

The central religious institutions of the Greek tradition were part of the city-state or *polis*. Each *polis* had a set of public cults honoring a selection of the great traditional Greek gods, especially Athena, Zeus, Apollo, Poseidon, Hera, Artemis, Demeter, Dionysos, and Aphrodite. For two or three of these deities the city built large public temples; others might receive smaller shrines, altars, or statues. Public cults always included sacrifices and sometimes other rituals as well, which could take a wide variety of forms. The most important public cults incorporated major festivals celebrated on a regular schedule, either annually or every few years. Such festivals normally involved one or more elaborate processions, in which priests, magistrates, and other representatives took part, and sometimes included athletic, theatrical, or musical competitions as well. The entire citizen body was expected to participate in major public cults, mostly as spectators but in some cases more directly; civic officials, particularly priests, presided and offered the sacrifices on behalf of the people as a whole. Important cults often had their own sources of income that helped defray the costs of maintaining temples and funding sacrifices and festivals, such as user fees, rent from land owned by the temple, and gifts from wealthy benefactors. But it was ultimately a public responsibility to ensure that a public cult received proper funding.

Polis religion was the main structuring device in the Greek religious tradition. But participation in the public cults of his or her city by no means constituted the entirety of a person's religious life. On the one hand, individuals could and did pray to the gods and make offerings on their own behalf, as I stressed in chapter 1, even to gods who did not have a public cult in their city. On the other hand, there were important religious institutions in the Greek tradition whose scope extended far beyond the individual city. Three of these require particular comment.

In some cases, the cult of a city's major deity was opened to the citizens of other city-states, who could make offerings in the temple and participate in the chief festival; this was especially true when the festival involved athletic or musical competitions. The oldest and most famous of these was the cult of Zeus at Olympia in southern Greece, whose great festival, the original Olympic games, was according to tradition first held in 776 BCE. In the sixth century BCE three other cults acquired a similar standing: those of Apollo at Delphi (the Pythian games), Zeus at Nemea in the Peloponnese, and Poseidon near Corinth (the Isthmian games). These four sanctuaries and their associated festivals were "Panhellenic" (from Greek *pan*, "all," and *Hellenes*, "Greeks"), in that they were open to all Greeks; as Greek horizons expanded, even non-Greeks were allowed to make offerings in the temples and eventually compete in the games. Although by the beginning of the imperial period the ancient Panhellenic festivals were in decline, imperial patronage and cultural nostalgia led to a revival, so that by the second century CE Olympia in particular was a major tourist attraction. Moreover, their prestige was such that other Greek cities both in the Greek homeland and elsewhere desired to have their own Panhellenic games; in the Hellenistic and imperial periods, especially the third century CE, the number of such festivals multiplied almost to the point of absurdity, many of them proudly proclaimed to be "isolympian" or "iso-pythian," equal (Greek *isos*) in status to the Olympian and Pythian games.

The sanctuary of Apollo at Delphi was famous not only for the Pythian games, but also as the seat of one of the most important oracles in the Greek world. Oracles allowed people to receive from a god answers to specific questions. The means by which this was done varied considerably. In some cases, a priest or more often a priestess spoke as the mouthpiece of the god; this was what happened at Delphi and at the two major oracles of Apollo in Asia Minor, Didyma and Claros. Other oracles made use of lots, somewhat in the manner of the Chinese I Ching, and the travel writer Pausanias describes a minor oracle of Herakles that employed dice (*Description of Greece* 7.25.10). At the oracle of Trophonios at Lebadea, in central Greece, the petitioner lowered himself through a small hole into an underground cave and received the god's response in person, although exactly how is not recorded; Pausanias, however, who himself consulted Trophonios and reports on the process in detail, describes it as an awesome experience, so that the questioner was afterwards "paralyzed with terror and wholly unconscious both of himself and his surroundings" (*Description of Greece* 9.39.5–14). In earlier times it had been common for cities and rulers to consult the oracle at Delphi on political matters, but by the second century BCE that had largely come to an end. Indeed, Plutarch, who served as a priest there, wrote an entire dialogue discussing why oracles were no longer as active as they once were (*On the Cessation of Oracles*). In fact, oracles continued to be popular, but their scope was now largely restricted to the everyday concerns of private individuals: marriage, children, money, travel, and health. There were also inquiries about proper cult procedures and increasingly, it seems, about the nature of the divine. In the third century CE, the philosopher Porphyry gathered together many responses on the latter subject in his work *Philosophy from Oracles*, which suggests a convergence of this traditional cult practice with philosophical beliefs.

The third type of institution whose significance went beyond the individual *polis* was the mystery cult, a cult that involved secret initiatory rituals and the bestowal of particular blessings. By far the most famous mystery cult was that of Demeter and Kore at Eleusis near Athens, but there were others as well, such as those at Andania in the Peloponnese and those on the island of Samothrace in the northern Aegean. Because the rituals were secret, our knowledge of the details is necessarily limited, but in the case of Eleusis we have at least a fairly good idea of the general outline. The rites, which took place every fall, began with the new initiates purifying themselves by bathing in the sea and probably fasting. They then processed along the Sacred Way from Athens to Eleusis, where the mysteries themselves took place in the Telesterion, the great "hall of initiation" that could hold several thousand people at a time. There, in a darkness illuminated only by torchlight, certain things were said, done, and revealed; the only specific reports come from Christian writers of the second and third centuries CE, who had no qualms about profaning the secret, but they are brief and difficult to reconcile with one another. We can nevertheless deduce from these and other sources that the rites had some connection with fertility, death, and rebirth. Initiates were thought to receive great benefit; as it says in the *Homeric Hymn to Demeter*, "blessed is the mortal on earth who has seen these rites; but the uninitiate who has no share in them never has the same lot once dead in the dreary darkness" (480–2; trans. H. P. Foley). Mysteries, both at Eleusis and elsewhere, were open to people beyond the local community, initially to other Greeks and eventually to all civilized people, and they remained popular well into the imperial period. Eleusis in particular retained great prestige, and many members of the elite, including the emperors Augustus and Hadrian, were initiated there.

Panhellenic games, oracles, and mysteries were all to a greater or lesser extent part of *polis* religion: the shrines and cults remained the peculiar possessions of the host city, and non-citizens participated in them as guests. But some traditions existed outside the system entirely, and served as potential rivals or complements to it. As I have already discussed, philosophical views on the nature of the divine world diverged sharply from those implicit in *polis* religion. Most of the time the two coexisted peacefully, and many philosophers actually endorsed traditional cult practices. But on occasion there was tension, most notably in Athens in the late fifth century BCE, when several philosophers were prosecuted for holding opinions about the gods contrary to those of the city; Socrates is the most well known of these. There was also in the Greek tradition a range of free-lance religious specialists who claimed to have access to secret wisdom and who offered special services to private individuals; the best known of these employed writings attributed to the mythical poet Orpheus. In some cases there was overlap between these religious specialists and philosophers; many Orphic ideas, for example, seem to have been absorbed into the shadowy and ill-defined tradition that claimed to stem from the early philosopher Pythagoras. In chapter 6 I will discuss these phenomena in more detail, but it is important to remember that they too formed part of the Greek religious tradition.

2 Asia Minor

In the Graeco-Roman period the large area that corresponds to modern Turkey was inhabited by a bewildering mix of peoples: Bithynians, Phrygians, Lycians, Pisidians, Isaurians, Cilicians, and Cappadocians, just to name some of the most prominent. In addition, peoples from elsewhere had added to its diversity. Some two centuries of Persian rule (from the mid-sixth to the mid-fourth centuries BCE) had left their mark, particularly in the eastern areas, and in the mid-third century BCE invading Celtic tribes had settled the west central area that became known as Galatia (the Greek word *Galatai*, "Galatians," like Latin *Galli*, "Gauls," presumably came from the Celtic word that these people used for themselves). As noted in the previous section, Greeks had settled the Aegean coast at a very early date, and Greek influence had expanded more or less steadily ever since, especially in the west.

Despite this great cultural variety, however, it is possible to make a basic distinction between the largely Greek areas of the western coasts and the vast interior region known as Anatolia. This is by no means a sharp divide: even in the most Hellenized areas we can detect connections with the traditions of Anatolia, and the zones of interaction between the two were many and complex. It is nevertheless true that religious life along the Aegean coast tended to fall into the patterns that I described in the previous section, and so I have included it with that of the Greek mainland. In Anatolia, by contrast, cities on the Greek model became common only in the imperial period. Traditionally, the cultural and religious landscape was dominated instead by villages on the one hand and major shrines or "temple states" on the other, both of which I will discuss in more detail. It will be useful, however, to look first at some of the major regional deities or, rather, types of deities.

The type of deity most commonly associated with ancient Anatolia is the mother goddess, often called "the Mother of the Gods" (*Mêtêr Theôn* in Greek): a goddess especially of fertility and the wild whose powers were thought to extend over all aspects of life. Worshippers frequently identified the goddess they honored with an epithet linking her to a specific locale, often mountains; for example, we hear of a Mother Sipylene (for Mount Sipylos near Smyrna) and a Mother Dindymene (for Mount

Dindymon in western Anatolia). The cult of the latter goddess, also known as Cybele, is by far the best known. It originally centered on a major temple at Pessinus, where the chief priests were eunuchs, but was introduced into Rome and then spread throughout much of the Roman world. In Asia Minor itself, however, the worship of mother goddesses remained more localized and diverse. There are traces of it even in the Greek cities of the Aegean coast, where the great Artemis of Ephesus shows some parallels with Anatolian mother goddesses: she was depicted not as the virgin huntress of the mainstream Greek tradition, but in a rigidly hieratic pose with a headdress, heavy necklaces, numerous round protuberances over her upper body (probably part of her clothing rather than breasts, as often thought), and a tightly wrapped skirt covered with figures of animals (see Figure 2.1). Another Anatolian goddess of a very different sort was Ma, a goddess of war whose worship was popular especially in eastern Anatolia and whom the Romans identified with their own war goddess Bellona.

Even more popular than the mother goddess was Zeus. In most cases this Zeus was evidently not an import from Greece, but an indigenous deity given the name of the Greek god. He often had the character of a sky or weather god, as his epithets and iconography make clear, but is also found as a war god or a fertility god. Another deity whose worship was very widespread in central Asia Minor was the moon god Men, typically represented in a "Phrygian" cap (a soft cap folded over in front, associated by the Greeks and Romans with eastern peoples; for an example, see Figure 6.1) with the crescent moon behind him. In Phrygia, the most distinctive gods were *Hosios kai Dikaios*, "Holy and Just"; their cult was particularly widespread in villages. By contrast, the inhabitants of the mountainous southern regions of Pisidia and Isauria, known for their warlike character, worshipped warrior gods whom they typically portrayed as armed and mounted on horseback, and whom they variously identified with the Greek gods Ares, Poseidon, or Apollo (see Figure 5.1 for an example).

The Greeks were not the only foreign people to influence the religious traditions of Asia Minor. Unlike the Galatians, who apparently abandoned their native deities for those of the land in which they settled, the Persians left behind many reminders of their rule. According to the geographer Strabo, writing under the emperor Augustus, there were in his day still many *magoi*, members of a Persian priestly caste, active in the region of Cappadocia in eastern Anatolia, where they maintained traditional Persian fire-temples (*Geography* 15.3.15). More widely spread were the cults of Persian deities. The goddess Anahita (Hellenized as Anaitis) was worshipped well into the Roman period. More sporadically attested, but ultimately more important, is Mithra, a martial protector of covenants,

Figure 2.1 Alabaster and bronze statue of Artemis of Ephesus. Naples, Museo Nazionale inv. 6278, Cat. R 0665. Reproduced by permission of Alinari Archives, Florence

whose worship in Asia Minor was probably the source for the Roman mystery cult of Mithras.

Although similar sorts of deities were worshipped throughout Asia Minor, that worship took place in very different social contexts and consequently took very different forms. As noted above, the two main types of traditional social organization were temple states and villages. The latter were communities that tended to lack the defining institutions of the Greek *polis*, including civic cult of the sort described in the previous section. The absence of civic cult, however, did not mean the absence of worship. On the contrary, the gods were thought to be not merely present but actively involved in people's lives. The inhabitants of western and central Anatolia in particular, who were noted for their strict morality, often invoked the gods as dispensers of justice and enforcers of proper behavior. A type of inscription distinctive to this region is what is usually called a "confession stele," an account of a malefactor's punishment by a deity. A wide variety of misdeeds are represented, including criminal offenses like petty theft as well as infractions against the god. The following is a typical example of the latter kind: "To Zeus Sabazios and Mother Hipta; Diokles son of Trophimos: because I made an attempt on the gods' doves [presumably sacred doves kept in a sanctuary], I was punished in my eyes and inscribed [on this stele] an account of the gods' power" (Petzl 1994: no. 50). The idea that human misdeeds were an offense against the gods and brought down divine punishment is much more developed here than in the mainstream Graeco-Roman tradition, and seems very close to the idea of sin in the Jewish and Christian traditions; some scholars have seen a link between this local tradition and the morally rigorous form of Christianity, conventionally known as Montanism, that developed in western Anatolia in the latter half of the second century CE.

In addition to villages, there were large independent temples in Asia Minor, especially in central and eastern Anatolia, known in modern scholarship as "temple states"; among the most notable were those of Ma at Comana, Zeus at Venasa, Men at Cabeira, Anaitis at Zela, and Cybele at Pessinus. Here is how Strabo describes the first of these, in what at the time was the tributary kingdom of Cappadocia: "It is a notable *polis*, although populated mostly by the divinely inspired and by *hierodouloi* [sacred slaves]. Its inhabitants are Kataonians [a local people], ruled in general by the king [of Cappadocia], but subject in most respects to the priest [of Comana]. He is the master of the temple and the *hierodouloi*, who at the time of our stay numbered more than 6,000 men and women. A considerable territory also belongs to the temple, and the priest enjoys the revenue; this man is second in honor in Cappadocia after the king" (*Geography* 12.2.3). As Strabo's description suggests, a temple state like this differed from a typical city-state not so much in size as in the nature of the community and its relationship to its chief god: in the Graeco-Roman city state, the god is conceived almost as an especially honored fellow-citizen, whereas in a temple state the god, represented by the chief priest, functioned more as an absolute ruler or master.

Nevertheless, we should see temple states and *polis* cults in Asia Minor not as two sharply distinct categories but rather as the two ends of a spectrum. In many cities there were important civic cults that were based in temples outside the city proper, that owned significant property including slaves, and whose priests had interests distinguishable from those of the *polis*; even the cult of Artemis in Ephesus, as closely bound up with civic identity as it was, displays many of these features. Such powerful suburban sanctuaries might constitute an intermediary form between a temple state and a prototypical *polis* cult like that of Athena Polias in Athens. The picture is made even more complex by developments in the imperial period, when many formerly independent temples were either assigned to newly-founded cities or transformed into cities themselves. All the same, the idea of a "temple state" remains useful as a way to think about a type of cultic organization found both in Asia Minor and elsewhere.

3 Syria

Although the name "Syria" is now attached to a single Middle Eastern country, Greeks and Romans frequently applied it to the entire swath of territory stretching from the Taurus mountains in southern Turkey to the deserts of southern Israel and Jordan. The perception of cultural unity that underlay their use of the term had some basis in fact. Not only were there religious customs and conceptions common to the whole region, as we shall see, but there was also a more or less common language. Although the inhabitants traditionally spoke separate but related Semitic languages, starting in the early first millennium BCE, one of these, Aramaic, had gradually spread to become the lingua franca of the entire region. In the imperial period different dialects of Aramaic continued to be the language of the common people and even, in more remote areas, of public life. As elsewhere in the eastern Mediterranean, however, Greek had become the language of cities and the upper classes. One of the successors of Alexander the Great had taken Syria for his kingdom, resulting in both the foundation of new Greek cities, most notably Antioch in the north, and the general spread of Greek culture among the local elites; over time, many old Near Eastern cities reinvented themselves as Greek-style *poleis*.

Yet if Greeks and Romans had justification for the general term "Syria," they also recognized numerous sub-groupings. In the eastern fringes of the region, in what is now central Syria, was the caravan city of Palmyra, which retained its distinctive culture, deities, and language throughout the imperial period; Palmyrenes were in fact almost the only people who used their native language in inscriptions even when they were elsewhere in the empire. To the southeast were the Nabataeans, whose territory in what is now Jordan and southern Syria was annexed in the early second century CE as the province of Arabia; their national god Dushara, known in Greek and Latin as Dusares, was traditionally represented not by an anthropomorphic image but by abstract symbols. Two of these sub-groupings are particularly important in the present context: the Phoenicians, who inhabited the ancient cities along the Mediterranean coast from southern Syria to northern Israel, and the Jews or Judaeans, whose homeland was the area around Jerusalem, with related populations to the south in Idumaea and to the north in Samaria and Galilee. In what follows I first consider some general patterns of religious life, and then look briefly at these two sub-groupings.

One notable characteristic of this region was a tendency to worship a dominant high god, sometimes together with a female counterpart and sometimes alone. Worshippers frequently referred to their high god not by a proper name but by the title "Baal," a Semitic word that meant literally "master" or "lord." The nature of the high god differed somewhat from place to place, although he was often imagined as a god of storms and rain and, by extension, agricultural fertility. In almost all cases, however, he was regarded as a cosmic ruler, as is clear in the popular title Baal Shamin, "Lord of Heaven." As with the Anatolian mother goddesses, people frequently distinguished a particular god by a local epithet, especially the name of a mountain, such as Baal Saphon, "Lord of Saphon," a mountain south of Antioch. These high gods were typically called Zeus in Greek and Jupiter in Latin, often again with a distinguishing local epithet, so that in the imperial period, for example, we hear of Zeus Kasios, "Kasios" being the Greek name for Mount Saphon.

Three particular cults require special mention. Worshippers around the town of Doliche distinguished their *theos Dolichênos*, "God of Doliche," by an iconography that showed him standing on a bull, wearing a peaked cap, with a thunderbolt in one hand and a double-headed ax in the other; what is striking is that the same iconography is found in local reliefs dating to the period 1200–700 BCE. In the imperial period, the cult of this god, under the name Jupiter Dolichenus, spread widely, mostly among soldiers. Another cult that became popular in the Roman army was that of Jupiter Heliopolitanus, the god of the town called Heliopolis in Greek and Baalbek in Semitic. A massive temple was built here during the imperial period, the impressive remains of which survive to this day. Two other deities, named Venus and Mercury in Latin inscriptions, had temples in the same city; some scholars have argued that the three constituted a triad of native deities, but the evidence is slight and the cult can in fact be traced back only to the Hellenistic period. The third cult is that of the god Elagabal at Emesa, who was regarded as a sun god and whose cult image was not an anthropomorphic statue but a large black stone. The earliest evidence for his worship dates only to the first century CE, but the cult rose to prominence along with the local elite. Its fortunes reached their zenith when Julia Domna, from one of the elite families of Emesa, married Septimius Severus, who became emperor (193–211 CE); the eventual result was that a priest of the cult actually became emperor himself, conventionally called Elagabalus after his god (218–22 CE). During his brief reign he transferred the cult stone to Rome and tried to establish Elagabal as the chief deity of the empire, although his attempt had no lasting impact.

The people of this region worshipped not only a high god but also a high goddess, sometimes together with the god and sometimes independently. As with the god, the character of the high goddess varied from place to place, although she was normally associated with water and fertility; again like the god, she was frequently described as the "Queen of Heaven." By far the most famous such goddess was Atargatis, whom Greek and Latin speakers often simply called "the Syrian Goddess" and whose sanctuary was at Hierapolis in what is now northern Syria. The Greek satirist Lucian left a lengthy account of this shrine and its cult, which Atargatis shared with a consort whom Lucian calls Zeus and another god he calls Apollo. Here is part of his description of the inner sanctuary and the cult statues:

> All may enter the large temple, but only the priests the inner chamber: not, however, all the priests, but only those closest to the gods and whose every care is the temple. In it are enthroned the cult statues, Hera [Lucian's name for Atargatis] and the god, Zeus, whom they call by a different name. Both are golden, both seated, though Hera is borne on lions, the other sits on bulls. . . . In one hand she has a scepter, in the other a spindle, and on her head she wears rays, a tower, and the decorative band with which they adorn the Heavenly Goddess alone. (*On the Syrian Goddess* 31–2, trans. adapted from Lightfoot 2003)

Other evidence indicates that the Semitic name for the god of Hierapolis was Hadad, a weather god whose name can be traced back to the early second millennium BCE. The name "Atargatis," in contrast, dates only to the Hellenistic period, but apparently derives from the combination of two much more ancient names of goddesses, Ashtart and Anat.

In addition to characteristic types of deities, a few distinctive religious customs seem to have been widespread throughout Syria. One of these is the tradition of aniconic worship, the rejection of anthropomorphic images of the gods. I have already noted that Elagabal was represented by a large black stone instead of a statue, and the same custom is widely attested throughout the region; modern writers describe this sort of cult object as a betyl, from a Greek word that may derive from the Semitic *bethel*, "house of god." In other cases, the altar itself seems to have represented the god. Although anthropomorphic statues were clearly the norm, as we have seen with Jupiter Dolichenus and Atargatis, the widely scattered evidence for aniconic worship nevertheless suggests a distinctive regional tradition. The most famous example is of course Jewish cult, which strictly rejected all representations of the deity. Other customs that most people associate with Jewish tradition, such as circumcision and prohibitions against pork, were likewise found elsewhere in this region. For example, the historian Cassius Dio claims that the emperor Elagabalus circumcised himself and abstained from pork, explaining the former as a requirement of his priesthood (*History* 79.11.1); according to Josephus, circumcision was a general practice for the Arabs as for the Jews (*Judaean Antiquities* 1.214), and the philosopher Porphyry associates the Phoenicians with the Jews in rejecting pork (*On Abstinence* 1.14.4).

Of the two important sub-groupings that I mentioned at the start of this section, the Phoenicians display several striking parallels with the Greeks: they were divided into several independent city-states with distinct identities, of which the most important were Byblos, Sidon, and Tyre, and they were a great sea-faring people, trading and establishing settlements all over the Mediterranean in the early first millennium BCE. As with the Greeks, each city had its own chief deities who together formed a kind of pantheon. In Byblos the chief deity was a goddess called simply Baalat, "Lady," whose cult dated back to the early Bronze Age; Lucian calls her Aphrodite, and associates her with the young Adonis, whose death and rebirth the people celebrated annually (*On the Syrian Goddess* 6–8). The patron deity of Sidon was also a goddess, Astarte, with whom was associated the healing god Eshmun, and the god of Tyre was Melqart, called Herakles in Greek. All these cults had a presence in the broader Mediterranean as well. The cult of Adonis was celebrated in Athens already in the fifth century BCE, and is in fact better known in its Greek than in its Phoenician context; the other cults are found chiefly in areas of Phoenician settlement.

The most familiar religious tradition in this region is of course that of the Jews or Judaeans; the English word "Jew" derives via Latin *Iudaeus* from Greek *Ioudaios*, a Hellenized form of the Hebrew *Yehudi*, "member of the tribe of Judah." It is important to keep in mind that in antiquity the Jews were perceived, both by themselves and by others, as a distinct people with a national homeland, comparable to the Greeks or Romans or Egyptians. As a way of emphasizing that fact, I will in the remainder of this book refer to them by the ancient term "Judaeans" rather than the modern term "Jews." As I have already suggested, the Judaean tradition can to some extent be seen as a particular version of the larger regional tradition; at the same time, however, it had some special features that made it unique. Like other peoples of Roman Syria, the Judaeans worshipped a high god whom they regarded as the ruler of heaven and whose cult centered on a major temple; but unlike other peoples, they elaborated on the power and importance of their god to the point of denying that other gods had any significance whatsoever. The Judaeans also differed from other peoples in possessing a set of sacred writings that combined a historical account of their relationship to their god with a body of moral, cultic, and social regulations regarded as divine commands. It is in fact largely due to these sacred scriptures and to the Judaean writers who commented on them that we are more richly informed about the Judaean religious tradition than almost any other in the empire. Adherence to the divine commands contained in these scriptures was one of the defining features of Judaean identity in the Graeco-Roman period, and often put Judaeans at odds with their neighbors; I discuss this topic further in chapter 7.

4 Egypt

As with the rest of the ancient Near East, Alexander the Great conquered Egypt in the late fourth century BCE; after his death his general Ptolemy assumed the kingship of the country and founded a dynasty that endured until his last descendant Cleopatra was defeated by the Roman emperor Augustus in 31 BCE. These three centuries of Greek rule left their mark, but to a lesser extent than elsewhere. For one thing, apart from Alexandria, there were almost no Greek cities; the population instead lived mostly in towns and villages. Among the well-to-do, as elsewhere, Greek language and culture acquired considerable prestige, and papyri suggest that by the Roman period Greek was the normal language of business and personal correspondence. Yet native Egyptian traditions remained very strong, and we can trace continuity in language, religious practices and beliefs, and even particular cult sites more clearly in Egypt than anywhere else in the Roman Empire. In this section I survey a few major features of the Egyptian religious tradition and then briefly consider some of the changes that took place under Greek and Roman rule.

Because Egypt had for many centuries been a politically unified country, its pantheon too was in many ways much more unified than those in Asia Minor or Syria. One of the most important deities was the sun god Re, who from a very early period was closely associated with the Pharaoh. There was also a close link between the Pharaoh and Osiris, the god of the dead: the Pharaoh at his death was thought to become Osiris, while his son and successor was identified with Osiris' son Horus. Isis, the consort of Osiris and the mother of Horus, was the third key member of this group. Other major gods included Amun, sometimes regarded as king of the gods; the creator god Ptah, the patron deity of craftsmen; and Thoth, the god of language and learning. Yet the Egyptian pantheon was by no means stable and universal. In addition to the great gods, there were many important local gods, of whom one of the best attested is Sobek, the crocodile god worshipped in the Fayum. Even the great gods were in a significant sense local gods, whose worship centered on major temples: that of Re at Onu (called Heliopolis in Greek), Amun at Thebes (modern Karnak and Luxor), Ptah at Memphis, and Thoth at Khmunu (Hermopolis Magna in Greek). A counterweight to this localism was the tendency to link together the various deities: Amun and Re, for example, were sometimes regarded as different forms of the same god.

Like other peoples of the ancient Near East, the Egyptians imagined their gods in human form. But they also closely associated certain gods with animals, in some cases to the point that they regarded the animal as an embodiment of the god: Thoth, for example, was linked with the ibis and the baboon, as Horus was with the falcon. This tradition underlay the widespread practice of depicting certain gods with the heads of their associated animals; for example, Thoth with the head of an ibis or Horus with that of a falcon. A related practice that greatly increased in popularity during the Graeco-Roman period was the mummification of sacred animals, which took place on a staggering scale: upwards of half a million falcons at Memphis, for example. Many of the papyri that throw such invaluable light on Egypt in Graeco-Roman times come in fact from the wrappings of crocodile mummies found in towns of the Fayum. A few deities had no form other than that of an animal. The most famous example is the Apis bull, a fertility god in Memphis. An Apis bull was a living bull, distinguished by particular markings as the incarnation of the god; when one died, the priests buried it with great ceremony and sought out the calf that was to be its successor. The Egyptian tradition of depicting some gods in animal or mixed animal–human form was something that regularly aroused amusement or contempt among Greek and Roman observers; the disgust expressed by Tertullian in the passage cited at the beginning of this chapter was by no means limited to Christians. On the contrary, when Augustus declined an invitation to visit the Apis bull with the quip that he was accustomed to worship gods and not cattle (Cassius Dio, *History* 51.16.5), he was expressing an attitude widespread among the elite of the empire.

Traditional Egyptian cult took place largely in temples. The largest of these were vast complexes whose construction had extended over many centuries and which served as major population centers; the ruins of the temples of Amun at Thebes give some idea of the size that they could reach. Such immense temples were obviously exceptional, and some of them, including those in Thebes, were already in decline in the Roman period. But even small villages could boast numerous shrines, some of surprising size and complexity. In the village of Karanis in the Fayum, for example, with a population of perhaps 4,000 people, there were in the second century CE at least two major temples. The better preserved of these, dedicated to the crocodile god Sobek, was some 15 by 22 meters in area and consisted of numerous small rooms surrounding two courtyards, in one of which was the actual sanctuary with an altar and the image of the god. The temple itself was located within a walled precinct some 75 by 60 meters that enclosed a variety of other buildings as well. Relative to the size of its village, this temple was clearly a major institution and, as the evidence of papyri indicates, the focus of considerable activity. Many temples owned significant amounts of land and sponsored associated commercial activities like weaving and brewing (Bowman 1986: 171–2).

But the chief business of a temple was of course the worship of the gods. In sharp contrast to the Greek tradition, this involved an elaborate daily ritual centering on the cult statue. The priests opened the sanctuary in the morning, greeted and praised the deity, cleaned and clothed the divine image, and offered it a sacred meal. After other rituals throughout the day, they closed the sanctuary again for the night. In addition to these daily services, there were periodic festivals in which temple attendants carried the cult statue in a public procession. These rituals, together with the administration of the temples and their property, were in the care of the priests, who formed a distinct caste within Egyptian society. The priesthood was hereditary, in that only the sons of priests could normally become priests. Candidates had to demonstrate proficiency in reading the ancient Egyptian language and scripts, were circumcised before taking office, and thereafter kept themselves ritually pure by shaving their heads, wearing only linen, and maintaining a special diet. In the Roman period, priests were forbidden to engage in private business, but instead received a salary. They were divided into different classes according to their particular roles: prophets, robers, sacred scribes, singers, and so forth. There was a sharp distinction between priests proper and other temple attendants, such as the *pastophoroi* who carried the divine image in the processions; the latter were forbidden by law from acting as priests.

The fact that the formal cult of the gods was conducted by ritually pure priests within temples meant that the general population mostly had little to do with it; people outside the temple normally saw the cult statues only during festival processions. To some extent, acting as spectators on these occasions was the limit of popular participation in formal cult. But this was by no means the limit of popular religion. As elsewhere, people sought blessings and oracular responses from the gods; sometimes there were mechanisms to allow such activities when the cult statue was publicly accessible during festivals, and sometimes people presented their petitions and inquiries at the temples themselves, often with the priests acting as intermediaries. There were also gods whose worship was found more among ordinary people than in the temples. One of the most popular gods in the Graeco-Roman period was Bes, depicted as a grotesque dwarf with goggle eyes, a protruding tongue, and a bushy tail. Bes was worshipped as a protective deity, providing safety from misfortune and evil influences, and invoked especially as a guarantor of safe childbirth. People could gain access to the blessings of Bes and other gods not only through private worship and prayer but also through representations of them in small figurines and amulets; the large numbers of these that have been found throughout Egypt indicate that the cultivation of the gods was by no means limited to the formal cult of the temples.

As I noted at the start of this section, the centuries of Greek and Roman rule certainly had an impact on traditional Egyptian religion, although it was more limited than in many parts of the empire. In some regions, particularly the Fayum, the worship of Greek gods became popular, with temples, priests, and rituals of the usual Greek sort existing alongside traditional Egyptian cults. As elsewhere, people made equivalencies between Greek and native deities, identifying Amun, for example, with Zeus, and Thoth with Hermes; in many respects, these equivalencies simply extended the long-standing tendency to make identifications among traditional Egyptian deities. One of the most important gods of the Graeco-Roman period, the god Sarapis, was apparently the product of this sort of process; his name is generally thought to derive from the combination of "Osiris" and "Apis." Despite this Egyptian derivation, Sarapis was from the first conceived largely in Greek terms; his cult was patronized by the Greek rulers of Egypt and eventually became popular throughout the Roman world. Even more popular was the cult of Isis, sometimes in association with Sarapis but more commonly on her own. In Egypt itself, the Greek kings and the Roman emperors took on the role of Pharaoh, and were honored as such by the priests according to traditional forms well into the third century CE. The emperors in turn upheld the traditional privileges of the priests. At the same time, they tended to curtail their wealth and subject them to strict regulation; imperial officials oversaw admission to the priesthood and supervised priestly activities. Nevertheless, priests maintained the influence they had as the chief intermediaries between people and the gods, and were even able to exploit to their advantage the romantic Graeco-Roman view of them as the guardians of secret wisdom, as we shall see in chapter 6.

5 North Africa

The Greeks and Romans made a sharp distinction between Egypt and the land they called "Africa," which for them meant the southern coast of the Mediterranean with its hinterland stretching into the desert. In contrast to the ancient civilization and political unity of Egypt, the native peoples of North Africa, whose language was related to modern Berber, maintained a tribal organization and in some regions a nomadic or semi-nomadic way of life. Unlike Egypt and the rest of the eastern Mediterranean, Africa had never been conquered by Alexander the Great or been under Greek rule. In fact, apart from Cyrenaica, there was no Greek settlement in Africa at all. Starting in the ninth century BCE, however, there had been extensive Phoenician settlement along the coast from what is now western Libya to eastern Algeria. The cities founded by the Phoenicians became major commercial centers, and the most important of them, Carthage, became Rome's greatest rival in the western Mediterranean. The Romans called these people *Punici* (the Latin form of the Greek term *Phoinikes*, "Phoenicians"); from this Latin name comes the modern term "Punic," which is used to describe the Phoenician culture of North Africa and the rest of the western Mediterranean. Just as Greek language and culture spread through Asia Minor and Syria, so Punic language and culture spread through North Africa. Although the Romans destroyed Carthage in the mid-second century BCE and assumed direct rule of the area around it, Punic culture remained dominant until the late first century BCE. Thereafter, with the refoundation of Carthage as a Roman colony and an influx of Italian settlers, local elites began to abandon Punic for Latin, and as a result much of the evidence for religion in the imperial period seems at first sight very "Roman."

In a few cases we encounter deities under their pre-Roman names. For example, two sites in Numidia have yielded dedications to a deity called Bacax, often associated with caves, and to Baliddir, a Latinized form of the Punic Baal Addir, "Powerful Lord." But such cases are exceptional. In general, as people began to adopt the Latin language, they adopted Roman names for their gods. At times we can trace this process in some detail. In Lepcis Magna, for example, where Punic was used in public inscriptions alongside Latin to the end of the first century CE, the chief cults were those of the old Phoenician deities Milk'Ashtart and Shadrapa; in the imperial period the cults continued, but the gods were called by the Roman names Hercules and Liber Pater. In other cases, distinctive features in the evidence indicate a regional cult with presumably a long history, even if we do not know the pre-Roman name of the deity.

For example, there are numerous dedications to Neptune at or near springs, suggesting that people used "Neptune" as the name for a local god of springs. The relative scarcity of rainfall meant that springs were important features of the landscape, and it is not surprising that spring-gods should be a focus of worship. Even more important were deities of agricultural fertility. For example, there is considerable evidence for the cult of Pluto, the Greek name for the god of the underworld conceived as the bestower of agricultural wealth. Similarly, there are numerous dedications to a god called only "Frugifer," a Latin adjective that means literally "crop-bearer." Since elsewhere in the Latin-speaking parts of the empire the cult of Pluto is unattested and the title Frugifer never occurs on its own, it seems clear that in both cases we have a local and no doubt pre-Roman god of agriculture. A particularly interesting case is that of the goddesses called the "Cereses." Ceres was an old Italic goddess of grain, but the plural form of the name is virtually unparalleled outside Africa. It seems to have been a local development of the Greek cult of Demeter and Kore, which the Carthaginians introduced from Sicily in the early fourth century BCE (Diodorus Siculus, *Library* 14.77.4–5). Over the centuries the cult became naturalized and spread widely, and by the imperial period was quite popular; a number of inscriptions survive which commemorate women described as *magnae sacerdotes*, "great priestesses," of the cult. All these cults reflect the crucial importance of agriculture in the economy and society of Roman North Africa.

By far the two most important deities of Roman Africa, however, were Saturn and Caelestis. In both cases there is clear continuity with the two major deities of Punic Carthage, Baal Hammon and Tanit. Since neither deity is well attested in the Phoenician homeland, the origins and meaning of their Punic names are disputed, although it seems likely that Tanit had some connection with Astarte. It is clear enough, however, that they were examples of the Syrian high god and goddess discussed above. In the Punic period, their worship centered on open-air sacrificial areas conventionally known as tophets. Although the one in Carthage is best known, tophets have also been found at other Punic sites in Africa, Sicily, and Sardinia. It was in the tophet that the most notorious rite in the cult of Baal Hammon and Tanit took place – that of child sacrifice: worshippers burned the bodies of small children and ritually buried their remains in urns, over which they erected carved steles commemorating their offerings to the gods. Although some scholars have argued strongly that these children died of natural causes before their bodies were burned, the evidence makes it overwhelmingly likely that many, if not all, of them were actually sacrificed. The Romans, however, regarded human sacrifice as barbaric, and by the end of the first century BCE the ritual seems to have been replaced by the "sacrifice of substitution," in which lambs and kids took the place of children.

The worship of Baal Hammon and Tanit itself continued to thrive. The Romans identified the great goddess of Carthage with their own Juno, as we see in Vergil's *Aeneid*. In Africa itself, however, her worshippers preferred the epithet Caelestis, "the Heavenly One," a usage that may reflect the ancient Semitic title "the Queen of Heaven." In the second century CE, the cult of Caelestis seems to have been officially re-introduced into Carthage, and by the end of the century, she had become its chief civic deity. Elsewhere in Africa, however, the cult of Saturn was more important. Although amply attested in the towns and cities, its chief centers were rural open-air sanc- tuaries, which have yielded hundreds of dedicatory steles: for example, some 600 from a sanctuary across the bay from Carthage and more than 500 from another further inland. We again find reminiscences of ancient Syrian tradition. The sanctuary near Carthage is on a distinctive double-peaked mountain that dominates the bay, and the dedications to Saturn there give him the distinctive epithet "Balcaranensis," a Latin adjective that derives from the Punic name Baal Qarnem, "Lord of the Two Horns": the high god here clearly took his name from the local mountain just as Baal Saphon/Zeus Kasios did near Antioch. That Saturn was worshipped as the bestower of agricultural fertility is clear from votive reliefs that depict him presiding over the prosperous farms of his devotees (see Figure 3.1 for an example). He was also regarded as the ruler of heaven and earth; his most common epithet in inscriptions is *dominus*, "lord," a Latin term that recalls the Semitic title "Baal." Caelestis and Saturn remained the chief gods of Africa throughout the Roman period, and seem to have aroused intense devotion on the part of their worshippers.

6 Western Europe

Although western Europe never constituted a unity in Roman times, certain distinctive features of religious life repeatedly appear in the territory from the Atlantic coast to the Rhine and the upper Danube, as well as Britain; for this reason it is convenient to treat this entire region together. In part, these shared features result from the spread of the cultural tradition usually labeled "Celtic." We can identify two main phases in this development. In the first half of the first millennium BCE, the Celtic language gradually spread through western Europe, so that by about 600 BCE it was spoken throughout much of this entire region. The second phase began about 450 BCE with the development of a distinctly Celtic material culture in what is now northeastern France and southern Germany. Rapid social and economic developments led to the mass movement of peoples from this homeland into northern Italy, eastern Europe, and even, as I have already mentioned, Asia Minor. As a result of these two phases of expansion, Celtic cultural traditions existed in many parts of Europe, although they were strongest in Gaul and Britain.

More or less simultaneous with Celtic expansion in the continent was the spread of Greek and Phoenician colonization along the Mediterranean coasts. The main area of Greek settlement was on the coast of southeastern Gaul, especially Massalia (modern Marseilles). The major Phoenician foundations were on the southwestern coast of Spain, notably Gades (modern Cádiz). This area of Phoenician settlement eventually fell under the sway of Carthage, which came to control much of southern Spain. As a result of its wars with Carthage, Rome took over this territory at the end of the third century BCE, and then gradually expanded into continental Europe. By the end of the first century, it controlled much of the Iberian peninsula as well as southern Gaul, and in the 50s BCE Julius Caesar extended Roman rule through the rest of Gaul up to the Rhine; a century later, under the emperor Claudius, the Romans began their conquest of Britain.

As a result of these historical developments, we can make a general distinction between the highly Romanized regions along the Mediterranean coast, where the influence of the Greek and Phoenician urban cultures extended back for centuries, and the less Romanized northern regions. In the coastal regions the evidence for indigenous religious traditions tends to be somewhat slighter than in the north, no doubt because imported religious traditions were much more firmly established. We may note for example the cult of the Tyrian god Melqart at Gades, who was known in Roman times as Hercules Gaditanus and whose temple was famous throughout the empire. In terms of religion, we can make another general distinction between the Iberian peninsula on the one hand, and Gaul and Britain on the other, which shared a number of characteristically Celtic traditions. In what follows, I will first discuss some religious traditions common to the entire region, and then look separately at the Iberian peninsula and at Gaul and Britain.

As in North Africa, the peoples of western Europe usually worshipped their gods under Roman names; unlike the peoples of North Africa, however, they frequently used indigenous names as well, either on their own or in combination with a Roman name (for example, Sulis Minerva or Apollo Grannus). As a result, it is often fairly clear when a deity has roots in local tradition. Yet even apart from the evidence of names, we can easily identify some characteristic regional traditions. Chief among these was a strong association of the divine with trees. A number of Greek and Roman authors refer to sacred groves as important centers for worship and assembly. The Celtic word for such a grove was *nemeton*, which shows up in place names from Nemetobriga in northwestern Spain to Nemetodurum in Gaul (now the Parisian suburb of Nanterre) to Aquae Arnemetiae in Britain (modern Buxton); according to Strabo (*Geography* 12.5.1), the Galatians of Asia Minor assembled at a place called Drunemeton, a word that apparently means "the sacred oak grove." Of equal importance was the veneration of water. The practice of depositing offerings in lakes and rivers, especially armor and weapons, was well-established and widespread in pre-Roman times, and in the Roman period water-deities continued to be widely worshipped. Particularly characteristic are goddesses associated with springs. A fairly typical example is the shrine of Coventina at Carrowburgh on Hadrian's Wall, consisting of a walled enclosure around a sacred well into which coins and other objects were thrown as offerings. Much more elaborate was the shrine of Sulis at Aquae Sulis (modern Bath), where the hot springs formed the center of an extensive complex that included both a temple and massive bath buildings; again, thousands of coins and other offerings have been found in the spring. A final example is the goddess Sequana, the personification of the Seine, whose shrine at the river's source northwest of Dijon was the site of an important healing cult, as indicated by the large numbers of carved wooden offerings representing various body parts that have been discovered there.

Other types of deities were also widespread. A number of native gods were identified with the Roman Mars, one of the gods most frequently invoked in dedications. In Gaul, he appears in a number of inscriptions as Mars Teutates (or Toutatis), a name that derives from *teuta*, the Celtic word for "tribe"; he is thus "the god of the tribe." In the area of Hadrian's Wall we find Mars Cocidius; in Noricum there is Mars Latobius, a name evidently connected with the tribe of the Latobici. Although the association with Mars makes it tempting to interpret these local deities simply as warrior gods, other evidence indicates that they had power over a range of areas, especially agriculture. Equally widespread are the goddesses called Matres ("Mothers") or Matronae ("Matrons"), often with an epithet linking them to a particular tribe or locale (for example, the Matres Aufaniae or the Matres Vallabneihiae); they are commonly depicted in reliefs sitting on thrones and holding baskets of fruits and other provisions, implying an association with agricultural fertility. Although they occur as individuals, in pairs, and in small groups, the most distinctive reliefs depict a set of three, calling to mind the characteristically Celtic interest in triads. The two main centers of their worship were northern Italy and the Rhineland, but dedications occur widely.

Another characteristic of religious life throughout much of western Europe is the important role of animals, both domesticated (bulls, horses, dogs) and wild (boars, deer). Animals are repeatedly depicted in religious contexts, sometimes in association with particular deities. Some evidence suggests that animals were thought to have a particularly close connection with the divine or the underworld. The rebel Roman general Sertorius, who built up a power base among the native peoples of Spain in the 70s BCE, kept a white deer that he claimed provided him with secret information about current and future events (Plutarch, *Sertorius* 11); although this was no doubt in some respects just a ploy on his part, he presumably developed it in response to genuine local beliefs. Like Greeks and Romans, the peoples of western Europe practiced animal sacrifice, and tended to sacrifice roughly the same sorts of animals. There were, however, some differences: in certain areas, for example, horses were sacrificed. The most spectacular deviation of this sort was the sacrifice of human beings, a practice that Greek and Roman writers repeatedly attribute to the indigenous peoples of western Europe; the poet Lucan, for example, provides a lurid description of a sacred grove in Gaul in which "the altars are set with dreadful offerings, and every tree is sanctified with human gore" (*Civil War* 3.404–5). Although these writers may have elaborated such stories in order to exaggerate the barbarism of the European peoples, archaeological evidence suggests that human sacrifice did indeed take place in pre-Roman times. Roman authorities, however, put an end to the practice, leading Pliny the Elder to exclaim proudly that "it is beyond calculation how much is owed to the Romans, who did away with unnatural rites, in which to kill a man was the most religious of acts" (*Natural History* 30.13).

Although the traditions that I have described so far existed in some form throughout western Europe, each region had its own characteristics as well. The religious traditions of the Iberian peninsula were in many ways quite distinct from those in the other parts of western Europe. Inscriptions have yielded the names of several hundred indigenous deities, most known from only one or two examples and not attested elsewhere. One rare exception is Conventena, a goddess known from dedications in northwestern Spain, whose name is strikingly close to the British Coventina.

Because of the scanty evidence, we can say little about most of these deities. The god Endovellicus, however, appears in some one hundred inscriptions from Lusitania; the imagery used on his altars suggests that he was a god of the underworld. Recent excavations at a major shrine of the god, at a site east of Lisbon near the Spanish border, indicate occupation only during the Roman period, despite the obviously pre-Roman origin of the deity. Distinctive to the eastern coast of Spain are sacred caves, which have revealed numerous offerings of coins and small ceramic cups; these may also have been associated with the worship of an underworld deity.

The evidence for the Celtic religious tradition of Gaul and Britain is much richer than for those of the Iberian peninsula. The distinctive nature of this tradition is apparent, for example, in the use of characteristic iconographic motifs, such as the human head, an image clearly imbued with great religious significance. It is also apparent in the distinctive forms of Romano-Celtic temples, consisting of a central tower-like building, often square but sometimes circular or polygonal, surrounded by a portico. Hundreds of such temples have been identified in Gaul and Britain, the majority in the countryside or small towns; a number of them had nearby theaters and hostels, suggesting that they served as places of pilgrimage and assembly.

Celtic deities are known from Greek and Latin literary sources, from Latin inscriptions, and from later Irish and Welsh myth, although the various types of evidence are not always easy to correlate. According to Caesar (*The Gallic War* 6.17), the Gauls worshipped Mercury in particular, followed by Apollo, Mars, Jupiter, and Minerva; inscriptions show that Jupiter and Mercury were indeed the gods most often invoked, with Mars and Apollo making impressive showings as well. I have already discussed the worship of Mars, and Caesar's Minerva was probably a goddess like Sulis at Bath, who was regularly identified with Minerva. Caesar describes the Gallic Mercury as the "inventor of all the arts," and some scholars have suggested a connection with the Irish god Lug, also a patron of the arts, whose worship is attested in Gaul by the place-name Lugdunum, "fortress of Lug." Caesar's Jupiter was presumably the sky god Taranis, whose name derives from the Celtic word *taran*, "thunder"; images of Jupiter in Gaul and Britain often depict him with a wheel, an ancient Celtic symbol of the sun. His Apollo was probably a healing god, such as Apollo Grannus, whose cult extended widely from northern Gaul to the Danube, and whose aid was sought by the emperor Caracalla during a serious illness (Cassius Dio, *History* 77.15.6). But not all Celtic deities were given Roman names. So, for example, the horse goddess Epona and the god Sucellus, characteristically depicted holding a hammer, kept their own distinct names and attributes. Indeed, Epona, whose name derives from the Celtic word for "horse," is one of the few Celtic deities to enter into the general Graeco-Roman pantheon, where she took on the role of a goddess of the stable; the Latin novelist Apuleius (*The Golden Ass* 3.27) mentions quite casually the presence of a shrine to Epona in a stable in central Greece, and just such a shrine has been found in the Italian town of Pompeii (see Figure 4.3).

The most distinctive feature of Celtic religious organization, and one of the most widely known aspects of Celtic civilization in general, was the class of men known as Druids. Etymologically, the word "Druid" seems to derive from the roots *dru-*, "oak," and *wid-*, "to know" (whence also English "wisdom"). The implication that the Druids were wise men is amply confirmed by the accounts of Greek and Roman writers, which are our main source of information. The most detailed is that found in Caesar's *Gallic War* (see Text Box 2.1). According to this, the Druids formed a separate and privileged caste in Celtic society; they derived their authority from

---

Text Box 2.1

Caesar, *The Gallic War* 6.13–14 (selections)

Throughout Gaul, anyone with any status and position belongs to one of two groups: [the Druids and the knights]. The former are involved in matters concerning the gods, oversee public and private sacrifices, and explain religious obligations. A large number of young men gather around them because of their teaching and hold them in great honor. They make the decisions in virtually all disputes, public and private, and if a crime has been committed, if a murder has been done, if there is a dispute about inheritance or borders, they are the ones who pass judgment and determine awards and punishments. . . . The Druids keep apart from war and do not pay taxes along with the rest. They are exempt from military service and immune from all public obligations. Enticed by such great benefits, many men come under their tutelage, either of their own accord or sent by parents and relatives. There they are said to learn by heart a great number of verses; consequently, quite a few continue in their training for twenty years. They do not think it lawful to entrust their teaching to writing, although in most other matters, both public and private business, they use the Greek script. . . . The most vital element of their doctrine is that souls do not die, but after death pass from one body to another; they believe that this is what most stimulates men to courage, causing them to dismiss the fear of death. Furthermore, they have many discussions about the heavenly bodies and their motions, the size of the universe and the earth, the nature of the physical world, and the essence and power of the immortal gods, and they pass on these teachings to their pupils.

specialized knowledge of the cosmos and the divine world, which could be acquired only through lengthy and laborious study. The Druids thus appear to have been religious authorities of a sort unknown in the Graeco-Roman tradition, combining what Greeks and Romans would have regarded as the different functions of priests, poets, and philosophers. But the accuracy of the Graeco-Roman accounts of the Druids is very uncertain, for they are all more or less heavily influenced by stereotyped ideas about "barbarian wisdom," a topic that I discuss further in chapter 6. Whatever the real nature of the Druids, it is clear from other sources that under Roman rule they soon either disappeared entirely or went underground, apparently as the result of a Roman ban on their activities. The reason for Roman hostility to the Druids has long been disputed, with some scholars emphasizing their association with human sacrifice and others regarding them as leaders of Gallic resistance to Roman culture. Whatever the reason for their disappearance, it is likely that much traditional wisdom disappeared along with them, although many other Celtic traditions survived, if often in new forms.

7 *Eastern Europe*

The indigenous peoples of the ancient Balkans are conventionally classed into two large groups: the Illyrians to the west and the Thracians to the east, with Dacians north of the Danube in what is now Romania. Greek colonization along the northern Aegean and Black Sea coasts from the eighth century BCE onwards led to increased interaction with Thracians; by the Hellenistic period, the southern part of Thrace was under Greek control. In the west, the Celtic migrations of the fourth and third centuries BCE led to a considerable admixture of Celtic culture among the Dacians and many Illyrian tribes. For the most part, however, the peoples of the Balkans remained fairly resistant to external influences and had a reputation for being very warlike. It was in fact Illyrian piracy that led to the first Roman campaigns in the late third century BCE; thereafter Roman military interventions in the region gradually increased, although it was only in the late first century BCE that the Roman presence began to be permanent. Things then developed quickly, and the emperor Augustus pushed the boundary of the empire all the way back to the Danube. After a major uprising in the early first century CE, the area remained peaceful enough, although Roman culture at first spread slowly. In the first decade of the second century, the emperor Trajan conquered Dacia, the last province to be added to the Roman Empire and, in 270 CE, the first to be abandoned.

Evidence for indigenous religious traditions in this region, and indeed for indigenous culture in general, is relatively slight. So little is known about the Illyrian language, for example, that some scholars have argued that the term is essentially meaningless. Inscriptions, which are almost entirely of Roman date, are always in Latin or, in the southeast, Greek. Likewise, virtually all the attested deities are apparently imports; there are very few examples of indigenous divine names or even local iconographic traditions. It seems that it was simply not customary for the peoples of this region either to represent the gods or to make dedications to them in permanent materials. Consequently, our knowledge of their religious traditions is very meager.

We know most about religious traditions in Thrace. According to Herodotus (5.7), writing in the fifth century BCE, the chief gods of the Thracians were Ares, Dionysos, and Artemis, by which he presumably meant a native war god, a god with an ecstatic cult, and a hunter-goddess. We know of one Thracian goddess under her original name, Bendis, whose cult was introduced into Athens in the late fifth century BCE; like Artemis, she was depicted as a hunter. It was under Greek influence that there developed the most famous Thracian deity of the Roman period, the so-called Thracian Rider God, a deity depicted on horseback and wearing a short cloak, often facing a tree around which a serpent is coiled; his Thracian name, if there ever was one, is unknown, and he is usually called Heros (Greek *hêrôs*), usually accompanied by a local epithet (see for example Text Box 0.1, no. 6). This title suggests that he was originally conceived of as a human who continued to exercise power after death, and many scholars think that the serpent provides another indication of his connection to the underworld.

For other parts of this region we know even less. There are some indications among the Illyrian tribes of an indigenous sun-cult, but little can be said about it. The most intriguing evidence concerns Dacia, where in the mid-first century BCE the powerful leader Burebista established a centralized kingdom; it was a renewal of strength in this kingdom in the late first century CE that led to Trajan's invasion. Archaeological work has revealed a number of distinctive native sanctuaries in Dacia, some consisting of unroofed sets of pillar-like stone bases, others of stone slabs set in elaborate circular patterns; the latter were almost certainly connected with the solar calendar. According to Strabo (*Geography* 7.3.5 and 11), Burebista was assisted in the creation of his kingdom by a powerful priest named Dekaineos, who claimed to know the will of the gods by reading celestial signs. The sanctuaries were destroyed at the time of the Roman invasion and not reused, and the priesthood disappears from knowledge; it thus seems likely that the Romans destroyed the religious structure of the old Dacian kingdom because it was too closely involved with the native kingship.

Despite the scanty evidence for indigenous traditions, we can deduce some regional tendencies from the relative popularity of various Graeco-Roman gods. Particularly striking is the tremendous popularity of the rustic god Silvanus, who is attested in some 450 inscriptions from this region, more than twice the number from the rest of the empire, excluding Italy, put together. Some scholars have explained this popularity by arguing that Silvanus was in these regions the Roman name given to an indigenous deity, although there is very little positive evidence to suggest this. Nevertheless, the popularity of this rustic woodland god must be indicative of local concerns. We may perhaps see some confirmation of this in the fact that Diana, another Roman deity with strong connections to woodlands, is also widely attested in dedications.

Along the Danube, the character of our evidence is strongly colored by the fact that this region, along with the Rhine and the eastern parts of Syria, had one of the largest concentrations of soldiers in the empire. As I will discuss further in chapter 6, there are certain religious tendencies characteristic of the Roman army, notably the popularity of initiatory cults like those of Mithras and Jupiter Dolichenus. An apparently similar cult peculiar to the Balkans was that of the so-called Danubian Rider Gods. This cult is known entirely from small votive reliefs that typically depict a goddess flanked by two gods on horseback, with a complex arrangement of other divine images and symbols above and below. Some system of beliefs presumably underlay this imagery, but in the absence of any written evidence we can say very little about its content or even about the cult's adherents. Yet the fact that it apparently originated in southern Dacia shortly after the Roman conquest and was almost entirely restricted to the lands around the Danube suggests that it in some way reflected regional traditions or concerns.

8 Italy

Rome began as just one of a group of cities in the region of Latium with shared traditions and a common language, Latin; peoples in the rest of the peninsula, with some exceptions, spoke a variety of related Italic languages and worshipped similar gods. Among the exceptions were the Etruscans, who lived just north of Rome in what is now Tuscany and spoke a language unrelated to any other now known. By the mid-sixth century BCE the Etruscans had developed a sophisticated culture that combined extensive Greek influence with distinctive characteristics of their own, notably an emphasis on the afterlife and a marked interest in divination. The Romans had close relations with the Etruscans and adopted a number of their traditions, although the extent of Etruscan influence on Roman culture is disputed.

Other peoples came to Italy from elsewhere in the Mediterranean. The Phoenicians, for example, established settlements in western Sicily and Sardinia, and also had close ties with the Etruscans. Far more important were the Greeks, whose earliest known colony was established in the Bay of Naples in the mid-eighth century BCE; by the fifth century BCE Greek settlements along the southwestern Italian coast were so numerous and prosperous that the region became known as Magna Graecia, "Great Greece." Greek colonization was equally successful along the coasts of Sicily, especially in the east. Trade relations with the Greeks (and to a lesser extent the Phoenicians) were in large part responsible for the economic and cultural development of Etruria and Latium; in studying Roman religion, it is important to remember that Greek influence began at a very early date. The last major group to arrive in Italy were the Celts; although they came far enough south to sack Rome in the early fourth century BCE, their area of settlement was confined to the Po valley in the north.

Rome began to expand its power in the late fifth century BCE, a process that greatly accelerated in the latter part of fourth century; by the mid-third century, all Italy south of the Po valley was under Roman control. A major war with Carthage at the end of that century extended Roman rule to Sicily, Sardinia, and Corsica, and the conquest of the Celtic region in the north was complete by the early second century BCE. Outside of a number of Roman colonies, however, the peoples of Italy maintained their local languages and traditions until a major revolt in the 80s BCE. Thereafter, Latin rapidly replaced all the other languages of Italy, apart from Greek, and Roman institutions became the norm. In terms of religion, not only do we know vastly more about Rome than the rest of Italy, but the Roman tradition had by the imperial period become dominant throughout the land. In this section, then, it is on Roman religion that I will focus, although I will call attention to elements that are characteristic of the broader Italian tradition.

As I noted in the introduction, the Roman religious tradition was in important respects very similar to the Greek tradition; this similarity was due in part to the very early Greek influence on Latin and Etruscan society and culture. As in a Greek *polis*, a certain number of deities received public cult in Rome: their temples were public monuments, and their rituals were performed by public magistrates and priests on behalf of the entire citizen population. These rituals included not only sacrifices but also more elaborate festivals, notably the great games for which the Romans are now famous. The usual components of the games were chariot races and theatrical performances; gladiatorial displays were originally not part of sacred festivals. The regular sacrifices and festivals were recorded in the public calendar, of which a number of inscribed stone copies survive from the reign of Augustus. The whole system was traditionally managed by the Senate, the body of current and former magistrates that oversaw public policy during the republican period.

Along with the general similarity between the Greek and Roman religious traditions, there were numerous differences. Two of these call for particular comment. In the Greek tradition, priests were typically individuals attached to a particular deity who oversaw the rituals of that deity's cult. Although this type of individual priesthood also existed in the Roman tradition, the norm was instead one of group priesthoods, conventionally called priestly colleges. The most important priests, moreover, were not attached to the cult of a particular deity, but had much broader roles and functioned to a large extent as experts in ritual tradition. The two most important priestly colleges were the *pontifices*, responsible for a wide range of sacred law, and the *augures*, responsible for the traditional Roman forms of divination. The institution of priestly colleges seems to have been characteristic of the Italian tradition. Several of the more specialized Roman colleges also existed in other Latin towns: the Salii, who performed ritual dances in archaic military garb, and the Vestals, the virgin priestesses devoted to the service of the hearth-goddess Vesta. Similarly, bronze tablets from the town of Iguvium in northern Italy, dating to the second and early first centuries BCE, preserve the ritual proceedings of a sacred fellowship called the Atiedian Brothers that was in some ways comparable to a group in Rome called the Arval Brothers.

Another distinctive feature of the Roman tradition was a strong emphasis on divination. The traditional Roman form of divination was augury, the interpretation of the calls and flights of birds; magistrates were required to employ augury before any public business in order to determine whether or not the gods approved. This concern with divination was something that the Romans shared with the Etruscans, who developed other forms of divination that were eventually also used in Rome: haruspicy, which involved reading the livers of sacrificial animals, and an elaborate system of interpreting thunder and lightening. In addition, Romans and Etruscans alike apparently regarded any untoward event as a possible message from the gods, and the Senate regularly authorized the consultation of either a Roman priestly college or the Etruscan haruspices in order to determine its significance. This concern for omens continued throughout the imperial period, when many other forms of divination seem to have faded away.

The gods who received public cult in Rome were for the most part common to all the Italic-speaking peoples. Jupiter, the great sky-god and patron of Rome, was worshipped throughout Italy, as was Mars, the war-god. Some of these deities, such as Diana, a goddess of the moon and the wilderness, were apparently introduced into Rome from elsewhere in Italy. As in the Greek world, these shared deities took different specific forms in different places. So for example in Rome the most important public cult was that of Jupiter Optimus Maximus ("Best and Greatest"), Juno, and Minerva, a grouping conventionally known as the Capitoline Triad from their joint temple on the Capitoline Hill in Rome; the Capitoline cult was a distinctive symbol of Roman identity, just as the cult of Athena Polias was in Athens. But although the Italic peoples had their own traditional gods, they began to assimilate them to comparable Greek gods at a very early date. Thus they identified Mars with Ares, Diana with Artemis, Minerva with Athena, and so on. In addition, the Romans imported some Greek deities outright, such as Herakles (who came to be called Hercules in Latin), Apollo, and Asklepios (Aesculapius in Latin).

This last point brings us to another important characteristic of the Roman religious tradition, its openness to new cults and rituals. The Senate could formally authorize a new public cult, and in some periods did so with surprising frequency. The deities whose worship was introduced into Rome in this way were usually either Italic or Greek in origin, but occasionally came from further afield. The most notable example was the Anatolian mother goddess Cybele, known in Latin as Mater Deum Magna Idaea, the "Great Idaean Mother of the Gods." The Senate officially introduced her cult into Rome in 204 BCE, although they restricted some of its more exotic elements, like the eunuch priesthood, to people who were not Roman citizens. During the last two centuries BCE the Senate seems to have been less inclined to establish public cults of foreign deities in this way, but Rome's new status as the capital of a far-flung empire meant that foreign cults appeared in the city all the same. Judaeans are attested in Rome by the mid-second century BCE, the worship of Isis by the early first century BCE, and that of the Syrian Goddess by the mid-first century CE. By that time, however, the traditional structures of Roman public religion were changing dramatically, as emperors displaced the Senate as the chief authority on matters of religion and, in death at least, became themselves official gods of the Roman people.

9 *Uniformity and Diversity in the Religious Traditions of the Empire*

Although this survey of regional traditions has necessarily been highly select-ive and condensed, it should nevertheless give some impression of the tremendous cultural and religious diversity that existed within the Roman Empire. Our grasp of this diversity is uneven, since the evidence is much richer for some areas than for others. The variability of the evidence is itself partly a consequence of cultural diversity, since some cultures (that of Egypt, for example) had long-standing traditions of writing and using non-perishable materials for religious artifacts while others (those of eastern Europe, for example) did not.

Some of these traditions differed significantly from the Graeco-Roman norm that I outlined in the previous chapter. For example, the Graeco-Roman practice of representing the gods in human form was not uniformly observed: in some cultures it was customary not to depict the gods at all, while the Egyptians sometimes represented them in mixed animal–human form. So too were there differences in sacrificial practice, so that in some cultures animal sacrifice was relatively unimportant, while others practiced even human sacrifice. For the most part, the ruling elite of the empire simply accepted this variety: it was an established principle in the Graeco-Roman tradition that each cult or shrine would have its own regulations, and this provided a precedent for diversity of cult practice that the elite could apply more widely. Although they regarded some customs as ridiculous or distasteful, it was only in extreme cases, such as that of human sacrifice, that their distaste determined actual policy.

More problematic was diversity in the social organization of public worship. A key element in the Graeco-Roman tradition was the integration of public cults into the social and political structures of the city, so that they were to some extent simply one facet of civic organization. But in many parts of the empire other forms of organization were normal. In continental Europe, for example, tribal rather than urban organization was the norm, with concomitant differences in the structures of public cult. In much of the ancient Near East, by contrast, there were wealthy and powerful temple complexes that functioned almost as substitutes for cities, as was the case in very different ways with the temples of Ma at Comana in Cappadocia, of the Judaean god at Jerusalem, and of Amun at Thebes in Egypt. A closely related issue is the nature of priesthoods. In the mainstream Graeco-Roman tradition, these were largely part-time public offices held by the same people who served as magistrates. Elsewhere, however, we can identify something much more akin to a priestly caste, whose members had highly specialized training and were set apart from the general population; this was the case with the Egyptian priests, Judaean priests, and apparently the Celtic Druids. Roman authorities were often more concerned with the organization of public cult and religious authority because these things were intimately bound up with the fundamental power structures of society. As I argue in chapter 7, to the extent that the rulers of the empire had a religious policy, it was largely in response to concerns of this sort.

More important than the diversity, however, was the uniformity that underlay it. Artemidorus, in his book on the interpretation of dreams, chose as his prime example of a custom common to all humanity that of venerating and honoring the gods: "For no nation is without gods . . . ; different people honor different gods, but they all have recourse to the same thing" (*The Interpretation of Dreams* 1.8). We have seen that virtually all the religious traditions considered here shared certain basic assumptions: that gods existed, that they were many in number, that they could affect people's lives for good or ill, that it was necessary to win their favor through offerings and rituals, and that different contexts required different offerings and rituals. Moreover, in virtually all these traditions we can observe similar dynamics, dynamics that were closely linked with these basic assumptions.

One of these dynamics was the ongoing creative tension between tendencies to particularization and generalization. By particularization I mean the tendency to identify gods very closely with specific locales and to give them distinguishing epithets that linked them to particular temples, cities, tribes, or topographical features. To a significant extent, people tended in practice to treat all gods as local gods. On the other hand, people with a shared language and common cultural traditions tended to use the same set of names for their local gods and to characterize them in similar ways; in doing so, they effectively acknowledged that in important ways the gods that one group worshipped in one place were "the same" as the gods another group worshipped in another. This is what I mean by the tendency towards generalization. This tendency accelerated when political or economic conditions encouraged greater regional unity and more extensive interaction between local communities. In the right circumstances, it even crossed cultural and linguistic boundaries, so that, as we have repeatedly seen, people could refer to a local Anatolian or British god, for example, as Zeus or Mars. In chapter 5 I discuss this phenomenon in more detail.

A closely related dynamic appears in the tension between continuity and change. The varying nature and quantity of the evidence makes this difficult to chart in some regions, particularly parts of Europe. But for those areas where there is extensive evidence from earlier periods (notably Asia Minor, Syria, and Egypt), it is possible to trace continuity in iconographic conventions, cult locations, divine names, and conceptions of the gods over many centuries. But in almost no case can we identify a tradition, a cult, or a deity that remains unaltered: continuity is always accompanied by change. In some cases these changes resulted from the influence of other cultural and religious traditions: as people came to associate a god worshipped in one place with one worshipped elsewhere, for example, they adjusted their practices and beliefs accordingly. But it is a mistake to think that religious traditions are like bodies in Newtonian physics, remaining static unless acted upon by external forces. On the contrary, change is just as inherent a feature of any cultural tradition as continuity.

These shared assumptions and common dynamics allowed for a relatively easy and effective integration of traditions across the empire. Enough common ground existed that people could find other regional traditions largely understandable, even if those traditions involved particular customs that they regarded as bizarre or objectionable. Moreover, most traditions were flexible enough that they could accommodate new elements while maintaining some continuity; adaptation to changing circumstances did not require a sharp break with the past. This is not to say that there were no points of tension; I have already indicated a few, and will discuss them in more detail in chapter 7. In general, however, there was enough uniformity underlying the regional religious traditions that the diversity rarely led to social or political instability. In chapter 5 I will examine more closely the specific processes of religious integration within the empire, but it is important first to consider the common underlying framework, people's experience of the gods in their day-to-day lives.

FURTHER READING

For the Greek tradition, Burkert 1985 provides a detailed and systematic survey, Bruit Zaidman and Schmitt Pantel 1992 a lively and thoughtful introduction; both are limited to the archaic and classical periods. Price 1999 is an excellent and wide-ranging introduction that includes the Hellenistic and imperial periods. Sourvinou-Inwood 2000a and 2000b provides the best succinct account of *polis* religion. On oracles, Parke 1967 is a general introduction; Lane Fox 1986: 168–259 discusses the imperial period. Mylonas 1961 remains the most thorough account of the Eleusinian cult, especially the archaeological remains; the major texts are translated in Meyer 1987: 17–32.

Mitchell 1993 is a comprehensive regional study of Anatolia, with sections on religion; Dignas 2002 deals with Asia Minor more broadly, but focuses on a particular set of issues. On Cybele, see Roller 1999; on Artemis of Ephesus, Oster 1990. Millar 1993 is a detailed and scrupulous regional study of Syria, with considerable discussion of religious traditions. Teixidor 1977 provides an introductory survey of Syrian religious traditions, now out of date. Lightfoot 2003 contains a wealth of information and astute analysis, with broad implications for the study of religion in Graeco-Roman Syria. The literature on the Judaean tradition in the Roman period is enormous: Cohen 1987 provides a stimulating introduction, Schürer et al.

1973–87 a comprehensive reference work, and Schwartz 2001 a brilliant analysis of Judaean religion and society in its imperial context; on the issue of Judaean identity in this period, see especially Cohen 1999.

On Egypt, Lewis 1983 and Bowman 1986 are general surveys, with chapters devoted to religious life. Dunand and Zivie-Coche 2004 provides an overview of religion that includes both the Pharaonic and the Graeco-Roman periods. Frankfurter 1998 is a detailed and complex work, focusing on popular religion and the later empire. MacKendrick 1980 is a general survey of Roman North Africa that highlights the material evidence; Rives 1995 concentrates on Carthage and its territory with a focus on issues of religious identity and authority.

Cunliffe 1997 provides a useful overview of the Celts; Green 1986 is clear and succinct on their religious traditions, and Piggott 1968 is a balanced account of the Druids. On religion in Roman Gaul, see especially Derks 1998; on Roman Britain, Henig 1984. Mócsy 1974 and Lengyel and Radon 1980 provide general surveys of eastern Europe, with some discussion of religion; Tudor 1969–76 is a comprehensive study of the Danubian Rider Gods.

Beard, North, and Price 1998 is indispensable for the study of the Roman religious tradition; the second volume is a valuable collection of sources. Scheid 2003 provides a concise and thoughtful introduction. Liebeschuetz 1979 and Feeney 1998, in very different ways, are concerned especially with the literary evidence; the latter also serves as an incisive discussion of general issues. Ando 2003 collects important papers and helpfully lays out areas of debate.

CHAPTER 3

The Presence of the Gods

ᒋᒋᒋᒋ

In the previous chapter, we saw that virtually all the religious traditions of the Roman Empire shared some fundamental beliefs: that the gods existed, that they affected people's lives, and that it was necessary to win their goodwill. As I indicated in chapter 1, these beliefs were rarely codified into formal dogmas or creeds, but instead found expression in people's behavior. The divine was not merely an abstract idea or something thought to exist "out there," but something deeply and intimately bound up with people's experience of the world. In this chapter I briefly explore three aspects of this experience. I first discuss the ways that people perceived the presence of the gods in the natural world. I then survey people's perception of divine power, and the way that they turned to the gods for protection and assistance. Lastly, I consider the widespread belief that the gods could and did directly manifest themselves in people's everyday lives.

1 The Gods in the World

In the Graeco-Roman tradition, the gods had long been perceived as a part of the natural world. According to Hesiod's *Theogony*, for example, Earth generates Sea and Heaven, and then in union with Heaven becomes the parent and ancestor of most other gods, including Sun, Moon, Dawn, and various rivers and winds as well as Olympian deities such as Zeus and Poseidon. In other words, the physical components of the world are not only divine themselves, but give birth to the other gods. Given this traditional view of the cosmos, it is not surprising that many people regarded the natural landscape as being charged with the presence of the divine. The Roman philosopher Seneca, writing in the mid-first century

CE, provides an evocative description of this widespread perception of the divine in nature (see Text Box 3.1).

Text Box 3.1

Seneca, *Epistles* 41.3

If ever you have come upon a dense grove of ancient trees rising to an unusual height and blocking the sight of the sky with the shade of branch upon branch, the loftiness of the forest, the solitude of the place, and the marvel of such thick and unbroken shadow out in the open generate belief in a divine presence. And any cave where the rocks have been eaten away deep into the mountain it supports, not made by human hands but hollowed out into a vast expanse by natural forces, will suggest to your spirit some need for religious observance. We venerate the sources of great rivers: the sudden eruption of a tremendous stream from its concealment causes altars to be built. Hot springs are worshipped, and the darkness and immeasurable depth renders certain pools sacred.

We could for the sake of analysis distinguish two different ways that people in the Roman world interpreted their awareness of the divine in nature. On the one hand, they might regard a particular topographical feature like a spring or a river as a deity in itself, and so make offerings to it; I noted a few examples of this practice in chapter 1. On the other hand, they might regard a certain place as the dwelling of a deity, as in traditional Greek myth Mt Olympus was the home of the gods. It is unlikely, however, that this distinction was one to which people at the time gave much thought. In most cases, they no doubt responded to perceptions of the divine through action rather than analysis, by making an offering or building a little shrine or in some other way acknowledging the divine presence.

Literary evidence suggests that such small markers of piety were very common throughout the countryside of the Roman Empire. Apuleius asserts that "it is the custom of pious travelers, whenever they come across a sacred grove or holy place along their way, to make a vow, offer fruit, and sit for a while," and he enumerates the variety of little sacred sites that they might encounter: "an altar wreathed with flowers, a cave shaded by leafy boughs, an oak weighed down with horns, a beech crowned with pelts, a little hill sanctified by an enclosure, a tree-trunk hewn into an effigy, a turf altar moistened with libations, a stone smeared with unguent" (*Bouquet* 1). The absence of such small offerings was evidently noteworthy. For example, when Apuleius was being tried on a charge of magic, he attacked his accuser's lack of piety by asserting that "no shrine has been erected on his country estate, no place or grove consecrated. But why am I talking about groves and shrines? Those who have been there say that they failed to see so much as a single anointed stone or garlanded branch on the entire property" (*Apology* 56.5–6). The implication here is that someone who does not even bother to acknowledge the divine aura of a special stone or tree must have utter contempt for the presence of the gods in his land.

As we saw in chapter 2, this perception of the divine in the natural world was common to virtually all the traditions within the Roman Empire. The specific topographical features associated with the divine varied somewhat from culture to culture, so that groves, for example, were more prominent in continental Europe, and mountains in the Near East. Yet the underlying belief was much the same throughout the entire area, and constituted an important unifying element among the various regional traditions.

Seneca suggests that woods were particularly associated with the divine. This was especially true in the Celtic tradition, as we have seen, but was by no means limited to it. Sacred groves existed also in the Italic tradition, such as the grove outside Rome where the Arval Brothers celebrated the cult of the goddess Dea Dia. We should note that this grove was not an untouched thicket of trees, but rather the site of several cult buildings; nevertheless, the fact that it is always described in the Arval records as a *lucus*, "grove," and that special rituals were necessary when removing damaged or fallen trees indicates that its status as a wood was central to the cult. Individual trees as well as groves could be regarded as sacred; the elder Pliny remarks that "trees used to be the temples of deities, and in accordance with ancient practice simple country places even now dedicate any outstanding tree to a god" (*Natural History* 12.3). Thus we regularly hear of people attaching garlands or other offerings (Apuleius mentions horns and animal pelts) to particular trees.

Seneca also mentions the divine aura of water, whether in springs or rivers or pools. This is again something we have already observed in many parts of the Roman world, particularly North Africa and western Europe; similarly, the Nile had a central place in the religious tradition of Egypt. Water was also very important in the Graeco-Roman tradition, as indicated by the high profile of springs and rivers in both myth and cult; Hesiod went so far as to advise people never to cross a river without first praying and washing their hands (*Works and Days* 737–41). Apuleius adds caves and rocks to the list of topographical features that might be linked to the divine. We have already seen evidence for sacred caves in North Africa and Spain, and they existed elsewhere as well. Greek tradition associated caves particularly with the rustic god Pan and with the underworld; in Rome, a cave called the Lupercal was revered for its connections with Romulus and Remus. As for rocks, many authors other than Apuleius refer to the practice of anointing particular stones with unguents, suggesting that it was widespread and familiar.

We must remember that the vast majority of people in the Roman Empire lived in much closer association with nature than most people in modern industrialized societies, and that forests, springs, rivers, and caves, even unusual trees and rocks, would have loomed much larger in their experience of the world. The tendency to sacralize such features of the landscape arose not only from the sense of the uncanny that Seneca expresses so well, but also from their role in shaping people's mental map of their environment. Mountains, for example, were obviously places where the earth came closer to the heavens, but they functioned also as major geographical markers. Islands and promontories played a similar role in navigation, and we find a similar association of these features with the gods. The most famous examples are the Pillars of Hercules at the passage between the Mediterranean and the Atlantic, but the elder Pliny notes many others: promontories named after Juno (*Natural History* 3.7), Saturn (3.19), Minerva (3.62), Apollo and Mercury (5.23), and Venus (5.92), and islands named after Diana (3.81), Hercules (3.84), Juno (4.120), and Apollo (6.32), in locations ranging from the Black Sea to the Atlantic coast of Lusitania.

The natural world, then, would for many people have been shot through with the presence of the divine. By acknowledging this presence through offerings and other demonstrations of piety, they were able to bring the natural world and the powers that animated it into a defined relationship with the human sphere, while at the same time demonstrating their respect for those powers. As we shall see in the following section, this respect for superhuman power was in an important sense the central issue in people's experience of the divine.

2 The Power of the Gods

As I argued in chapter 1, the idea of "god" in the Graeco-Roman world was flexible and wide-ranging. At its core, however, was the acknowledgment of power, power that had an actual or potential impact on day-to-day life; hence the importance of acknowledging that power when people felt that they had encountered it in the natural world. In a very real sense, people believed that the gods were what the gods did. The orator Aelius Aristides elaborates on this idea in his prose hymn to Sarapis when he says "Let it be left to the Egyptian priests and writers to say and to know who, indeed, the god is and what is his nature. But our praise would be sufficient for the present if we should tell of the number and nature of the benefits he is shown to have given to mankind. And at the same time through these very acts it will be possible to consider his nature. For if ever we declare his powers and gifts, we have more or less stated his identity and nature. For he is not different from what he appears to be and is shown to be by his deeds" (*Orations* 45.15, trans. C. A. Behr). To understand what the gods meant to people, then, we should consider the contexts in which people supplicated their power.

Almost immediately, however, we run into problems, because the evidence is relatively scarce. The ancient literary texts that survive are rarely concerned with the ordinary concerns of everyday people, and votive dedications of the sort described in the introduction often reveal little or nothing about the specific context: the dedicator and the deity knew what was at stake, and that was enough. Nevertheless, it is clear that people turned to the gods whenever they felt themselves at the mercy of forces beyond their control. Travel, for example, by land and even more by sea, was always fraught with danger. It does not require much imagination to envision the circumstances behind this dedication from Rome (the name of the dedicator is lost): "Sacred to Neptune; . . . [so-and-so] discharged the vow that he undertook in the straits of Sicily" (*ILS* 3280). Similarly, a new recruit in the Roman army, writing to his father in Egypt, reported that his arrival in Italy had been a close call: "I thank the lord Sarapis that when I was in danger at sea he straightway saved me" (trans. Hunt and Edgar 1932: no. 112). For merchants, financial as well as personal safety could be at stake; a chalk merchant based in Britain erected a votive dedication to the goddess Nehalennia on the coast of Lower Germany "because of the complete preservation of his merchandise," presumably after a rocky crossing of the channel (*ILS* 4751). The cult of Isis included an entire rite to invoke her protection of seafarers, celebrated every spring at the start of the sailing season (for a description, see Apuleius, *The Golden Ass* 11.16). Although the perils of sea-travel were undoubtedly greater, travel by land could also be dangerous, especially in more remote and inhospitable regions. There was in Roman times a shrine in the St Bernard Pass dedicated to Poeninus, the god of the Mont Blanc range, from which several bronze votive dedications have survived; a certain Gaius Julius Primus explicitly states in his dedication that it was "for his journey and return," presumably because the god had granted him a passage free from snowstorms and landslides (*ILS* 4850a).

People invoked the gods not only in times of crisis, but also for ongoing aid in areas of crucial concern. Given the importance of agriculture in the Roman world, it is not surprising that they looked to the gods for the prosperity of their crops and herds. We may consider, for example, this

Figure 3.1 Votive stele from North Africa dedicated to Saturn. Tunis, Musée du Bardo inv. 3119. Reproduced by permission of akg-images/Erich Lessing

votive relief from Africa dedicated to Saturn by a man named Cuttinus (see Figure 3.1). The brief inscription says merely that "Cuttinus, together with his dependents, discharged his vow," but the images tell a more detailed story. The central panel depicts a scene of sacrifice, with a man, presumably Cuttinus himself, to the right of the altar and a woman, probably his wife, holding a basket of produce to the left; two other female figures, possibly his daughters, hold additional baskets on either side. In the two panels below we see farm workers plowing, reaping, and transporting grain. Presiding over all is Saturn himself, sitting on a bull and accompanied by two attendants. Cuttinus, we may infer, was the owner of an estate, and had prayed to Saturn for an abundant harvest; this relief records both the god's bestowal of this blessing and Cuttinus' own offerings to the god in return. One final detail is worth noticing: Saturn holds in his right hand a bill-hook, a farm implement with a curved blade used especially for clearing brush. Is this a way of representing the god's ability to clear away the threats to a good harvest? After all, the threats to crops were many, and care had to be taken with regard to them all. In the mountain pass between Cilicia and Anatolia, for example, someone erected a statue of Mercury with the following inscription: "Mercury of the powerful staff . . . , ward off the clouds of locusts from these places with your holy rod: for your likeness stands in this spot, erected for the increase of the crops and the healthful cure of these places and peoples; be merciful and well-disposed to people and give increase of crops and all things" (trans. Horden and Purcell 2000: 417–18). Livestock as well as crops needed the protection of the gods, as in this dedication from Phrygia: "Gaius the son of Manes, for the well-being of his cattle and of all his dependents, [dedicated this] votive offering to Hypsistos" (*MAMA* 5.212).

Health was another major concern. Private letters preserved on papyri in Egypt often contain a declaration to the effect that "I pray always for your health; every day I make supplication for you before such-and-such a god" (for example, Hunt and Edgar 1932: nos. 120–1, 125, 133–4, 137, 155). This was obviously a stereotyped expression, and we may wonder whether in every case the writer actually did supplicate the gods each day. Yet stereotyped phrases like this do not develop unless they to some extent reflect actual practice. And indeed, other letters contain more spontaneous expressions of the same idea: for example, a man named Serenus reports to his brother that "with the help of the gods our sister has taken a turn for the better, and our brother Harpocratian is safe and well; for the gods of our fathers help us at all times, giving us health and safety" (trans. Hunt and Edgar 1932: no. 136). A certain Gaius Julius Libosus in Mauretania Caesariensis dedicated an altar to Caelestis, "Restorer and Preserver of his home, because he found his parents Gaius Julius

Victoricus and Caecilia Namphamina safe and unharmed," perhaps after his absence from home on a journey (*ILS* 4431). Some health issues, then as now, were rather less than life-threatening, as with the woman in northern Italy who erected a dedication to "Mindful Minerva" for the reversal of her hair loss (*ILS* 3135). Others were more serious: a soldier in Apulum in Dacia gave thanks to Aesculapius and Hygia ("Health") for the recovery of his vision (*ILS* 3847), and a woman in Thrace similarly gave a gift to Demeter "for her sight" (*IGBulg* 3.932).

Certain gods were especially associated with healing, such as the Celtic deities Sequana and Apollo Grannus mentioned in chapter 2, and their shrines became centers of pilgrimage for people seeking cures. A distinctive feature of such shrines was the presence of votive offerings depicting the body parts for which people had sought healing, such as the carved wood offerings dedicated to Sequana that have been recovered from the source of the Seine. This practice was widespread in the Greek and Italic traditions as well: an inventory of the shrine of Asklepios in Athens, for example, lists among other offerings two pairs of eyes, a pair of ears, two individual breasts, a set of genitals, a pair of legs, and a thigh (van Straten 1981: no. 1.32). Asklepios was the healing god *par excellence* of the Roman Empire (see for example Text Box 0.1, no. 4); his cult was widespread throughout the Mediterranean, with his most important temple sited at Pergamum in Asia Minor. Central to this cult was the practice known as incubation (literally, "sleeping in"): people seeking cures spent the night in a sacred hall attached to the temple, where the god was thought to appear to them in their dreams and either heal them forthwith or prescribe a course of treatment. These cures were sometimes recorded in compendious inscriptions kept in the temples, like this one from Rome: "To Lucius, who suffered from pleurisy and had been despaired of by all men, the god revealed that he should go and from the threefold altar lift ashes and mix them thoroughly with wine and lay them on his side; and he was saved and publicly offered thanks to the god, and the people rejoiced with him. To Julian, who was spitting up blood and had been despaired of by all men, the god revealed that he should go and from the threefold altar take the seeds of a pine cone and eat them with honey for three days; and he was saved and went and publicly offered thanks before the people" (trans. Edelstein and Edelstein 1945: no. 438).

Concerns for health, agricultural prosperity, and personal safety appear regularly in our evidence. Appeals for justice, like those that I briefly noted in chapter 1, are also common, and other concerns are occasionally attested as well; slaves, for example, might pray for their freedom, like the man in the Bay of Naples who proudly noted in his dedication to

Hercules that he had "made his vow as a slave, discharged it as a free man" (*ILS* 3427; see also Text Box 0.1, no. 5). But what we most often find in dedicatory inscriptions are very general references to divine support and assistance. Many dedications in both Latin and Greek contain a phrase indicating that they were made "for" or "for the well-being" of someone, without revealing anything more specific. Indeed, it may well be that in many cases there was no specific context, and that the dedicator was instead simply making a blanket appeal for divine blessings and protection. Sometimes the dedicator specifies by name the people for whom he or she has made the offering. So for example a relief of the Thracian Rider God from Odessus on the coast of Lower Moesia bears the inscription "To Heros Manimazos; Hestiaios the son of Neikios [dedicated this] thank-offering for his sons Neikios and Agathenor" (*IGBulg* 1^2.78). Similarly, a small altar was dedicated in Spain to Juno Regina by the senatorial couple Licinius Serenianus and Varinia Flaccina "for the well-being of their daughter" Varinia Serena (*ILS* 3106). Even more common, however, are generalizing phrases like "for his/her own well-being and that of his/her dependents" or "for him/herself and his/her dependents." Noteworthy also are dedications "for" or "for the well-being of" the emperor and his family, often made by public officials or collectivities such as cities (see for example Text Box 0.1, no. 3): since the emperor was regarded as so crucial to the well-being of the empire and its population, it was only reasonable that people invoke the gods to preserve him.

People also frequently asked the gods not for a tangible benefit, but simply for advice. In chapter 2 we saw the role of oracles in the Greek religious tradition, and similar institutions existed in other parts of the empire as well. Plutarch noted that in his day people made inquiries of oracles on "minor and everyday matters . . . : whether one should marry, or embark on a sea-voyage, or lend money," and "about the yield of crops and the increase of livestock and bodily health"; in other words, the same sort of everyday concerns that also feature in votive dedications (*On the Oracles of the Pythia* 28, 408c). This sort of question is precisely what we find in Egyptian papyri that preserve questions put to Zeus Helios Sarapis: "Nike asks whether it is to my advantage to buy from Tasarapion her slave Sarapion" (trans. Hunt and Edgar 1932: no. 194); "Menander asks, is it granted me to marry?" (*POxy* 1213); "should I employ Hermeinos of Hermopolis as a doctor for the treatment of my eyes?" (*POxy* 3078). In cases like these, people looked to the superior wisdom of the gods for guidance in negotiating the uncertainties of their day-to-day lives.

In all this we see a general acknowledgment of the gods' power, and a desire to win the gods' favor so that people might benefit from that power.

But did this awareness of divine power also cause people to fear the gods? Did worshippers make offerings to the gods simply in order to propitiate them and avert the evils that they might otherwise inflict upon them? In the vast majority of cases it is impossible to recover the specific emotions and beliefs of the individuals who left behind memorials of their devotion. Some literary texts, however, suggest that there were people whose interactions with the gods were motivated primarily by fear. Plutarch, for example, devoted a treatise to the problem of *deisidaimonia*, a Greek word often translated as "superstition" but which means literally "fear of the divine." Plutarch saw this as an even worse error than atheism, since atheists "do not see the gods at all, while [the superstitious] think that they exist but are evil; the former dismiss them, while the latter regard the kindly as terrifying, the fatherly as tyrannical, the providential as harmful, and the slow to anger as savage and brutal" (*On Superstition* 6, 167d).

Although individual beliefs no doubt varied from person to person, it is worth noting that inscriptions tend to highlight the gods' beneficence and so to reflect what Plutarch obviously regarded as the correct attitude towards the divine. The epithets that people attributed to various gods are also suggestive of their attitudes. One common epithet in Greek dedications is *epêkoos*, "he/she who listens." From Athens, for example, there is a model of the lower part of a male body with the inscription "Athenodoros dedicated [this] votive offering to Asklepios Who Listens" (van Straten 1981: 10.1; see also Text Box 0.1, no. 6). The Latin equivalent is less common, but we may note a dedication to Jupiter Optimus Maximus from Numidia that describes him as "the hearer of the prayers of the human race" (*ILS* 2996). Another common epithet in dedications is *sôtêr* (Greek) or *conservator* (Latin), "savior" or "preserver." In the port of Rome, for example, a man dedicated a statue to "the ever-present *numen* of Minerva Augusta, preserver and protector of the Most Illustrious Guild of Tow-Workers" (*ILS* 3129). Epithets like these suggest that people generally regarded the gods as a source of blessings and protection: the gods heeded people's prayers, aided them in times of need, and bestowed security and prosperity.

The survival of so many votive dedications indicates that it was normal for people to turn to the gods for assistance and protection in matters affecting their day-to-day lives. They did not, however, conceive of divine power solely in passive terms, as something that impinged on their lives only when they sought it out. As we saw in the previous section, there was a widespread tendency to perceive divine power as an inherent part of the natural world, which one might encounter at any time. Moreover, as we shall see in the following section, many people also believed that the gods could actively intervene in their lives.

3 Manifestations of the Gods

I noted above that Asklepios was thought to exercise his powers of healing through the medium of dreams, sometimes accomplishing the cure directly, but more often, as in the examples quoted above, advising a course of treatment for the suppliant to carry out on his or her own. We should note the immediacy of the contact between human and divine in these cases: the patient did not simply recover, but had a personal interview with the deity as with a consulting physician. The valetudinarian orator Aelius Aristides, who for a while lived almost full time in the temple of Asklepios in Pergamum, has left a lengthy and fascinating account of his experiences with the god, known as the *Sacred Tales*, in which he relates in great, if sometimes confused, detail the various ways that Asklepios, and other gods as well, intervened in his life. These interventions involved all aspects of his life, although health concerns are naturally the most prominent. Two examples will be enough to give some flavor of his account.

One of the therapies that Aristides adopted on the god's advice was drinking wormwood; this came about in the following way. Aristides dreamed that he and other worshippers, all dressed in white, stood before the god's temple and that he called out to the god.

> And after this there was the wormwood, made clear in some way. But it was made as clear as possible, just as countless other things also clearly contained the presence of the god. For there was a seeming, as it were, to touch him and to perceive that he himself had come, and to be between sleep and waking, and to wish to look up and to be in anguish that he might depart too soon, and to strain the ears and to hear some things as in a dream, some as in a waking state.

On awaking, he consulted his doctor, who was concerned that Aristides was too weak to take wormwood. They then talked with the temple wardens, and discovered that one of them had also had a dream that night: he had watched Aristides giving a public speech in honor of Asklepios, in which he described "how many another time [the god] averted my fate, and recently when he found the wormwood and commanded me to drink it diluted with vinegar." Then, "since the dreams agreed, we used the curative, and I drank as much as no one before, and again on the next day, as the god gave me the same signs. Why should one need to describe the ease in drinking it, or how much it helped?" (*Orations* 48.28–35, trans. C. A. Behr).

On another occasion, during an epidemic, Aristides was so ill that he believed he was near death. After an initial intervention by Asklepios, "Athena appeared with her aegis and the beauty and magnitude and the whole form of the [statue of] Athena by Phidias [in the Parthenon] in Athens. There was also a scent from the aegis as sweet as could be, and it was like wax, and it too was marvelous in beauty and magnitude. She appeared to me alone." Aristides pointed to her and called out her name, causing those with him to fear that he had become delirious, "until they saw that my strength was being restored and heard the words which I had heard from the goddess. . . . She reminded me of *The Odyssey* and said that these were not idle tales, but that this could be judged even by the present circumstances. It was necessary to persevere. I myself was indeed both Odysseus and Telemachus, and she must help me." From this moment he began to recover (*Orations* 48.38–44, trans. C. A. Behr). Two things are noteworthy about this account. Firstly, Aristides perceived Athena's intervention not as a response to an appeal on his part (so far as we can tell), but rather as a spontaneous act on her own part. Secondly, his experience of the goddess was profoundly shaped by traditional myth and art: she appeared in the form of one of the most famous classical Greek sculptures, and described her relationship with him by reference to one of the foundational works of Greek literature. For someone as steeped in classical culture as Aristides, it is hardly surprising that he should envision the goddess in these terms.

Although Aelius Aristides' *Sacred Tales* are in many ways unique, Aristides himself was not at all unique in his conviction that the gods actively intervened in his life. Valerius Maximus, who compiled a collection of edifying anecdotes in the early first century CE, told the following story about the future emperor Augustus. On the night before the battle of Philippi, one of the major battles of the Roman civil wars, "a vision of Minerva appeared to [Augustus'] doctor Artorius [in a dream] and instructed him to advise his patient, who was at the time in the throes of a serious illness, not to let his ill health prevent him from being present at the battle on the next day. When [Augustus] heard this, he gave orders that he be carried in a litter into the battle; while he remained active, pushing his bodily strength to the utmost in order to obtain victory, his camp was captured by [his enemy] Brutus"; in this way Minerva's warning saved his life (*Memorable Deeds and Sayings* 1.7.1). This tale undoubtedly had propaganda value for Augustus, who could use it to demonstrate that he was favored by the gods, and it may accordingly have been improved in the telling. At the same time, since propaganda is effective only insofar as it appeals to widely held sentiments, we may deduce that many people would have accepted the underlying premise that the gods could intervene in people's lives through dreams.

One area in which the gods were often thought to intervene was in matters of their own worship. Pausanias, for example, reports that near the city of Tithorea in central Greece "is a precinct and holy shrine of Isis. . . . Entrance into the shrine is impossible for anyone other than those whom Isis herself has honored by calling them in dreams. The underworld gods in the cities above the Maeander [a river in Asia Minor] do the same thing; to whomever they wish to enter their shrines, they send visions in dreams" (*Description of Greece* 10.32.13). In other words, Isis and the unnamed gods of the underworld were believed to choose their own worshippers. Similar sorts of dream-instructions play an important role in Apuleius' novel *The Golden Ass*, in which Isis rescues the hero Lucius from the donkey form that he had brought upon himself by dabbling in magic. Lucius is afterwards eager to be initiated into the goddess's mysteries, but the priest explains that only those whom she has herself summoned could be initiated. The call eventually comes in the form of a double revelation similar to that which led Aelius Aristides to the wormwood treatment. Isis appears to Lucius in the night and tells him that the day for his initiation is now at hand; when in the morning he goes to inform the priest, it is clear that the priest too has already learned the news from the goddess (*The Golden Ass* 11.21–2). Christians also believed that God could communicate with people through visions and dreams, and *Acts of the Apostles* has an account of a double revelation not unlike those already described. A Roman military officer named Cornelius had a vision in which an angel of God instructed him to seek out the apostle Peter; at about the same time, Peter himself had a vision in which the Lord urged him to eat food that according to Judaean law was unclean. While he was puzzling over the meaning of this vision, messengers arrived from Cornelius. Peter then understood that his vision was a message that he should not refrain from interacting with non-Judaeans, with the result that Cornelius and all those with him became Christian converts (*Acts of the Apostles* 10.1–11.18).

Inscriptions also provide ample evidence for the belief that the gods could appear to mortals and give them direct messages, although they naturally provide much less detail than the literary accounts. We may consider, for example, this inscription from Lower Moesia: "Good Fortune! To Zeus Keraunios the Most Manifest, in accordance with the command of a dream, Dekmia Epiktesis erected [this offering] for herself and her husband Dekmios Sapios and her children and dependents, for the sake of her vow" (*IGBulg* 2.670). We cannot know what exactly Dekmia dreamed, but it presumably involved an appearance of Zeus Keraunios ("of the Thunderbolt"), whom she describes as a "most manifest" god. Phrases indicating that an offering was made at the command of the god are in fact relatively common in inscriptions from across the empire. We may briefly consider three further examples (see also Text Box 0.1, no. 1). From a small town in Africa: "By order of the Lord Aesculapius, Lucius Numisius Vitalis, the son of Lucius, has built a shrine at his own expense; whoever wishes to ascend into the shrine, let him abstain from woman, pork, bean, barber, and public bath for three days; do not enter the enclosure wearing shoes" (*ILAfr* 225). On a relief in Cologne depicting the three Mothers: "To the Matronae Afliae, Marcus Marius Marcellus [has made this offering] for himself and his dependents, at the goddesses' own command" (*ILS* 4798). From the shrine of Endovellicus in Lusitania: "Sacred to Endovellicus; in accordance with *religio* and by order of the deity, Pomponia Marcella has willingly erected this altar" (*ILS* 4513c). How these worshippers received their commands is not clear: possibly through dreams, as Dekmia Epiktesis explicitly states, possibly through oracles (another dedication to Endovellicus, *ILS* 4513e, was erected "in accordance with the response," presumably of an oracle), or even through an actual epiphany of the deity. Although the last seems to have a less common type of divine manifestation, it was certainly not unknown.

We have already seen that Aelius Aristides beheld Athena while awake, and he was by no means the only one to have such a direct encounter with the divine: Cornelius saw the angel of the Lord in the middle of the afternoon. Another episode from *Acts of the Apostles* is equally instructive. When Paul and Barnabas arrived at the city of Lystra in southern Anatolia, Paul healed a lame man. "When the crowds saw what Paul had done, they shouted, in their native Lycaonian [language], 'The gods have come down to us in human form.' And they called Barnabas Zeus, and Paul they called Hermes, because he was the spokesman. And the priest of Zeus, whose temple was just outside the city, brought oxen and garlands to the gates, and he and all the people were about to offer sacrifice"; it was only with considerable difficulty that Paul and Barnabas were able to prevent them (*Acts of the Apostles* 14.8–18, trans. adapted from the New English Bible). Whatever the historical value of this anecdote, the author clearly thought that his readers would find these people's belief that the gods had appeared in human form entirely plausible. Nor was this sort of belief limited to the less educated: after all, Aelius Aristides, one of the most cultivated men of his age, saw Athena, and Maximus of Tyre, another highly educated orator of the second century CE, claimed to have seen Asklepios and Herakles as "not a dream, but a waking vision" (*Discourses* 9.7i). Such epiphanies may lie behind the numerous dedications that were erected "in accordance with a vision," such as this one from Augusta Vindelicum (modern Augsburg) in Raetia: "To Pluto and Proserpina; Flavia Veneria Bessa, in accordance with a vision, [constructed this] shrine at her own expense, discharging her vow willingly and deservedly" (*ILS* 3972; for other examples, see Text Box 0.1, nos. 3

and 5). Again, however, the brevity of inscriptions tends to conceal details of the context, so that the visions to which they refer may have been dreams rather than epiphanies.

The gods were thought to manifest themselves in other ways as well. There are, for example, numerous stories of miracles connected with divine images. To take just one example, an Egyptian papyrus preserves a highly tendentious account of an Alexandrian embassy to the emperor Trajan, appealing to him to uphold their rights against the resident Judaeans. The ambassadors took with them a bust of their ancestral god Sarapis, presumably to lend them divine support, and when their leader Hermaiskos urged Trajan to aid them instead of the Judaeans, the bust of Sarapis broke into a sweat, astounding Trajan and apparently causing a near riot (*POxy* 1242). Other divine manifestations were less obvious. An inscription from Dacia runs more or less as follows (errors in spelling and grammar make it somewhat difficult to interpret): "To Jupiter Optimus Maximus. Aurelius Marinus Basus and Aurelius Castor Polydeuces(?) were standing around when they saw the divine presence of an eagle descend from a mountain upon three serpents; one very powerful viper squeezed the eagle. These men, named above, freed the eagle from danger. They placed [this] votive offering willingly and deservedly" (*ILS* 3007; see further MacMullen 1981: 69–70). The eagle is well attested as the bird of Jupiter (as we see in Figure 1.2), but apart from that it is not entirely clear what led these men to believe they had encountered the divine; the fact that they made and fulfilled a vow, however, indicates that this was indeed how they interpreted their experience.

4 Conclusion

The two Dacians' encounter with the eagle brings us back to the perception of the divine in nature, although in this case embodied in an animal rather than a topographical feature. Throughout this chapter, we have seen a considerable variety in the ways that people felt that they encountered the divine. Yet they all experienced the gods as a real presence in their lives: Gaius Julius Primus, to whom Poeninus granted safe passage through the Alps; Gaius the son of Manes, who thanked the Most High God for the well-being of his cattle; Lucius, whom Aesculapius cured of pleurisy; Nike, who asked Zeus Helios Sarapis whether she should buy a particular slave; Cornelius, to whom the angel of the Lord appeared; Dekmia Epiktesis, who encountered Zeus Keraunios in a dream; Flavia Veneria Bessa, who had a vision of Pluto and Proserpina; Hermaiskos, whose bust of Sarapis broke into a sweat.

It would be a mistake, however, to deduce that everyone in the Roman Empire was, so to speak, constantly bumping into gods. Although the evidence for people's personal experience of the divine is both extensive and varied, it was by no means a universal phenomenon. Then as now there were undoubtedly those who gave little or no thought to the divine, and who consequently did not perceive it as impinging on their lives. More importantly, people's experience of the divine was not simply a personal and individual phenomenon. We must keep in mind the fact that virtually all the evidence I have cited in this chapter comes from public documents, especially inscriptions; they are thus not immediate expressions of personal experiences, but were instead shaped by social conventions and concerns. As I argue in the next chapter, the social side of religious life in the Roman Empire was at least as important as the personal.

FURTHER READING

On people's experience of the gods, see in general Nock 1972: 33–48, MacMullen 1981: 49–62, and Lane Fox 1986: 102–261. On religion and the landscape, see Horden and Purcell 2000: 401–60. On the cult of Asklepios, see Edelstein and Edelstein 1945; on anatomical votive offerings, van Straten 1981. On Aelius Aristides, see Festugière 1954: 85–104 and Behr 1968.

CHAPTER 4

Religion and Community

卍卍卍卍

Dekmia Epiktesis was one of the thousands of people in the Roman Empire about whom we would know nothing at all if she had not set up an inscription that happened to survive into our own times; even as it is, we know very little. What we do know is that at some point in her adult life she received a divine directive in a dream that led her to dedicate an offering to Zeus Keraunios: it is this monument that provides us with our information (*IGBulg* 2.670). In the previous chapter I quoted the inscription from this monument to illustrate the sorts of individual encounters with the divine that a person in the Roman Empire might experience. We know something else about Dekmia Epiktesis as well: she was not simply an individual, but belonged to a number of groups. She was first of all part of a household, since it was on behalf of her husband, children, and dependents, as well as herself, that she offered her gift to Zeus Keraunios. She was also part of a wider community, in this case the city of Nicopolis ad Istrum in the province of Lower Moesia. Her inscribed votive offering was clearly intended for public display, and as such it served not only as a gift to Zeus, but also as a demonstration to her fellow-citizens of her piety, her financial resources, and her family solidarity. It is thus a good reminder that religion in the Roman Empire was as much a social phenomenon as it was a matter of personal experience.

Many people today tend to assume that personal experience, what an individual feels or believes in his or her heart, constitutes the real essence of religion. Some scholars, however, have argued that this assumption reflects the modern western tendency to privilege the individual over the wider community; they suggest that in the Graeco-Roman world people instead viewed themselves above all as members of groups. We can get some sense of this from the Greek philosopher Aristotle, writing in the fourth century BCE, who argued that communities develop from two types of natural and integral human relationships: the union of male and female, without which the species could not survive, and the union of ruler and subject, which is as necessary as the relationship between mind and body. Out of these two relationships arises the household, "the natural association established for our daily needs," and out of the household develops the village. When several villages merge into a single community that is large enough to be more or less self-sufficient, they form a *polis* or city-state. "Therefore, since the primary associations exist by nature, so too does the *polis*," and "man is a living being who by nature belongs to a *polis*" (*Politics* 1.2).

If we were to follow Aristotle and regard communities rather than individuals as the natural constituents of society in the Roman world, our analysis of religion would shift accordingly. For example, we can interpret Dekmia Epiktesis' dedication in two different ways, depending on whether we regard religion as primarily a personal or a social phenomenon. If the former, we would interpret Dekmia's encounter with the divine as the significant religious fact, and see her inscribed votive offering as merely a byproduct. If the latter, we would instead interpret Dekmia's monument as the important thing, since it publicly encapsulated the nexus of relationships that linked her with her family, her fellow citizens, and her god. Whether the real essence of religion lay in individual experience or collective activity is a question that is both difficult to answer and perhaps in the end not very meaningful. What is clear enough is that the social dimension of religion in the Roman world was extremely important in its own right. Building on Aristotle's analysis, we may distinguish two aspects of this social dimension, although these were in practice closely intertwined: on the one hand, the role of religion in defining group identity and, on the other, its role in articulating social hierarchies.

The role that religion can play in defining communities is familiar enough. For example, a particular set of beliefs and practices distinguishes Roman Catholics from other Christians, while attendance at a particular church presided over by a particular priest distinguishes the members of one Catholic parish from those of others. The same principle held true in the Graeco-Roman world, although as we shall see it took some distinctive forms. But something more needs to be said about social hierarchies, since the status categories of the Roman Empire were in some ways very different from those of modern western societies. There were two fundamental social distinctions. Men were assumed to be naturally superior to women, and women were consequently barred from active participation in political life and even to some extent restricted in the management of their own affairs. The other distinction was that between free people and slaves. Slavery was a widespread institution, and even people of very modest means might own one or two slaves to act as servants and assistants. Although slave owners had the authority to free their slaves if they saw fit, these former slaves, known as freedmen or freedwomen, retained low social status. Beyond these two fundamental distinctions the situation could become quite complex. As in many other societies, two of the most important factors in determining status were wealth and access to power, whether the latter came with a formal position or informally through influence and connections. It is important to keep in mind that wealth and power were not always associated with other markers of superior status; women and freedmen, for example, although in other respects inferior to freeborn males, might well hold positions of social influence because of their financial resources or access to power. Moreover, a willingness to use one's wealth and power in order to bestow benefits on those of lesser status could in itself increase one's social standing still further. This point is crucial for understanding social relationships in the Roman Empire. People who employed their resources to benefit others were in effect demonstrating their superior status; those whom they benefited then acknowledged their dependent status through a public display of gratitude towards their patrons. This exchange of benefactions and honors between people of unequal social status, known as patronage or euergetism (from Greek *euergetês*, "benefactor"), was fundamental to social life in the Roman world.

In this chapter I examine in more detail the role of religion in defining group identity and structuring social hierarchies in the Roman Empire. I discuss in turn three different types of communities, starting with what Aristotle regarded as the perfect and complete form of society, the city-state. The city-state was central to Graeco-Roman culture, although perhaps more as an ideal than a reality. For one thing, the cities of the imperial period differed in several respects from the model *polis* that Aristotle had in mind: they lacked the autonomy that made it a state as well as a city, and also to some extent the cultural homogeneity that made it so cohesive a community. For another, the vast majority of the empire's population lived not in cities but in rural areas and small villages; as we saw in chapter 2, in some areas of the empire alternative forms of social organization, such as powerful temple complexes or tribal associations, retained their importance. Nevertheless, the old ideal of the city retained tremendous cultural prestige, with the result that both Roman authorities and ambitious local elites tended to encourage the development of cities in areas where they were not traditional, such as Gaul and Anatolia. It is the cultural significance of cities that makes them central to any understanding of religion in the Roman Empire.

All the same, the city was not the only type of community. In this chapter, I discuss two other smaller-scale types of community: the household and the voluntary association. The household, as Aristotle observed, was the most basic form of community and existed in all parts of the empire. Voluntary associations, by contrast, had no part in Aristotle's analysis of "natural" communities, but nevertheless played an important part in many people's lives. In all cases, religion was an important medium for defining and structuring communities, while at the same time allowing for complex and overlapping identities.

1 The City

As I noted in chapter 2, it was traditional for every Greek city-state to have its own patron deities whom the community as a whole worshipped. This was more or less also the case in the two other major urban cultures of the ancient Mediterranean, the Phoenician and the Italic. We have already come across some examples of these civic patron deities: Athena in Athens, Artemis in Ephesus, Melqart/Herakles in Tyre, Caelestis in Carthage, Jupiter in Rome. In each case, identification with the city was closely bound up with devotion to its chief deity.

As one particular example, we may consider in more detail the relationship between Ephesus and Artemis, for which we have abundant and varied evidence. I will here cite just a small sample of it. First, Artemis regularly appears on the local coinage of Ephesus from the reign of Augustus onwards. The example shown here (see Figure 4.1) dates to the reign of Domitian (81–96 CE). The legend "Artemis Ephesia" on the reverse of the coin is hardly necessary, since the distinctive image of the goddess, despite being both minute and worn, is instantly identifiable (compare Figure 2.1). She is moreover accompanied by two deer, one of her usual attributes. Even today, of course, countries use their coinage for the display of images and emblems that symbolize national identity. In the Roman Empire, although imperial mints produced all the gold and silver coinage, some cities continued to mint their own bronze coinage for minor transactions. That the authorities of Ephesus chose to adorn their coins with the local cult image of Artemis is a strong indication of her importance to Ephesian identity. Her significance is similarly stressed in decrees of the city council and letters of imperial officials. For example, a civic resolution declaring that the entire month Artemision be sacred to the goddess includes the observation that "the goddess Artemis, defender of our city, is honored not only in her own land, which she has rendered more glorious than all other cities through her holiness, but also by Greeks and barbarians, so that holy places and precincts are everywhere established for her" and that "the greatest sign of her cult" is "that we have called a month after her name, Artemision . . . , during which festivals and holidays are held" (*SIG*³ 867, trans. MacMullen and Lane 1992: 41). We see very clearly here how the glory and renown of Ephesus was bound up with that of its chief deity.

Lastly, we get a vivid illustration of the sentiment that she could arouse among Ephesians from an anecdote found in *Acts of the Apostles*. When the apostle Paul was in the city, urging people to put their faith in Christ, he attracted the attention of a man named Demetrius, "a silversmith who made silver shrines of Artemis and provided a great deal of employment for the craftsmen." Demetrius organized a meeting of craftsmen, and argued Paul's activities posed a threat to them: "it is not only that our line of business will be discredited, but also that the sanctuary of the great goddess Artemis will cease to command respect; and then it will not be

Figure 4.1 Bronze coin of Ephesus: cult image of Artemis on reverse. Paris, Bibliothèque nationale 647. Reproduced by permission of Bibliothèque nationale de France, Paris

Figure 4.1   Bronze coin of Ephesus: head of Domitian on obverse

long before she who is worshipped by all Asia and the civilized world is brought down from her divine pre-eminence." On hearing this, the crowd became furious and began shouting "Great is Artemis of the Ephesians!"; it took two hours before one of the local magistrates was able to calm them down, reminding them that "all the world knows that our city of Ephesus is temple-warden of the great Artemis" (*Acts of the Apostles* 19.24–36, trans. adapted from the New English Bible). This anecdote reveals an intertwining of civic pride, economic interests, and religious devotion that to many people today might seem strange and even improper. In the civic cults of the Roman Empire, however, it was absolutely typical.

The significance of civic cults lay not only in the strong attachment that the inhabitants of a city might have to its chief deities, but also in the way that they shaped people's experience of life in that city. For example, the spatial organization of most cities in the Roman Empire was profoundly affected by the location of its major temples. As just one striking illustration, we may consider the Imperial fora in the city of Rome (see Figure 4.2). The original forum was an open area in the city center used as a general public gathering place and for more formal activities such as political meetings and judicial proceedings. By the mid-first century BCE it was becoming too crowded, and Julius Caesar constructed a new public space nearby: a paved rectangular area with porticoes on the two long sides and at one end a monumental temple dedicated to Venus Genetrix ("the Ancestress"), from whom Caesar claimed descent. His forum thus provided the same sort of public space as the old forum while at the same time serving as the forecourt of a temple. His successor Augustus adopted the same basic design for his own even more elaborate forum. The temple in this case was dedicated to Mars Ultor ("the Avenger"), whom Augustus

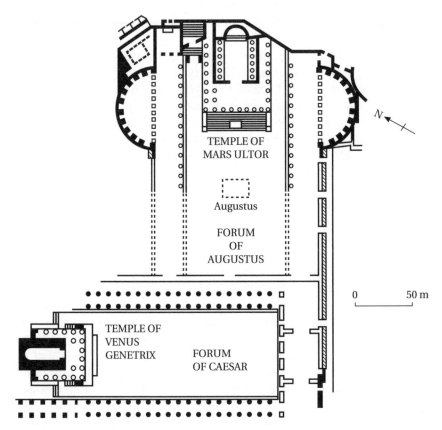

Figure 4.2 Plan of the fora of Caesar and Augustus in Rome

had invoked in his struggle against Caesar's assassins. The pediment of the temple featured an image of Mars in the center, flanked on one side by Venus and Romulus, the founder of the city, and on the other by Fortuna and Roma, the personification of the city. The porticoes that enclosed the forum on its two long sides, with their two large apses, contained statues of great heroes from Rome's past, and in the center of the forum was a monumental statue of Augustus himself. The whole space thus constituted a monumental visual lesson about the relationship between the city, the gods, and the emperor, while at the same time serving as the site for much public and private business. Later emperors built similar fora, and variations on the pattern eventually appeared in many other cities of the empire as well. Many other patterns for the organization of public and religious space also existed; that in traditional Greek cities was quite different, although in them as well the Roman model of the temple with its associated forum began to appear. But in all cases the temples of the major local deities constituted a significant element in the overall urban layout.

Just as the placement of temples and shrines helped shape the organization of civic space, so too the rituals of public cult helped determine the rhythms of the civic year. Because there was no such thing as a "weekend" in the Roman world, religious festivals provided the main opportunities for rest and relaxation. Most of these took place annually according to a regular calendar; one of the best known is that of the city of Rome, which we may consider as a representative example. The Roman calendar included a mixture of folk traditions, sacrifices to particular deities, and elaborate festivals involving chariot races and other types of spectacles. I will here mention just a very small selection. On February 15 was the festival of the Lupercalia, when a group of men known as the Luperci sacrificed goats and then raced through the city, naked except for the goatskins, striking the bystanders with goatskin thongs; the festival was very ancient, and endured to the end of the fifth century CE. Also ancient were the rituals in honor of Mars during March (which took its name from the god); on various days of the month, most importantly the first and the nineteenth, another fellowship known as the Salii ("Leapers") processed through the city in archaic armor, pausing periodically to perform a ritual war dance. On April 21 was the ancient agricultural festival of the Parilia, which in the imperial period was reinterpreted as the birthday of the city. In September came the great Ludi Romani, the "Roman Games" celebrated in honor of Jupiter Optimus Maximus, which at their height lasted 16 days and included as their chief attraction chariot races in the Circus Maximus, attended by upwards of 150,000 people. The festivities opened with an elaborate procession, led by the chief magistrates of the city and including statues of the gods carried shoulder high above the crowds; it began from the great temple of Jupiter on the Capitoline Hill, wound its way through the old forum, and ended at the Circus Maximus, where the magistrates and priests presided over sacrifices. At the end of the year was the Saturnalia: sacrifices and a public banquet at the temple of Saturn on December 17 inaugurated a week-long period of merry-making, during which people exchanged presents and masters waited on their servants.

Many of these festivals involved an official suspension of public business, and we may reasonably suppose that most people were happy to take a break from their personal business as well. Of course, then as now, popular celebrations were not to everyone's tastes, and there must have been those who deliberately avoided them; we know, for example, that some members of the elite retired to their country estates for the duration of the Roman Games. Yet regardless of the way individuals responded to these festivals, they inevitably loomed large in the lives of everyone who resided in Rome. The same was true for all the cities of the empire: each had its own calendar of festivals that shaped the annual rhythm of life. As with the Ludi Romani in Rome, the most important festivals honored the chief patron deities, and many involved athletic competitions or musical and theatrical performances; this was especially true in the eastern half of the empire, where as I noted in chapter 2 festivals modeled on the traditional Panhellenic games of the Greek tradition became very widespread. Yet public cults were not simply excuses for holidays and mass entertainment; they also entailed rituals that in certain respects encapsulated what it meant to be part of a particular city. We may consider two specific examples as an illustration.

In Athens, the Panathenaia, the celebration of the birth of Athena, was traditionally celebrated every year on the twenty-eighth day of the month Hekatombaion, which apparently took its name from the hecatomb, or sacrifice of one hundred oxen, that was offered to Athena at that time. The festival began with an elaborate procession that formed on the outskirts of the city, passed through the Agora (the ancient center of social and political life), and climbed the Acropolis. The procession included groups of old men, young men, and young unmarried women as representative segments of the citizen population, and ended at the great altar before the Parthenon, where the priests and magistrates presided over the hecatomb. Part of the meat from these extensive sacrifices was distributed on the spot to the city officials and those who had taken part in the procession; the rest was distributed at another location to the entire citizen population, each city ward receiving an allotment in proportion to the number of its residents in the procession. Every four years the city celebrated a more elaborate version of the festival, known as the Great Panathenaia, which included athletic and musical competitions and the presentation to the goddess of an elaborately woven robe.

Very different was a procession of statues in Ephesus, endowed in the early second century CE by a wealthy citizen named Gaius Vibius Salutaris and known from a lengthy and detailed inscription (*IEph* 27, trans. in Rogers 1991). No sacrifices were associated with this procession, and it took place not annually but during all significant civic events, such as meetings of the assembly and important festivals: on average, about every two weeks. First came images of the emperor and empress, followed by 27 other statues in groups of three; each group included a statue of Artemis, one representing a division of the Ephesian citizen body, and one representing either a Roman political body or an important figure from Ephesian history. The statues were kept in the great temple of Artemis on the outskirts of the city; from there the procession entered the city proper, where it was met by the ephebes, the young men enrolled in the official civic youth organization. They escorted the procession through the heart of the city with a stop in the theater, where the statues were displayed on nine pedestals especially erected for this purpose; the procession then exited the city, at which point the ephebes left it, and returned to the temple of Artemis. Including the ephebes, the procession would have involved between 200 and 300 participants, and so could not have failed to attract the attention of anyone in the vicinity.

In their different ways, both these rituals functioned to define and reinforce the civic and religious identity of the populace. The processions physically and visually tied the temple of the chief deity to key public spaces in the city. In the Panathenaia, the participation of representative groups in the procession and the elaborate formula for the distribution of the sacrificial meat symbolically united the entire citizen body in the worship of its patron goddess while at the same time affirming the distinct social roles that the different parts of the population were supposed to play. In Ephesus, the statue procession constituted a symbolic figuration of local civic identity, in which both the Roman present and the Ephesian past had their place but which centered on identification with the goddess Artemis; it thus provided the city's residents, especially the ephebes who participated in it, with a lesson about Ephesian identity in the second century CE. In all cases, it was through public rituals like these that people learned what it meant to be part of their city. And these public rituals, in turn, were inevitably grounded in the relationship between the city and its chief patron deities.

In addition to shaping civic identity, public cults also played a part in articulating social hierarchies. The elite of a city not only represented the citizen body by presiding over religious rituals as magistrates and priests, as at the Panathenaia and the opening ceremonies of the Ludi Romani, but they also to a large extent determined what deities received public cult. This role is clearly laid out in the civic charters that governed the foundation of new Roman cities. For example, a charter from Spain stipulates that the chief magistrates of the new foundation shall "raise with the city councilors, when not less than two-thirds shall be present, which and how many days it may be agreed shall be festivals and which sacrifices shall be publicly performed and who shall perform those sacrifices"; whatever the majority of councilors decides "is to be legal and binding, and there are to be those sacrifices and those festival days in that colony" (*Lex Coloniae Genetivae* 64, trans. adapted from Crawford 1996: 1.422). In a long-established city like Athens or Ephesus, where most public sacrifices and festivals were traditional, there would have been no need for this kind of initial establishment. Yet even in these cities, it was the council that authorized any additions or changes to the public cults.

It is important to keep in mind that a city's magistrates, priests, and councilors were not so much its elected representatives, as they are in modern democracies, as its socio-economic elite. It is of course true that in modern democracies the wealthy have a significant practical advantage when it comes to seeking high office, but in the end it is a person's election and not his or her wealth that makes that person a public official. In the cities of the Roman world the correspondence between wealth and public office was much more direct. For one thing, it was necessary to pay a substantial fee on taking up most public offices, including priesthoods. Moreover, while in office people were expected to perform other benefactions as well; priests and magistrates who presided over festivals, for example, would normally help finance them out of their personal resources, and some would in addition fund distributions of food and money or the construction of public amenities. Wealth was thus a formal requirement for holding public office, and an important part of serving as a magistrate or public priest was using that wealth on behalf of the populace. In these ways the public cults of a city were intimately bound up with the system of euergetism, the relationships of patronage that I sketched in the introduction to this chapter. The elite used their wealth and influence to benefit the city in exchange for the social prestige and authority that their offices conferred upon them, including the implicit right to regulate the city's relations with its gods.

The merging of the civic, religious, and economic spheres that we saw in Demetrius the silversmith's defense of Artemis was thus a pervasive feature of civic cult in the Roman Empire. Yet we should be careful not to dismiss civic cults as nothing more than a branch of city administration.

The fact that they were closely integrated with other aspects of civic life did not prevent them from having their own distinctive dynamics as well. For example, the city was not involved in all interactions with the gods, even when there was a public cult of the deity in question. As we saw in the previous chapter, people frequently had personal reasons of their own to pray and make offerings to a particular deity; if that deity had a public temple, that was no doubt often considered a particularly appropriate place in which to do so. Public temples thus served the needs of private individuals and groups as well as the community as a whole. Nor was the significance even of public rituals necessarily limited to their communal role. It was the job of public priests and other officials to ensure the correct performance of the rituals, not to dictate their interpretation. As a result, people might well participate in them for reasons that had nothing to do with the wider community, and interpret them in terms of their own religious ideas and values. For all these reasons, even public cults could have a private dimension.

Moreover, the identity between a city and its public cults was rarely total, since magistrates and priests might at times have distinct interests. Tensions over finances provide a particularly good example of this. It was normal for there to be a clear distinction between general public funds and sacred funds, which could include public funds earmarked for particular cultic expenses as well as separate sources of income that were under the direct control of cult officials. For example, some temples owned property, from which they received rental income, and all temples received income from the fees that they charged private worshippers for the use of their facilities, as well as donations and votive offerings from the devout. Although it was generally accepted that civic officials could draw on these funds in time of need, there were also instances of abuse that sometimes led local priests to appeal to Roman officials for support against local magistrates. In situations like these, the disjunction between city and cult becomes apparent. If civic cults played a crucial role in establishing civic identity and were consequently integral to civic organization, we must keep in mind that they were at the same time semi-autonomous.

We must also remember that there was no formal mechanism to enforce participation in civic cult, although there were informal social pressures, and that some people evidently chose not to take part. In Galilee, for example, Judaean rabbis argued that when there was an "idolatrous festival" in a city and some shops were "adorned" while others were not, observant Judaeans could do business at the unadorned shops without involving themselves in idolatry (Mishnah, *Abodah Zarah* 1.4, trans. H. Danby). The "adorning" in question was presumably the common practice of decorating one's doors with garlands and lamps as a way of acknowledging a festival. The rabbis clearly regarded the absence of such decorations as a sign that a person was not participating in the festival; equally clearly, the fact that they bothered to rule on this issue suggests that such lack of participation was common enough to warrant particular discussion. To a large extent, however, the importance of civic cults lay not in the enthusiasm that they might or might not have inspired in people, but rather in their banality, in the familiar way that temples shaped public space and festivals shaped the year. The fact that Salutaris' procession of statues in Ephesus took place an average of once every two weeks must have meant that most people gave it little conscious thought, and perhaps even regarded it as an interruption and an annoyance. Yet they would have absorbed its underlying message all the same: the centrality of Artemis was part of what it meant to be an Ephesian. In this respect, as I argue in chapter 7, it was not the shopkeepers who were uninterested or too busy to take part in a public festival that presented a problem, but rather the resident Judaeans, who deliberately rejected the entire tradition on which the festival was based.

2 The Household

In most western societies of the last century or so, the household has been largely equivalent to the nuclear family: husband, wife, and children, perhaps with the addition of a widowed parent or an unmarried sibling. This was not the case in the Roman Empire, where many or even most households would have included slaves and sometimes freedmen and freed-women as well. Free or slave, all members of a household were organized in a set of hierarchic relationships. Aristotle analyzed three basic relation-ships within the household: master and slave, husband and wife, father and children (*Politics* 1.3), with the first member of each pair being the superior. Thus in theory a free adult male acted as the head of every house-hold; in practice, however, this was not always the case, and in some cases single women acted as the heads of their own households.

The main objects of household cult were, on the one hand, the house-hold gods and, on the other, the family dead. When a member of the family died, the survivors were naturally responsible for ensuring that he or she received a proper funeral and burial. But their obligation towards the deceased did not end there: they were also expected to honor the dead person for years to come by making regular offerings at the grave site. In the city of Rome, the festival of the Parentalia, which lasted for nine days in February, was the traditional time for families to pay cult to their forebears, and similar festivals existed elsewhere in the empire. People also made offerings on private anniversaries, such as the birthday of the deceased. Offerings could include foodstuffs, lamps, and incense, although the most typical were flowers and libations. The practice of placing flowers on graves continues to this day, although that of offering libations has disappeared; in antiquity, however, it was so common that some graves were even equipped with special tubes into which people could pour the liquid. The ritual offerings were often accompanied by a meal, which in a sense united in fellowship both the living and the dead members of the family.

The cult of the dead was especially important in maintaining the identity of the family over time. We can see this very clearly in an inscription from Rome, dating probably to the mid-second century CE. A freedman of the emperor named Titus Aelius Faustus and his wife Aelia Arete had a tomb constructed "for themselves and their children, and likewise for their freedmen and freedwomen and their descendants" with the express stipulation that it not "pass out from their name or household," so that "sacrifices may be made to their memory for as long as possible" (*ILS* 8274). The inclusion of the freedmen and freedwomen, often found in inscriptions of this kind, is significant: since in Roman law freed slaves took the family name of their former owners, they could play an important part in maintaining the family, and the cult of its deceased members, over the years. But just as the family maintained the cult, so too the cult helped to maintain the family, by defining it in relation to earlier generations.

Although household gods existed in many cultures of the empire, I will here limit my discussion to the Greek and Roman traditions, which are the best known and which spread with Greek and Roman culture. In the Greek tradition, one important household god was Zeus Herkeios, "Zeus of the Courtyard," at whose altar the head of the family performed regular sacrifices on behalf of the household. Another was Zeus Ktesios, "Protector of Property," whose presence was marked by a pot filled with foodstuffs in the pantry. But the most important was Hestia, whose name was simply the ancient Greek word for "hearth" and whose identification with the physical hearth of the home was very close: offerings were placed there at mealtimes, and rituals performed there transformed newborn babies, brides, and new slaves into official members of the household. The cult of Hestia thus played a crucial part in defining the household community.

The Roman tradition likewise bestowed a central role on the goddess of the hearth, called Vesta in Latin, who similarly received offerings at mealtimes. In place of the domestic forms of Zeus, however, we find two groups of deities, the Lares and the Penates, whose precise nature is uncertain. The name "Penates" (found only in the plural) is probably connected with the Latin word *penus*, "larder"; they were thus apparently the protectors of the household property. The name "Lares" (also found in the singular "Lar") is more obscure, and their function seems to have been less specific, since Lares also appear as guardians of crossroads. It was to the household Lares that young men dedicated the symbols of their boyhood on their assumption of adult status, and young women dedicated their toys and girlhood clothes when they married. Distinctive to the Roman tradition was the *genius*, or divine alter-ego, of the head of the family; the other members of the household made offerings to the *genius* on important occasions, and it was not uncommon for slaves and freedmen to erect dedications to the *genius* of their master (or the *iuno* of their mistress, in households headed by women). The cult of the *genius* is a very clear example of the way that domestic cult reinforced the social hierarchy within the household.

Although the hearth was the most common focus for domestic cult, many houses also contained household shrines or altars. Our best evidence for domestic shrines comes from the Italian towns of Pompeii and Herculaneum, where excavators have discovered many examples not only in private homes but also in taverns and shops. They take a wide variety of forms, from miniature temples to wall paintings to simple niches in which statues could be placed. The paintings typically depict two young men, often dancing, who represent the Lares, an adult male in a toga, usually offering a libation, who represents the *genius*, and a large serpent, regarded in both the Greek and the Italic traditions as a guardian spirit. The example shown here (see Figure 4.3), from a stable in Pompeii, consists of a small niche decorated with wall paintings. On either side are the Lares, each holding a cornucopia and a small dish for making libations, and below is the serpent. On a wall of the niche itself we find instead of the *genius* an image of the Celtic horse goddess Epona, an appropriate guardian for a stable.

As we saw in the introduction to this chapter, Aristotle identified the household as the basic building block of the city-state: both were part of the "natural" structuring of human society. Not surprisingly, there were significant interconnections between the household and the city. First, the city often functioned in cultic terms as a household writ large, so that the traditional cults of the household also existed on the civic level. In many Greek cities, for example, there was a public cult of Hestia, represented by a communal hearth in one of the major civic buildings. In some there were also public cults of Zeus Herkeios and Zeus Ktesios, as in Athens, where Zeus Herkeios had an altar on the Acropolis. Similarly, in the Roman tradition there was a public cult of Vesta in a small round shrine on one side of the original forum, where the famous Vestal Virgins ensured that her fire never went out; the Vestals likewise maintained the public

Figure 4.3 Domestic shrine from a stable in Pompeii, depicting Epona (center) and the Lares (left and right). Pompeii IX, 2, 24. Reproduced by permission of DAI Rome, Inst.Neg.Nr. 31.1770

Penates. We may also note that when the emperor Augustus received the title *pater patriae*, "father of the fatherland," his *genius* became an object of cult, especially among slaves and freedmen. Secondly, civic officials had an interest in upholding and even regulating the traditional forms of domestic cult. A candidate for public office in Athens, for example, was traditionally asked whether he had family tombs and a cult of Zeus Herkeios (Aristotle, *The Constitution of the Athenians* 55.3). In Rome, Cicero regarded it as an essential part of an ideal city-state that heirs be required to maintain family cults (*On Laws* 2.48), and the *pontifices*, one of the chief groups of public priests, did exercise some authority in matters of household cult such as burial law and the inheritance of religious duties.

It would thus be misleading to see household cults and civic cults as an opposition of "private" and "public": although they existed in different spheres, there were significant links between them. At the same time, they did not fit together into a seamless and all-embracing system. Just as individuals could pursue their own religious interests with little or no interference from public authorities, so too could households worship whatever deities they liked. The deities attested in the household shrines of Pompeii and Herculaneum, for example, are not limited to the traditional Lares and *genius*, but also include Jupiter, Minerva, Fortuna, Hercules, Liber Pater, Mercury, Venus, Isis, Aesculapius, and others. A house in Ostia had a niche-shrine with a mosaic image of Silvanus, and as we have already seen, there was a domestic shrine of Epona in Pompeii (see Figure 4.3). Excavators have discovered numerous figurines and statuettes of deities in virtually every region that once formed part of the Roman Empire: were these objects of domestic cult, placed in small house shrines, or were they merely objets d'art used for decoration? The evidence from Pompeii suggests that at least some of them were used in worship, although as I suggested in chapter 1 the distinction between cult object and art object was never hard and fast. So just as it would be wrong to see domestic cult as completely isolated from the public sphere, so too would it be wrong to assume that it was simply an extension of public cult.

In all cases, however, domestic cult was a group activity in which all members of a household normally participated and over which the head of the household normally presided; the votive relief of Cuttinus from Africa provides a vivid image of a household acting as a cultic unit (see Figure 3.1). Some people went so far as to assert that the subordinate members of a household should not engage in separate cult activities of their own. Plutarch, for example, was of the opinion that "it is fitting for a married woman to honor and recognize only those gods whom her husband acknowledges, and to bar the door against superfluous devotions and foreign superstitions; for with no god do the stolen and secret rites of a woman find any favor" (*Conjugal Precepts* 19, 140d). The very fact that Plutarch felt he had to insist on this suggests that it was in reality not uncommon for wives and the other subordinate members of a household to engage in their own religious activities. At the same time, however, it encapsulates the idea that the household was a corporate body with a defined internal hierarchy, and that the religious lives of those who belonged to it should ideally be determined by its collective worship.

3 Voluntary Associations

Along with cities and household, there also existed in the Roman Empire a wide range of groups that modern scholars usually describe as "voluntary" or "elective" associations. People formed groups like this for a variety of reasons: because they lived in the same area, or pursued the same line of work, or shared a common ethnic or cultural background, or were devoted to the same deity, or were simply interested in the opportunities for fellowship and support that went with being part of an organized group. For the sake of convenience, I here distinguish three basic kinds of associations, ethnic, occupational, and cultic, although it is not always easy or even appropriate to make sharp divisions between them. As we have already seen, communal identity, economic concerns, and religious devotion were often deeply intertwined, and this was as true in voluntary associations as it was in cities. In fact, all associations tended to engage in much the same types of activities, which we may broadly group under the headings of fellowship, mutual support, and common worship. They varied, however, in their relations with the wider society: some were virtually official civic bodies, whereas others were fundamentally opposed and offered a radical alternative. Between these two extremes there was a spectrum of groups that were distinct from but not necessarily at odds with society as a whole. In what follows I briefly discuss each of these topics in turn, beginning with the different types of associations.

The Roman Empire encompassed a wide range of peoples and cultural traditions, which I briefly surveyed in chapter 2; as we will see in chapter 5, there was considerable movement of people from one part of the empire to another, and these people frequently brought the worship of their traditional deities along with them. Just as in our own culture, immigrants often associated with one another and at times even established formal societies. Not surprisingly, an important activity of these ethnic associations was the worship of ancestral deities. For example, a certain Karpion son of Anoubion dedicated an altar to Sarapis and the emperor Septimius

Severus on behalf of the "household of Alexandrians," probably a group of resident Alexandrian merchants, in Tomis on the coast of Lower Moesia (*IGR* 1.604); a similar group was perhaps responsible for a small shrine of Sarapis in Carthage. An inscription from Pompeii refers to a "corporation of Phrygians," whose priest made a dedication to Phrygian Zeus (*IGR* 1.458), and at Puteoli, an important port south of Rome, a group of people from Berytus in Phoenicia described themselves as "worshippers of Jupiter Heliopolitanus" (*ILS* 300).

Although all these associations may have been made up of people only temporarily resident abroad, in a few cases we can identify more or less permanent communities of immigrants. In Puteoli, for example, there was also a community of Tyrians, who in the year 79 CE transferred a statue of their god Sarepta from Tyre to Puteoli; another inscription indicates that the group still existed a century later, although financial difficulties had forced them to appeal to the city council of Tyre for assistance in maintaining their community center and their ancestral worship (*IGR* 1.420–1). But by far the most important example of permanent immigrants who formed associations for the worship of an ancestral deity were the Judaeans, who formed communities not only in much of the eastern empire but in North Africa and Italy as well. The organization of these Judaean communities varied. In many eastern cities, such as Ephesus, Smyrna, Antioch, and apparently Alexandria, they seem to have formed single corporations within the city, whereas in Rome they made up a number of apparently separate synagogues.

Some ethnic associations apparently consisted of resident businessmen from particular cities, and thus to some extent doubled as professional associations. There were also many associations of people who shared an occupation but not necessarily any ethnic bond; among the numerous examples attested in all parts of the empire are societies of physicians, traders, shipbuilders, ferrymen, sailors, carpenters, weavers, fullers, bakers, and silversmiths. Professional associations of this sort also engaged in group religious activities and had their own patron deities. Although the latter could be any deity the group liked, we frequently see an obvious connection between deity and worshippers. Craftsmen, for example, often honored Minerva, the goddess of handicrafts: as I noted in the previous chapter, the patron of "the Most Illustrious Guild of Tow-Workers" at the port of Rome dedicated a statue to Minerva, the group's "preserver and protector" (*ILS* 3129). Mercury similarly received the devotion of people involved in trade or retail operations: in Volubilis in Mauretania Tingitana, an association of clothes merchants who called themselves "the college of Mercury" paid for the gravestone of an eleven-year-old boy, presumably the son of one of the members (*ILS* 7291), and in Rome a group of wine-merchants shared their devotion between Mercury and Liber Pater, the god of wine (*ILS* 7276). The association of grain-measurers in Ostia named themselves for Ceres, the goddess of grain (*ILS* 6146), and included a shrine of the goddess in their headquarters. At Ephesus the physicians' guild described themselves as "those who sacrifice to ancestor Asklepios and the emperors" (*IEph* 719), and in what is now Turin a group of doctors took the title "worshippers of Asclepius and Hygia" (*ILS* 3855a). More unusual is an inscription found in Zurich with a votive dedication to the woodland deities Diana and Silvanus made by a group of bear-keepers (*ILS* 3267).

The most widely attested associations of this kind consisted of the athletes, musicians, and actors who competed in the games at major religious festivals. The theatrical performers took as their patron Dionysos, the god traditionally associated with dramatic and musical performances, and the athletes similarly adopted Herakles. These associations are widely attested, and they apparently took their devotion to their patron deities very seriously. In an inscription that probably originated in Rome, for example, the Dionysiac artists record a benefaction to their god made by a certain Lucius Septimius Trypho, twice priest, chief priest for life of Dionysos the Leader, and chief priest for life of "Marcus Aurelius Antoninus Augustus the New Dionysos," the emperor Caracalla (Merkelbach 1985).

Lastly, there was a wide range of groups defined above all by devotion to a particular deity. I will here give just a small sampling. In Ephesus there were the initiates of Dionysos and the Demetriastai, worshippers of Demeter (for example, *IEph* 275, 1595, and 4337). In Athens was a group of devotees of Bakkhos who called themselves the Iobakkhoi and who had as their meeting place a fairly large hall (11 by 18 meters) with an apse containing an altar at one end; a column found near the altar is covered by a lengthy inscription of the association's by-laws (*SIG*³ 1109, trans. Meyer 1987: 96–9). In Tarsus, the *therapontes*, "servants" or "attendants," of Demeter likewise had their own meeting place (*IGR* 3.883). An inscription in Belgrade records a dedication made by "the worshippers of the God Heros" (*ILS* 4065). At Lanuvium, in central Italy, another long inscription preserves the by-laws of "the worshippers of Diana and Antinous," the young lover of the emperor Hadrian who was deified after drowning in the Nile (*ILS* 7212). Groups of "worshippers" of Hercules and of Silvanus are known from sites in Italy and elsewhere, while in Africa we find the "worshippers of the Cereses" and a cult association of Caelestis (*ILS* 4462 and 9294). Groups of *dendrophori*, "tree-bearers" who had specific duties in the cult of the Great Mother, existed in many cities, notably Ostia in Italy, and in Pompeii the Isiaci, devotees of Isis, endorsed a candidate for local public office (*ILS* 6420b). Throughout the empire, especially in

Italy and the provinces along the Rhine and Danube, were small groups of initiates of Mithras, who met in distinctive underground shrines conventionally known as mithraea, but which they themselves apparently called "caves." Last but not least were the communities devoted to the worship of Jesus Christ, who seem generally to have described themselves as *ekklêsiai* (whence modern English "ecclesiastic"), a Greek word that meant "assembly," particularly the public assembly of a city-state.

As I noted above, virtually all associations shared the same basic features. One of these was a concern for mutual support, especially at the time of death. For example, when one of the worshippers of Diana and Antinous in Lanuvium died, the association sent three representatives to arrange for his burial and paid all the expenses; if a member who was a slave died and his owner refused to hand over the body, the association performed the funeral ritual all the same, with an image of the deceased representing the body. Some associations even had their own burial grounds: the worshippers of Hercules in Pisa presumably paid for theirs themselves (*ILS* 7320), whereas those in another Italian town received theirs as a gift (*ILS* 7324). It is clear that associations like these, made up of people from the poorer segments of society, functioned in part as burial societies, guaranteeing a proper burial for their members. For this reason some scholars have distinguished "funerary associations" as a distinct type of group in the Graeco-Roman world. Yet many groups that would not be classed as "funerary associations" were also concerned with the deaths of their members. The Iobakkhoi, for example, contributed a wreath to the funeral of a deceased associate, and those who attended shared a jar of wine. Christian groups also became involved in the burials of their fellows, and by the beginning of the third century CE had their own burial grounds, such as the famous catacombs in Rome. Moreover, even if for many people the guarantee of a proper burial was in itself a good reason to join an association, that does not mean that they regarded its other activities as secondary.

Many associations also put considerable emphasis on fellowship, and their members enjoyed regular group meals and festivities. The Athenian Iobakkhoi met once a month and on all festivals of Bakkhos; these meetings could apparently become quite rowdy, since the by-laws forbid members to sing or create a disturbance and specify the procedures to follow if two members quarrel or come to blows. The worshippers of Diana and Antinous in Lanuvium likewise had regular group dinners; the regulations specify that the annual *magistri cenarum*, "dinner-masters," were to provide good wine, bread, sardines, tablecloths, hot water, and service. A monument from northwestern Turkey, set up by the men and women of a *thiasos*, a cult association, in honor of a priestess of Mother Cybele

Figure 4.4 Honorific relief for a priestess of Cybele and Apollo. Athens, National Museum, inv. no. 1485. Reproduced by permission of National Archaeological Museum, Athens/photo Archaeological Receipts Fund

and Apollo, shows us what these meals could be like (Figure 4.4). At the top is a relief depicting a woman, presumably the priestess, approaching an altar with her attendants to offer a sacrifice; to the right of the altar are Apollo with his harp and Cybele, seated and wearing a high headdress. In the lower register is a scene of the cult members enjoying a feast: they recline at their tables while below them musicians play the pipes and servants mix wine in large bowls and attend to the meat that is roasting on spits. Common meals like these, repeated at regular intervals through-out the year, were not merely a form of entertainment; they also played a crucial role in fostering a sense of fellowship among the members of an association. The close ranks and almost identical profiles of the *thiasos* members constitutes a visual expression of this group identity.

This monument is not only a vivid depiction of the festivities that were so important to many associations, but also a reminder of the close con-nection between sacrifice and feasting that was typical of the Graeco-Roman tradition. Every meal shared by the members of an association, except in Judaean and Christian groups, also involved an offering to the gods, whether a full animal sacrifice or a simple libation. There was thus an inextricable bond between fellowship, group identity, and communal worship. But sacrifice was only the most common ritual means of reinfor-cing group identity. Some cult groups required prospective members to undergo an initial period of instruction followed by a ritual of initiation; this was true, for example, of the worshippers of Christ and of Mithras. We know almost nothing about initiation into the cult of Mithras, although a series of frescoes from a mithraeum in Italy depicts the initiate as nude and blindfolded, with his hands tied behind his back. Further rituals allowed cult members to ascend through a complex hierarchy of seven grades, from "Raven" to "Father." Worshippers of Mithras also took part in a common meal, during which they ritually reenacted an episode from their god's history. We know a great deal more about the religious activities of Christian groups. The younger Pliny, for example, who as governor of Bithynia interrogated some Christians, reported to the emperor Trajan that they regularly met before dawn in order to sing hymns in honor of Christ, and then reassembled later in the day in order to share a meal (*Letters* 10.96.7). A Christian manual that dates probably to the early second century CE discusses in detail the two main Christian rituals: the initiation ritual of baptism with water and the Eucharist, the sharing of wine and bread that commemorated the sacrificial death of Jesus Christ (*Didache* 7–10).

In all types of associations, participation in shared religious rituals played a crucial part in creating a sense of group identity. And for cultic associations, the relationship with a particular deity was the only thing that defined them as a group at all: whatever else they might do, "the Iobakkhoi" or "the worshippers of Diana and Antinous" was who they were.

4 Conclusion

To belong to a community in the Graeco-Roman world meant to worship the deities of that community and to participate in its rituals, especially sacrifice and the accompanying meal. As a distinguished scholar of Greek religion has put it, religion served "not just to embellish but to shape all essential forms of community: the definition of membership [was] participation in a cult" (Burkert 1985: 255). We have seen how this principle operated in the city, the household, and the voluntary association. Participation in shared religious rituals also helped to articulate social hierarchies: those of higher status, for example, normally represented their groups in collective worship, as civic magistrates and priests did in civic cults and the heads of households did in household cults, while those of lower status frequently expressed gratitude to patrons and benefactors through prayers and dedications on their behalf. But while these various religious practices were highly effective in defining communities and structuring social relationships, they also allowed for considerable flexibility.

For example, although religion frequently served to reinforce traditional social hierarchies, it also provided opportunities for marginalized groups to advance their social status in ways that would otherwise be denied to them. Women, for example, who were generally barred from political office, could nevertheless hold public priesthoods. This was especially common in the Greek tradition, in which female deities were typically served by female priests; even in the Roman tradition, in which there were fewer female priests, the Vestals enjoyed extremely high public status. In the imperial period some elite women used their priesthoods to establish themselves as public benefactors on the same level as men, and consequently received the same forms of public recognition. Similarly, freedmen, who were also excluded from political office, might become Augustales, a formal civic rank common especially in the western empire that seems to have been connected with the worship of the emperor. If public cult offered opportunities for women and freedmen to acquire and display social status, voluntary associations offered even more. As we have seen, many associations drew their membership from the lower strata of society; in associations of this sort freedmen and even slaves could hold important positions. For example, the officials of an association of fullers who made a dedication to Minerva in a town of central Italy consisted of three freedmen and a slave (*ILS* 3127). It was similarly not uncommon for women to serve as officials of cult associations, such as the "mother of the *dendrophori*" and the female "chief staffbearer" of a group of *dendrophori* in Tomis on the Black Sea coast (*IGR* 1.614). Women in such positions often received public expressions of gratitude, such as the monument in honor of the priestess of Apollo and Cybele discussed above (see Figure 4.4).

In terms of group identity, the fact that worship of one deity did not preclude the worship of others meant that it was possible for people to belong simultaneously to a number of different groups. In some cases their group identities could be mutually reinforcing. I noted above, for example, the significant links that could exist between the household and the city. Some voluntary associations also had more or less close connections with the larger community. For example, in Ephesus both the initiates of Dionysos and the Demetriasts describe themselves as *pro poleôs*, "for the city," presumably because they saw themselves as in some sense acting for the city as a whole. The Demetriasts on at least one occasion actually obtained an official civic decree in support of their activities (*IEph* 4337). Other groups also sought and received official decrees in support of their activities. For example, a priest in the cult of Sarapis in Carthage, which was probably organized by a group of resident Alexandrians, made an offering to the god "by decree of the city council" (*ILS* 4388; see further Rives 1995: 185). Similarly, a group of worshippers of Mithras in what is now Milan obtained the land for their shrine by a grant from the city council (Clauss 2001: 43). Participation in collective worship was the key. Even if the worshippers of Mithras felt a primary identification with their cult association, as seems likely, they did not for that reason reject the community cults. They consequently remained a part of the larger community and could even, as happened in Milan, receive some measure of formal recognition from that community.

There were, however, some groups who understood their relationship with their god to exclude any participation in other religious activities; this was true above all of Judaeans and Christians. I noted above the concern of the Judaean rabbis to demarcate very carefully what did and did not constitute involvement in "idolatry," prescribing that observant Judaeans do business only with shops that gave no sign of participating in a public festival. Many Christian leaders were equally concerned with keeping the followers of Jesus Christ away from other religious activities; Tertullian wrote an entire treatise *On Idolatry* to enumerate all the ways that a person might even unwittingly participate in the worship of other gods. Both the members of these groups and those outside them were aware that rejecting collective worship meant rejecting group identity, and that the refusal to take part in public cults was in effect a refusal to belong to the larger community. It was for this reason above all that people could at times become violently hostile to Judaeans and Christians, a topic that I discuss in more detail in chapter 7.

Among Judaeans and Christians themselves, attitudes varied. There was often a sense of pride in constituting a separate group, and external hostility in many cases must only have reinforced internal solidarity. "The assembly of God that sojourns in Rome," for example, is how some Christians in Rome described themselves in the heading of a letter that dates probably to the 90s CE and is conventionally known as *1 Clement*. The Greek verb translated here as "to sojourn" means literally "to live somewhere as a foreigner," implying that this Christian group saw itself as being in Rome but not a part of Rome. The author of a brief defense of Christianity develops the idea in more detail: "[Christians] inhabit their own cities, but as foreigners; they participate in everything as citizens, but endure everything as aliens" (*Epistle to Diognetus* 5.5). Yet at the same time as he asserts the separation of Christians from the larger communities in which they lived, he also implies participation. Despite the rigorous prescriptions of someone like Tertullian, Judaeans and Christians could never remove themselves from their communities entirely, and many did not want to. Instead, there are signs that some advanced the radical idea that they could still be members of the wider community without taking part in public cults. Some Judaean communities seem to have taken this position, for example, and met with some success; in the very late second century or early third century CE, the emperors Septimius Severus and Caracalla ruled that Judaeans should be allowed to hold civic offices in the cities where they lived without undertaking any duties that conflicted with their religious obligations (*Digest* 50.2.3.3). Some Christians made similar appeals. As I mentioned at the start of chapter 2, writers like Athenagoras and Tertullian noted the wide variety of religious practice and devotion within the empire and argued that Christians should likewise be free to follow their beliefs without penalty or restriction. The irony with that, of course, is that once Christians became dominant, they in turn sought to penalize heretics, pagans, and Judaeans: the old principle that full membership in a community entailed participation in collective worship did not disappear, but was simply transformed.

FURTHER READING

On civic cult in the Greek tradition, see Bruit Zaidman and Schmitt Pantel 1992 for a stimulating introduction and Sourvinou-Inwood 2000a and 2000b for an incisive discussion; for the Roman tradition, see North 1976 and 1979, two crucial papers; Wardman 1982, a historical overview; and Scheid 2003, a valuable introduction. Woolf 2003, Bendlin 2000, and Dignas 2002 offer important critiques and qualifications. Scullard 1981 provides a convenient guide to the calendar of Rome; Rogers 1991 is detailed study of the Salutaris inscription from Ephesus, with valuable insights into civic cult and civic identity. On euergetism and civic cult, see especially Gordon 1990. Klauck 2003: 55–80 provides a brief overview of domestic cult; on the household shrines of Pompeii and Herculaneum, see Boyce 1937 and Orr 1978. On voluntary associations, see the papers in Kloppenborg and Wilson 1996; Harland 2003, although focused on Asia Minor, also provides a very useful general discussion. Clauss 2001 is an excellent guide to the practices and organization of the worshippers of Mithras.

CHAPTER 5

Religion and Empire

רּרּרּרּ

As we saw in the previous chapter, religion played a crucial role in creating group identity, to the point that being a member of a group meant participating in the cults of that group. Most of the groups that I discussed were strictly local, whether cities, households, or voluntary associations. Religion, however, was important not only in defining local identities, but also in forging links that bound together the multiplicity of local groups. At the end of chapter 2 I argued that, despite the considerable variety of religious traditions that existed within the Roman Empire, there was also enough common ground to allow for a relatively easy and effective integration. People throughout the empire would have agreed that a number of gods existed, that they could affect human lives, and that it was important to win their goodwill. These assumptions helped shape the way that they responded to the religious traditions of foreign groups. To put the matter somewhat simplistically, when people encountered a deity worshipped by foreigners, they could conclude either that this was a deity previously unknown to them or that it was a familiar deity worshipped under another name; in either case, the proper thing to do was to acknowledge and honor the deity, so as to win divine goodwill. Other possibilities of course existed: a person could dismiss foreign deities as non-existent, the delusions of uncivilized peoples, or accept them as real but evil, as demons or devils, and in either case reject their worship. But there is little evidence for either of these positions in the Graeco-Roman world, outside the Judaean and Christian traditions, a fact that in itself is highly revealing of the common ground shared by most religious traditions in the empire. As we will see in chapter 7, people could and did have strong ideas about the proper way to worship the gods; but the gods themselves were in a sense accepted by everyone, so that there was no need to convert people from one "religion" to another. The general recognition of multiple gods was thus the foundation for the religious integration of the empire. In this chapter I examine four particular phenomena that served to promote that integration by creating links between localities: the mobility of worshippers, the mobility of gods, the tendency to identify gods from different traditions as the same, and the unique role of the emperor as the religious center of the empire.

1 Mobility of Worshippers

According to the Judaean historian Josephus, at the festival of Pentecost in 4 BCE, "an endless crowd" of people poured into Jerusalem, not only from its immediate vicinity, but also from the neighboring districts of Galilee, Idumaea, Jericho, and Peraea (*The Judaean War* 2.43). Although Josephus says that on this particular occasion it was not so much the traditional ceremony that drew them as tension with their Roman overlords, it was evidently normal for large crowds to congregate at the temple in Jerusalem during major festivals. The author of *Acts of the Apostles* claims that at a Pentecost festival some 35 years later there were visitors from Persia, Mesopotamia, various parts of Asia Minor, Egypt, Libya, Crete, and Rome (2.9–11). Although he may well have exaggerated this list for his own purposes, it nonetheless gives a vivid impression of pilgrimage in the ancient world.

Pilgrimage within the Judaean tradition was by no means typical. For one thing, Judaean law required all Judaean men to assemble for the three great pilgrimage festivals, of which Pentecost was one (*Deuteronomy* 16.16–17). For another, most Judaeans regarded the Jerusalem temple as a uniquely holy site, the only place where sacrifices could legitimately be offered to their god and the only true locus for his worship. There was nothing like this in most other traditions within the Roman Empire. Instead, as we have seen, anyone could worship the gods at almost any place, so that even in the countryside a traveler might often encounter small altars or offerings. Since the gods were present everywhere, most people would not have felt a need to travel to a particular holy site, in the way that many Judaeans, even those resident elsewhere in the empire, wanted to visit the Jerusalem temple. There was nevertheless considerable travel for religious purposes within the Roman Empire. Even though anyone might pray to the gods and engage in simple forms of divination, it was only natural that in times of crisis people would want to avail themselves of more specialized services. As I noted in chapter 3, two of the most common benefits that people sought from the gods were help with health problems and advice in making decisions. Not surprisingly, then, sanctuaries with particular reputations as oracles or healing shrines tended to draw regular visitors from the general vicinity and in some cases more distant regions. People also traveled to take part in less common types of religious ceremonies, such as initiations into mysteries, or to attend major festivals. Lastly, some people traveled simply in order to see famous temples and visit other notable holy places. In such cases it is not always clear where we should draw the line between religious travel and tourism; but it is perhaps even less clear whether that line had any real meaning in the ancient world. In this section I look briefly at these various kinds of travel for religious purposes.

As I noted in chapter 2, oracles were an ancient part of the Greek tradition. Although in earlier centuries the oracle of Apollo at Delphi had been the most renowned, in the imperial period that at Claros in Asia Minor, near Ephesus, seems to have superseded it; inscriptions from the temple indicate that cities throughout Asia Minor as well as Thrace sent ambassadors to make inquiries there. There were many other oracles as well, not only in Greece and Asia Minor but also in Italy, Syria, and Egypt. At the oasis of Siwa in western Egypt, for example, was the famous oracle of Amun, called Zeus Ammon by Greek speakers, that had been consulted by Alexander the Great and in the 120s CE was still receiving inquiries from as far away as the northwest coast of Asia Minor (Merkelbach and Schwertheim 1983). In addition to these ancient foundations were more recently established oracles. The satirist Lucian composed a biting account of a certain Alexander, who founded an oracle of a god named Glykon on the northern coast of Asia Minor. Although Lucian regarded the whole thing as a complete fraud, many people did not, and Lucian describes how visitors began to pour into the town, first from the nearby areas of Bithynia, Galatia, and Thrace, and eventually from more distant regions, including even Rome (*Alexander the False Prophet* 18 and 30).

As with oracles, people were often willing to travel considerable distances in order to visit the shrines of deities regarded as particularly effective in curing health problems. As I noted in chapter 3, the most famous of these was Asklepios, whose great sanctuary in Pergamum attracted the infirm from as far away as Rome. Asklepios had many other shrines as well, notably at Epidaurus in Greece and at Leben on the southern coast of Crete; according to Philostratus, writing in the early third century CE, "just as Asia flocks to Pergamum, so Crete flocks to this shrine [at Leben], and many Libyans also cross over to it" (*Life of Apollonius of Tyana* 4.34.3). But Asklepios was by no means the only healing god, and many other sanctuaries attracted those seeking cures. These were often located at springs, just like modern health spas. For example, the quantity of offerings found at the shrine of the goddess Sequana at the source of the Seine suggests that it attracted many worshippers from the surrounding parts of Gaul. In Britain, the hot springs of Sulis Minerva at Aquae Sulis (modern Bath) seem also to have had visitors from Gaul, as well as Britain. Well-known healing shrines expected such a regular stream of visitors that they sometimes incorporated inns or hostels into their complexes.

Another common reason to travel was to attend a major religious festival. The most celebrated were the ancient Panhellenic games of Greece, especially those of Zeus at Olympia and the Pythian games of Apollo at Delphi. As I noted in the previous chapter, however, almost every significant city had its festivals, and these would have attracted large crowds from the surrounding territory. It was not only in cities that such festivals took place. A number of rural sanctuaries in northern Gaul, for example, were equipped with monumental theaters whose size suggests that they attracted worshippers from a large surrounding area. We may reasonably assume that ceremonies connected with the public cults of the local tribe took place there, and that people from the entire region traveled to these sanctuaries for the festivals. People attended religious festivals for a variety of reasons: devotional, recreational, and not least economic. Any large gathering of people, of course, provides an excellent opportunity for trade, and it was not uncommon for important festivals to include formally organized markets and fairs; the calendar of Rome, for example, sets aside four days for a market after the great Roman games in September. Some people made the rounds of festivals over a wide area, as for example Artemidorus, who says that he collected the material for his book on dream-interpretation by consulting marketplace diviners at major religious festivals throughout Greece, Asia Minor, and Italy (*The Interpretation of Dreams*, preface).

Lastly, there were people who traveled in order to visit and worship at famous temples. According to Lucian, many people undertook formal pilgrimages to the great shrine of Atargatis in Hierapolis in northern Syria; since he also claims that the temple contained treasure from Arabia, Phoenicia, Babylonia, Cappadocia, and Cilicia, we may deduce that pilgrims came from all these regions (*On the Syrian Goddess* 10 and 55–6). The temple of Artemis at Ephesus was accounted one of the seven wonders of the world, and was undoubtedly a major destination. The silversmith Demetrius, whose story I told in the previous chapter, presumably made his living by selling small silver shrines of the goddess as souvenirs to visitors (*Acts of the Apostles* 19.24). But even less famous and accessible sites could attract worshippers from afar. The emperor Hadrian (117–38 CE), for example, while staying in Antioch, climbed nearby Mt Kasios and offered a sacrifice there to Zeus Kasios, the ancient Baal Saphon (*The Augustan History, Hadrian* 14.3). Even at the southernmost edge of the Roman Empire, the temple of Isis at Philae in Egypt received travelers from considerable distances; in 191 CE a certain Serenus visited from Alexandria, after being instructed by an oracle of Apollo to make the pilgrimage, and left an inscription attesting to his belief that "he who has worshipped Isis in Philae is blessed, not only in wealth but likewise in long life" (Bernand 1969: no. 168).

While travel for religious purposes must have been fairly common, the bulk of it was no doubt local or regional, simply because healing shrines and festivals existed throughout the empire, and there was no need to travel great distances in order to enjoy their benefits. But as we have seen, there was a certain amount of long-distance travel as well. In some cases, people who for other reasons happened to be near a notable sanctuary took advantage of that fact in order to pay a visit, as was presumably the case with Hadrian and Mt Kasios. Others, however, traveled simply for the sake of sightseeing. Whether or not their motivations were primarily religious is usually difficult to determine, and in most cases probably not important. Just as there was no sharp line between "religious" art and "secular" art, as I argued in chapter 1, so too there was no clear division between "pilgrims" and "tourists." Pausanias' account of the sights of old Greece, for example, focuses almost exclusively on the monuments of its past glory and so might be regarded simply as a guidebook for tourists. Yet he not only describes a number of temples, shrines, and images of the gods, but also provides information about a range of local myths and rituals; moreover, throughout the work his piety and devotion are much in evidence. If this is a guidebook, then, it is a guidebook for tourists with a keen interest in traditions about the gods.

The sort of people for whom Pausanias was writing might travel very widely indeed. Plutarch provides an intriguing account of how, just before the Pythian games in the early 80s CE, two men coming "from the opposite ends of the world" happened to meet at Delphi: Demetrios of Tarsus, on his way back home from Britain, and Kleombrotos of Sparta, who had journeyed extensively throughout Egypt and the territory of the Red Sea. Plutarch points out that Kleombrotos had not undertaken his travels for the sake of business; instead, being a man "who loved learning and sightseeing," he was gathering material for a philosophy that had as its main goal the understanding of the divine. Kleombrotos had recently visited the famous oracle of Ammon, and his report on that visit sparked the discussion about the decline of oracles that is the main topic of Plutarch's dialogue (*On the Cessation of Oracles* 2, 410a–b). Kleombrotos, it seems, was what we might call a seeker after wisdom, a type familiar from other Graeco-Roman sources. Regardless of their motivations, however, it is clear that people did travel in order to visit shrines and take part in religious ceremonies; even though much of this travel was undoubtedly much more circumscribed than the journeys of Kleombrotos, it nevertheless helped to expand people's religious horizons beyond their immediate locality.

2 Mobility of Gods

There was of course considerable movement of people within the Roman Empire for reasons other than religion, involving both permanent immigration and temporary relocation. It was not uncommon for slaves to be brought from their native land to another area, which thereafter became their permanent home even if they gained their freedom. On the opposite end of the social spectrum, the careers of imperial officials regularly took them all across the empire. Gaius Vibius Salutaris, for example, whose bequest funded the statue procession in Ephesus that I discussed in the previous chapter, held positions in Sicily, Mauretania Tingitana, northern Gaul, and the Rhineland, before settling down in his native Ephesus. Yet Salutaris' career in the imperial bureaucracy was low-level and undistinguished; men with successful careers often served even more widely. Similarly, soldiers and other military personnel could expect to experience some relocation in the course of their careers, despite an increasing tendency for legions to remain in one location for long stretches of time and recruit locally. Private individuals might also travel extensively, for the sake of either business or pleasure. Archaeological research has revealed the extent of the trade that took place between the various parts of the empire, trade that was necessarily accompanied by the movement of traders. In the previous chapter, for example, I mentioned groups of resident Alexandrian businessmen in various parts of the empire, including Carthage and the Black Sea coast. There were also itinerant craftsmen, who made their living by moving from place to place. *Acts of the Apostles* provides a vivid picture of the extensive travels that could be undertaken by even a relatively humble artisan like Paul of Tarsus, who worked as a tentmaker and yet was nevertheless able to journey through-out Syria, Asia Minor, and Greece.

People like these often brought their gods with them when they moved to a new place. Some gods, of course, were strictly associated with specific locations. As we saw in chapter 3, there was a widespread tendency to perceive divine presences in topographical features like woods, springs, mountains, and even rocks and trees. People honored these divinities, often giving them no more specific a designation than *genius loci*, "the guardian spirit of the place"; they normally did so, however, only when they were in the immediate vicinity. There would have been little reason, for example, to worship Poeninus, the god of the Mont Blanc range, except when one was traveling through the St Bernard Pass. Many deities, however, were not geographically defined in this way, and it was natural that people should continue to invoke those with whom they were familiar even when they were in a new place.

As an example of the role that a mobile group could play in the circulation of different cults, we may consider the Roman army, whose activities are richly documented. The army began simply as part of the Roman citizen body under arms, and even in the imperial period, when it was in fact fully professionalized, it remained in theory an extension of the Roman civic and religious community. A papyrus discovered at the remote outpost of Dura-Europos on the Euphrates river, known as the *Feriale Duranum*, preserves a copy of the official calendar of festivals that was presumably observed by all army units (trans. in Beard, North, and Price 1998: 2.71–4). Although the vast majority of the prescribed offerings are for emperors past and present, some mark ancient festivals of the city of Rome: for example, the sacrifice to Mars on March 1, the Parilia or birthday of Rome on April 21, the offering to Vesta on June 9, and the sacrifice to Neptune on July 23. Likewise, both individual soldiers and entire units frequently made offerings to the chief gods of Rome, above all the Capitoline Triad of Jupiter Optimus Maximus, Juno, and Minerva. There are for example dedications to the entire triad by a group of discharged veterans at Apulum in Dacia (*ILS* 2301) and by an army detachment in Numidia (*ILS* 2485); to Jupiter and Juno by individual soldiers at Aquincum (*ILS* 2410 and 2431); and to Jupiter Optimus Maximus alone by a soldier at Aquincum (*ILS* 2318) and by two different cohorts at Hadrian's Wall in Britain (*ILS* 2553–4).

Yet the army of the imperial period drew its personnel from all over the empire, especially its more remote and less urbanized regions, and soldiers often maintained worship of their ancestral deities wherever they were stationed. A small sampling will give some impression of this practice. The god Hercules Magusanus, for example, who was worshipped along the lower Rhine, received dedications in Rome from members of the imperial horse guard (*ILS* 2188) and from a soldier at the wall of Antoninus Pius in present-day Scotland (*ILS* 4628). Jupiter Heliopolitanus, the god of Baalbek, was honored in Rome by a detachment of Ituraeans, a people of Syria (*ILS* 2546), and in Nemausus, modern Nîmes in France, by a senior centurion from Berytus in Phoenicia (*ILS* 4288). A soldier from Palmyra made a dedication to his native god Iarhibol while serving in southern Egypt (*IGR* 1.1169), and an entire division of Palmyrene soldiers stationed in southern Numidia made a similar offering to their other chief deity Malagbel (*ILS* 4340).

Lastly, some cults had a particular appeal to military personnel regardless of their origin, and consequently spread throughout the Roman army. The most famous of these is the cult of Mithras, whose most common epithet, "the Unconquered," was no doubt particularly meaningful to soldiers. One of the seven grades of initiation was in fact that of "Soldier," and some scholars have persuasively argued that the cult attracted soldiers because it laid great stress on such military values as "submission to authority, acceptance of a specific rôle within an organisation, identification with the prescribed values, conformity, [and] fitting into the system" (Clauss 2001: 40). Soldiers and officers make up a significant percentage of the attested members of the cult, which was particularly common in heavily militarized parts of the empire like the Rhine and Danube frontiers. But the cult of Mithras was not the only "military cult." The percentage of military personnel among the attested worshippers of Jupiter Dolichenus is if anything even higher than that for Mithras, and the cult again thrived especially in regions where there was a significant army presence.

Although the evidence for the religious activities of soldiers is particularly rich, the army was not the only mobile group in the Roman Empire: officials, merchants, performers, artisans, even slaves might regularly end up far from their native land. Although we cannot always determine why a given individual or group had relocated, the relocation itself is often clear enough. In the previous chapter I noted several examples of ethnic associations that maintained the worship of ancestral gods: Alexandrians with Sarapis in Tomis and Carthage, Tyrians with Sarepta in Puteoli, Judaeans with their god in cities throughout the eastern Mediterranean. There is even more evidence of this sort of activity among individuals than among groups. We may consider a few examples taken more or less at random. In Lambaesis, a legionary camp in Numidia, a Roman official originally from Risinium, on the coast of southern Dalmatia, erected a statue of his native god, whom he addresses as "you who dwell in the Aeacian town of Risinium, the citadel of Dalmatia, public Lar of our people, holy Medaurus, holy at home and holy here" (*ILS* 4881). At Hadrian's Wall in northern Britain, a woman named Diadora dedicated an altar to Herakles of Tyre, the ancient Phoenician god Melqart, and a man named Pulcher dedicated a companion altar to Astarte (*RIB* 1.1129 and 1124). Titus Aurelius Heliodorus, who describes himself as a Palmyrene, dedicated a silver statue in Rome to Aglibol and Malachbel, his "ancestral deities," with a bilingual inscription in Greek and Palmyrene (*IGR* 1.45). In Sarmizegetusa in Dacia a man named Publius Aelius Theimes, apparently also a native of Palmyra, dedicated a temple to "his ancestral gods Malagbel and Bebellahamon and Benefal and Manawat" (*ILS* 4341). Lastly, we may note again the image of the Celtic goddess Epona in a domestic shrine in Pompeii (see Figure 4.3), far from the lands where she was originally worshipped.

This brief survey gives us some idea of the extent to which the mobility of people led to the mobility of gods. We find gods of the lower Rhine in Rome and Scotland; Syrian gods in Rome and southern Gaul; Dalmatian gods in North Africa; gods of Palmyra in Egypt, Rome, and the Balkans; Phoenician gods in Italy and northern Britain; Mithras, the Judaean god, and the gods of Rome almost everywhere. Yet this divine mobility was not all of the same kind. We may make a fundamental distinction between diaspora cults, the worship of ancestral deities by emigrants, and cults that spread beyond the limited circles of their native adherents. Although people in other parts of the empire no doubt became aware of the Germanic Hercules Magusanus, the Tyrian Sarepta, the Palmyrene deities, and even the obscure Dalmatian god Medaurus, there is little evidence that they took much personal interest; the worship of these gods remained essentially limited to those for whom it was traditional. In contrast, a wide range of people throughout the empire adopted the worship of Mithras, Jupiter Dolichenus, the Judaean god, Isis and Sarapis, and the Capitoline Triad of Rome. The reasons for the spread of these cults and others like them are diverse, complex, and much debated. Here I will note just a few of the issues involved.

Perhaps the most obvious reason for the spread of a cult is active proselytism, the deliberate attempt by worshippers of a deity to convince others to adopt that worship as well; the figure of the Christian missionary, active throughout so much of the world over so many centuries, tends to loom large in people's minds. It is widely assumed that this sort of missionary activity was typical of Christians from the beginning, and there is indeed some evidence for it. According to *Acts of the Apostles*, for example, early followers of Jesus "made their way to Phoenicia, Cyprus, and Antioch, bringing the message to Judaeans only and to no others. But there were some natives of Cyprus and Cyrene among them, and these, when they arrived in Antioch, began to speak to Gentiles as well, telling them the good news of the Lord Jesus; the power of the Lord was with them, and a great many became believers, and turned to the Lord" (11.19–21; trans. adapted from the New English Bible). But this sort of deliberate proselytism seems to have been fairly rare in the Roman world, and perhaps played a smaller role even in the spread of Christianity than is often supposed. Much more common was the general promotion of particular deities through the public advertisement of their abilities. Testimonials to a god's willingness to answer petitions, to the divine assistance that one had received, and more generally to a god's benevolence and power must have carried considerable weight; as we saw in chapter 3, many people turned regularly to the gods for help with their lives, and a deity with a proven track record could be very attractive. Thus, votive dedications, hymns, and laudatory speeches, even if they were not deliberately employed in the service of proselytism, no doubt all played a role in the spread of a cult.

Somewhat less obvious, but probably in practice more important, was the spread of a cult through pre-existing social networks, by word of mouth, so to speak. The cults of Mithras and Jupiter Dolichenus in the Roman army provide clear examples. Soldiers might naturally become curious about the devotions of the men with whom they worked and lived for long stretches of time, and the transfer of troops and officers from one area to another meant that awareness of a new cult would have been able to spread fairly quickly. Indeed, the worship of Mithras seems to have expanded with amazing speed: the earliest datable evidence comes from the end of the first century CE, and by the middle of the second century it had reached almost all the areas where it is ever attested. But the army is only the most obvious example of such a social network. Ethnic and professional ties constituted other cases. Although people often think of the apostle Paul as a Christian missionary, he was also a Judaean and a traveling craftsman; *Acts of the Apostles* suggests that most of the contacts he made were with either local Judaean communities or other artisans like himself. When he arrived in Corinth, for example, he came upon a Judaean named Aquila, originally from northern Asia Minor, who with his wife Priscilla had arrived there from Italy; because they also were tent-makers, Paul moved in with them and they all set up business together (*Acts of the Apostles* 18.1–4).

A very different dynamic was at work in the spread of Roman cults. Rome was of course the center of power, and it is not surprising that people, especially local elites, wanted to associate themselves with that power by worshipping Roman gods. This was true not only in the Roman army, in which Roman gods had an ancestral role, but also in many other contexts. The most universal objects of cult in the Roman Empire were in fact the emperors and their families. More than anything else, it was the figure of the emperor that united all the diverse peoples and traditions of the empire, as I discuss in more detail in the last section of this chapter. But the worship of other traditional Roman deities, especially Jupiter Optimus Maximus and the Capitoline Triad, was also widespread. In some cases, however, it is not entirely clear whether the worshipper had in mind the actual Roman deity, or was using the Roman name for a local deity, or even made a clear distinction between the two. This raises the issue of how people identified gods, a topic that requires separate discussion.

3 *Identifying Gods*

In the conclusion to chapter 2 I argued that one of the dynamics shared by the various religious traditions within the Roman Empire was a tension between tendencies to particularization and generalization. On the one hand, all worship was in a sense local, insofar as people tended to identify their gods as specific deities associated with specific places. The great patron god of Rome, for example, was not simply Jupiter, but Jupiter Optimus Maximus, worshipped together with Juno and Minerva in the temple on the Capitoline hill. The great goddess of Ephesus was not simply Artemis, but specifically Artemis of Ephesus, with her absolutely distinctive iconography. On the other hand, there were various counter tendencies that emphasized the identity of gods worshipped in different places. Among people who spoke the same or closely related dialects, the very language promoted this process: because both Spartans and Ephesians called their local goddess "Artemis," for example, they naturally saw her in some important sense as the same goddess, even though the cults themselves were quite distinct. This tendency to identify local deities with one another was further enhanced in a number of ways: by the spread of myths, which typically concerned a generic Zeus or Artemis rather than their specific local manifestations; by the development of a conventional iconography of the various deities, often tied to their role in myth; and by the growth of philosophical speculation about the divine world, which in various ways emphasized its order and unity.

The tendency towards generalization was often so well established that when people from different traditions came into contact with one another, they generally seem to have had little difficulty in recognizing gods across linguistic and cultural boundaries. Thus Greeks and Romans began from a very early date to identify their deities with one another, regarding the god whom Latin-speakers called Jupiter as the same as that whom Greek-speakers called Zeus, Mars the same as Ares, Diana the same as Artemis, and so forth. The name that a person used was thus determined not so much by the deity as by the language: a Roman, for example, would never refer to the great goddess of Ephesus as Artemis, but rather as Diana (unless, of course, he or she was speaking Greek). The recognition that their deities were the same meant that the Romans adopted traditional Greek myth and iconography as well.

But it is important always to keep in mind the complexities generated by the ongoing tension between particularization and generalization. We may consider, for example, this dedication from southern Thrace: "Hadrianios Demetrianos and Asklepiades erected this altar and statue to

Zeus Kapitolios at their personal expense. With good fortune!" (*IGR* 1.703).
By "Zeus Kapitolios" they meant the Zeus of the Capitoline temple in Rome,
the god whom Latin-speakers called Jupiter Optimus Maximus. In using
this particular name, they were implying both that this god was Zeus and
at the same time that he was a distinctive form of Zeus, not simply identical with, for example, the Zeus worshipped at Olympia. The possibility
that people could view deities as simultaneously the same and distinct
allowed for considerable complexity in the identification of gods across
cultures.

Another important point to remember is that this process of identification and distinction was not subject to any formal control. As I argued in
chapter 1, people were to a large extent free to pursue their own religious
lives, especially in their ideas about the divine world. Public authorities
had little interest in dictating an official set of identifications between
the deities of different traditions, and the process was instead largely left
to individual initiative. For practical reasons, many equivalents quickly
became conventional, and some, those between the Greek and Roman
traditions in particular, were so firmly established that there were few
exceptions to the standard identification: Zeus in Greek was Jupiter in Latin.
But between Greek and Latin on the one hand and other languages and
cultures on the other there was almost always room for debate. Lucian,
for example, says of the Syrian Goddess worshipped at Hierapolis that
"in general she is undoubtedly Hera," which is the name he regularly
gives her, "but she has something also of Athena, Aphrodite, Selene,
Rhea, Artemis, Nemesis, and the Fates" (*On the Syrian Goddess* 32); in fact,
many people preferred to call her Aphrodite. The scope for debate and
discussion about the identification of deities across cultures further
increased the complexity of the process.

For the sake of convenience, we may distinguish between two chief
forms of this process of identification: a simple and practical recognition
that "the god called X in this language is called Y in that," and a more
deliberate equation of two or more deities for specific philosophical or
theological reasons. In practice, it is difficult to maintain a rigorous distinction between these two types, but they provide a helpful framework
for thinking about the issues. The word "syncretism," from the Greek noun
synkrêtismos, "union," is often used for this whole range of phenomena,
but I will here restrict it to identifications of the latter type.

Identifications of the first type most frequently involved the substitution of a Greek or Latin name for the indigenous name of a deity. In
modern scholarship, the use of a Latin name is often called *interpretatio
Romana*, "Roman translation," a phrase borrowed from the Roman historian
Tacitus (*Germany* 43.3); the use of a Greek name is correspondingly called

interpretatio Graeca. We have already come across many examples of this practice in chapter 2: Zeus in Asia Minor, Hermes in Egypt, Saturn in Africa, Mars in western Europe. In some cases people joined the Greek or Roman name with the indigenous name; this was common in western Europe, where we find among others Sulis Minerva, Mars Cocidius, Mars Teutates, and Apollo Grannus. In other cases a distinguishing epithet served to identify a particular local or regional deity: so for example Hermes Trismegistos was the god whom the Egyptians called Thoth, and Aphrodite Ourania, "Heavenly Aphrodite," usually indicated a Syrian goddess like Astarte or Baalat of Byblos. In still other cases, the Greek or Latin name is used on its own, but the iconography suggests that the deity in question was local rather than imported. For example, the inscription on this small votive relief from Asia Minor, probably Phrygia or Pisidia, informs us that it was dedicated by Atimetos the son of Heraklidos to Apollo (see Figure 5.1). In the Graeco-Roman tradition, however, Apollo was virtually never depicted on horseback, and he carried a bow rather than a double-headed ax, a weapon more commonly associated with Anatolian and Syrian gods such as Jupiter Dolichenus. In short, this seems to be the image of a local warrior god, whom the dedicator, for reasons that we can no longer recover, identified as Apollo. In all cases, however, we must remember that the question of whether a given deity was indigenous or Graeco-Roman was not one that the worshippers themselves would normally have asked. The whole point of *interpretatio* was the recognition that different peoples worshipped the same gods: the names, images, myths, and cult practices were what varied, not the deities.

The process of *interpretatio* was thus essentially one of cultural trans-formation, and must be seen as part of the broader interrelation between the Graeco-Roman culture of the imperial elite and the myriad indigenous cultures that existed throughout the empire. Because the most obvious result of this interrelation was the adoption of Graeco-Roman cultural practices by local populations, modern scholars have conventionally labeled it "Romanization" or, with emphasis on Greek influences, "Hellenization." Certainly much more was involved in *interpretatio* than simply the sub-stitution of a Greek or Latin divine name for an indigenous one. As I noted above, the name that a person gave to a deity was largely determined by the language that person was using, so that someone speaking Latin would naturally refer to the great goddess of Ephesus as Diana. The use of Greek and Latin divine names was thus part of the more general use of the Greek and Latin languages in place of the local indigenous languages. With the languages came other aspects of Graeco-Roman culture. An education in Greek or Latin meant the study of the literary classics, which were steeped in traditional Graeco-Roman myths about the gods. As

Figure 5.1 Votive relief to Apollo. Marble, 24.3 × 18.5 – 20 × 5 cm. Museum of Fine Arts, Boston, 69.1255. Gift of Mathias Komor, Esq. Photograph © 2006 Museum of Fine Arts, Boston

people began to call their local gods by Greek and Latin names, then, they also began to apply to them the stories, associations, and iconography of the Graeco-Roman gods.

They likewise began to adopt other Graeco-Roman religious conventions, such as the erection of inscribed votive offerings and the use of anthropomorphic images to depict the gods. In many areas, notably parts of Syria, North Africa, and western Europe, it had not been traditional to represent the gods in human form or even in any form at all; with the spread of Graeco-Roman culture, anthropomorphic images were gradually adopted almost everywhere. Similarly, although it had been normal in many cultures to make offerings to the gods, these were not necessarily accompanied by inscriptions in stone or some other permanent medium. For this reason it is difficult to gauge how common *interpretatio* was in any given area, because of a circularity in our evidence: the evidence for *interpretatio* comes almost entirely from votive inscriptions; since the practice of erecting votive inscriptions was largely a Graeco-Roman one, it was natural to use Greek or Latin rather than the local language; and since the dedicator was writing in Greek or Latin, it was natural to use the Greek or Latin rather than the indigenous name of the deity. What names people may have used in other contexts is impossible to know.

The significance of Romanization/Hellenization in general, and in the area of religion in particular, has in recent years been hotly debated. Was it essentially a gradual and easy development, or did it involve struggle and resistance? Was it due to the attempts of local elites to assimilate themselves to the new ruling class, or did Roman authorities take an active role in promoting or even enforcing the spread of Graeco-Roman culture? Did it involve the eradication of indigenous traditions and their replacement by a generic Graeco-Roman culture, or did it result in complex negotiations and the creation of hybrid cultural forms? There are no simple answers to these questions, since the process was complex and varied, and took different forms in different contexts. In chapter 7 I will discuss in more detail the role of Roman officials in regulating religious practices; here I will make only three general observations.

Firstly, as I have already argued, a balance between continuity and change was part of all the religious traditions within the empire. Even where we can trace long-term continuity in iconographic conventions, cult sites, and divine names, we can also identify ongoing change, resulting from both internal developments and external influences. To a certain extent, Romanization and Hellenization in matters of religion was simply a further, if often more dramatic, stage in a long-established process. Secondly, it would be a mistake to think of this process as uniform even in a single location. People's religious lives, as we have seen, were largely under their own control; public cults and the fashions of the elite had considerable influence, often at an almost subconscious level, but they did not determine the sum of people's religious practices and beliefs. As I argued in chapter 4, this was the case even in the context of the Graeco-Roman city, where participation in public cults did not preclude other identities and devotions. Hence, we should expect the same or even greater diversity of responses in the interaction between Graeco-Roman and local religious traditions. Lastly, the cultural meaning of a given practice is not necessarily inherent in the practice itself. In some cases, it appears that local adoption of Graeco-Roman cultural forms gave new impetus to local cults and provided new tools for the articulation of local religious devotions. The great temple of Jupiter at Heliopolis/Baalbek in Syria and the shrine of Endovellicus in Iberia were alike constructed only in the Roman period; the worship of these local deities extended back into pre-Roman times, but acquired new force under Roman influence. These various considerations suggest the difficulties involved in making generalizations about the process of *interpretatio*, which is perhaps best studied on a case-by-case basis.

As I noted above, there is no sharp line dividing *interpretatio* from the type of identification that I am here calling syncretism, the deliberate equation of deities for philosophical or theological reasons. Nevertheless, it is clear that in some cases more was at stake than simply determining the appropriate Greek or Latin name for a local god. Some people were apparently motivated by a desire to aggrandize certain deities by subsuming others under them. This was especially true of the goddess Isis, one of whose regular epithets was precisely *myrionomos*, "many-named." In Apuleius' novel *The Golden Ass*, for example, when Isis appears to the hero, she announces that "the whole world worships my single godhead with multiple images, rites, and names," and goes on to claim identity with the Phrygian Mother of the Gods, Minerva, Venus, Diana, Proserpina, Ceres, Juno, Bellona, and Hecate (11.5). Already in the 80s BCE, a man named Isidoros, in one of the four hymns to Isis that he had inscribed on the wall of an Egyptian temple, says that "the Syrians name you Astarte, Artemis, Nanaia; the Lycians call you Leto, Lady; Thracian men name you Mother of the Gods; the Greeks call you great-throned Hera and Aphrodite and good Hestia and Rhea and Demeter; the Egyptians call you Thiuois, because you singly are all other goddesses named by the peoples" (Vanderlip 1972: no. 1, lines 18–24). But Isis was not the only deity to inspire such multiple identifications. A military officer stationed at Hadrian's Wall in northern Britain erected an inscription in which he claims that a goddess whom he describes only as "the Heavenly Virgin" is "likewise the Mother of the Gods, Peace, Virtue, Ceres, the Syrian Goddess, weighing life and laws in the balance; Syria brought forth a constellation seen in heaven to be honored by Libya" (*RIB* 1.1791). The last line suggests that he further identified this great goddess with Julia Domna, the Syrian-born wife of the African-born emperor Septimius Severus, a fact that if anything underscores the use of syncretism as a means of glorification.

In other cases we find attempts to systematize and simplify the multiplicity of divinities in the Roman world. Under the influence of philosophical speculation, these often verged on a kind of theoretical monotheism. Plutarch, for example, writing in the early second century CE, says that he does not regard the gods "as different among different peoples nor as barbarian and Greek nor as southern and northern; but just as sun and moon, heaven and earth and sea are common to all, but differently named by different peoples, so too, although there is one reason that orders these things and one providence that manages them and assistant powers that are assigned to all things, different honors and appellations are given them according to local customs" (*On Isis and Osiris* 67, 377f–378a). Similarly, his contemporary Dio Chrysostom allows that "some say that Apollo, Helios, and Dionysos are the same . . . , and many combine absolutely all the gods into a single strength and power, so that it makes no difference whether one honors this one or that" (*Orations* 31.11). Somewhat earlier, the Roman philosopher Seneca, arguing that Nature and God are the same, asserts that "you may address this author of our world by different names as often as you wish," noting that it is appropriate to call him Jupiter Optimus Maximus and that some people also name him Liber Pater, Hercules, and Mercury. "So say 'Nature', 'Fate', 'Fortune': they are all names of the same god using his power in different ways" (*On Benevolent Deeds* 4.7–8).

As we saw in earlier chapters, the diversity of deities within the Roman Empire was practically endless; so too, however, were the strategies that people could use to bring them together. Although that process was uneven and deeply complex, it nevertheless contributed greatly to a certain religious unity within the empire, insofar as most people could be held to recognize the great gods, even if they worshipped them in different ways and under different names. Yet there was one set of gods that was common to all inhabitants of the empire: these I discuss in the next section.

4 Emperors and Gods

Despite all the mechanisms that promoted religious integration, the Roman Empire remained in essence an amalgam of diverse traditions. What united it more than anything else was the figure of the emperor: the emperor was the concrete embodiment of what was otherwise an almost unimaginable abstraction. Although it would be accurate to say that the emperor symbolized the unity of the empire, he was in fact much more than a symbol. As the supreme commander of the imperial army and the center of the imperial bureaucracy, he directly controlled those aspects of imperial power that most people were likely to encounter. He was also at the peak of the social hierarchy, the culmination of the complex network of patronage mentioned in the previous chapter: the emperor was the only person in the empire who could bestow benefits on everyone without himself receiving benefits from anyone. In a very important sense, then, the emperor was the empire. Given the close intertwining of religious, political, and cultural concerns in the Graeco-Roman world, it is not surprising that the emperor played a central role in the religious life of the empire. So too, in a derivative sense, did other members of the imperial family, both male and female; much of what I say in this section applies to them as well, although for the sake of simplicity I restrict myself to the emperor.

The nature of the emperor's religious role, however, varied tremendously. For this reason, the conventional term "imperial cult" can be rather misleading, since it implies an organized and coherent system of worship that focused on the emperor as a god. In fact, there was a wide range of diverse strategies for integrating the emperor into religious life. Some of these treated him unambiguously as a god, others equally unambiguously as a mortal, and still others were deliberately ambiguous; in many specific cases different strategies were combined. Some strategies were established and promoted by Roman authorities, others developed locally, and still others arose through the interaction of imperial and local initiatives. In what follows, I first survey some of the ways in which the emperor was integrated into religious life, and then discuss in more detail the complexities and ambiguities in his position.

The religious role of the Roman emperor has its origins both in the traditions of the Greek world, where Alexander the Great and his successors were in various ways the objects of cult, and in republican Rome, where the great generals of the last century BCE claimed special connections with the divine. Although Julius Caesar apparently experimented with various modes of self-deification, it was his heir Augustus who established the main practices followed by most later emperors. We may briefly note two of these in particular. The first is the inclusion in the calendar of an increasing number of imperial anniversaries: the emperor's birthday, the anniversaries of his accession and major military victories, and other notable occasions. These were marked by public sacrifices and celebrations, just like the festival days of traditional deities. The second practice is the formal deification of deceased emperors. Whatever had occurred in Caesar's lifetime, after his death Augustus carefully promoted the cult of Divus Iulius, the "Deified Julius," for whom he constructed a temple and appointed a priest. With Augustus' own death in 14 CE, a formal procedure for deification began to take shape. The Senate decided whether the deceased emperor should be recognized as a god (unpopular emperors often were not); if so, there was a splendid funerary ritual, in which an effigy of the emperor was burnt on a pyre and an eagle released from it in order to mark the new god's ascent into the heavens. Like Caesar, deified emperors were given the title "Divus" (for example, Divus Augustus, Divus Claudius, and so forth) and received a temple, a priest, and annual public offerings.

Among Roman citizens and in official contexts, Roman authorities made some attempt to maintain a distinction between deceased and deified emperors, who were worshipped as gods, and the living emperor, who was not; only tyrannical emperors like Caligula and Commodus demanded that they be treated as gods while alive. We can see the traces of this distinction in a range of evidence. The *Feriale Duranum*, for example, the festival calendar of the Roman army from the third century CE, marks the anniversaries of deified emperors with sacrifices to those emperors themselves, but marks those of the current emperor with sacrifices either to the emperor's *genius* or to traditional deities like the Capitoline Triad. The same distinction occurs in official oaths. For example, the municipal charter of a town in southern Spain, dating to the reign of the emperor Domitian, specifies that public officials shall swear oaths "by Jupiter, Divus Augustus, Divus Claudius, Divus Vespasianus Augustus, Divus Titus Augustus, the *genius* of Domitianus Augustus, and the Penates" (*ILS* 6088, section 26); a military document of the same date from Egypt records the very similar oath "by Jupiter Optimus Maximus and the *genius* of the most sacred emperor Caesar Domitianus Augustus Germanicus" (*ILS* 9059). Outside these officials contexts, however, the distinction between deified emperors and living emperors was not necessarily upheld; a man in Egypt who filed an official death certificate, for example, vouched for the truthfulness of his information by swearing "by the emperor Caesar Marcus Aurelius Commodus Antoninus Augustus," just as though that emperor were a god (*POxy* 79). As in other areas of religious activity, there was in general little attempt at regulation.

The chief exception to this lack of regulation concerns what is conventionally called provincial cult. Each member city in a province sent one or more representatives to an annual assembly; in some provinces these assemblies had been instituted even before the reign of Augustus, and in all provinces they handled a variety of business. But from Augustus on, the primary focus of all provincial assemblies was the worship of the emperor: they met at a provincial temple of the emperor, they elected one

of their number as chief priest, and they celebrated a festival in honor
of the emperor. Within this general pattern there was some variation.
Although most provinces had only one provincial temple, Asia had several:
since hosting the provincial cult contributed greatly to local prestige, the
three chief cities of Ephesus, Smyrna, and Pergamum vied with each other
for imperial permission to construct additional provincial temples. The
specific object of the cult also varied. Initially, imperial authorities tried
to restrict the worship of the living emperor to non-citizens and in more
Romanized areas promoted the cult of deified emperors instead. Over time,
however, most provincial cults came to honor "the emperors" in general,
both past and present. Provincial cults were largely unprecedented and
unparalleled institutions in the Roman Empire: no other cult was organized
in this way on a regional level. Moreover, because they provided opportunities for members of the elite to extend their prestige and patronage
beyond their own cities, they tended to attract the most eminent and
ambitious men in the province. It is not surprising, then, that imperial
authorities were keen to exercise some control over provincial cult.

Public cults of the emperor also existed in cities throughout the empire,
with shrines, public priests, and a regular schedule of ceremonies. For
example, an inscription from an altar in Narbo (modern Narbonne in
southern France) dating to 11 CE indicates that every year on Augustus'
birthday and other significant dates, six representatives of the populace,
including three freedmen, were to offer animal sacrifices to the emperor's
numen, "divine power," and provide the people with wine and incense
for individual offerings (*ILS* 112). Although it was not necessary to obtain
imperial permission for civic cults of the emperor, any more than it was
for other public cults, an official endorsement brought prestige. The town
of Gytheon in southern Greece, for example, sent envoys to the emperor
Tiberius to win his blessings for a proposed imperial festival; Tiberius
supported the honors for Divus Augustus, but not those for himself.
Nevertheless, the townspeople proudly engraved his response right above
the regulations for their elaborate cult, which included six days of games
in honor of Divus Augustus, Tiberius, and other members of the imperial
family, an elaborate procession, and a set of sacrifices offered by the civic
magistrates on behalf of the rulers' well-being (trans. in MacMullen and
Lane 1992: 74–6).

Voluntary associations as well might center on the emperor just as they
did on other gods. A dedication to the emperor Hadrian was made in a
town in Numidia by the "Roman citizens, worshippers of the emperor's
Lares and Images" (*ILS* 6778), and an inscription from a town in Upper
Pannonia refers to "the great association of the Lares and Images of Our
Lord Caesar" (*ILS* 7120). As I noted in the previous chapter, in many cities

of the western empire wealthy freedmen served as Augustales, a formal rank in some way connected with the worship of the emperor. But other voluntary associations might also offer cult to the emperor. The physicians in Ephesus described themselves as "those who sacrifice to ancestor Asklepios and the emperors" (*IEph* 719), and a group of initiates in the same city performed annual "mysteries and sacrifices" for Demeter Karpophoros and "the divine emperors" (*IEph* 213). Even private individuals participated in the worship of the emperors. For example, an inscription from Carthage records a dedication to "the Family of Augustus" made by one Publius Perelius Hedulus, who took the title "priest for life" and built a shrine for them "on his own property and at his own expense" (*ILAfr* 353).

As even this small sampling of the evidence reveals, the emperor was not always worshipped in the same way as traditional deities. This did occur: the physicians of Ephesus apparently sacrificed to the emperors just as they did to Asklepios, and the initiates of Demeter performed their mysteries for the emperors along with their goddess. Officially deified emperors were in all cases treated the same as other gods. But the worship of living emperors was frequently more indirect. People often swore by the living emperor's *genius*, as though he were the master of a household, and not by his person, as though he were a god; the public cult in Narbo was directed to the *numen* of Augustus, and not to Augustus himself. Even in Gytheon the sacrifices were offered not to Tiberius, as they would be to a god, but instead "on behalf of his well-being," as they would be for other people. Offerings and dedications "on behalf" of the emperor in fact seem to have been the rule in provincial cults and typical in civic cults as well. Phrases like this, which as we saw in chapter 3 were by no means limited to the emperor, seem to imply that he was not himself divine, since gods had no need of divine blessings. The younger Pliny, for example, reporting to the emperor Trajan on the vows that the populace of the empire undertook every January 3 on behalf of the emperor's well-being, says that "we have entreated the gods to keep you and the state prosperous and safe, with the good will that you have earned, over and above your many great virtues, by your exceptional piety, devotion, and respect for the gods" (*Letters* 10.100). Here the difference between the emperor and the gods is very clear-cut.

Cult was not the only medium for expressing the religious role of the emperor. Images of the emperor, for example, like those of the gods, were omnipresent, ranging from larger-than-life statues in public spaces to small figures in private residences to images on coins. And like the images of the gods, their constant presence helped to shape people's sense of who they were. As I argued in the previous chapter, the distinctive image of the great goddess Artemis on the local coins of Ephesus was a marker of

Ephesian identity. Yet these same coins bore on their other side images of the Roman emperor, in this case Domitian, suggesting that his status was in some way analogous to hers: just as Artemis symbolized their local identity, so too the emperor symbolized their Roman identity (see Figure 4.1). At times emperors were depicted in the guise of specific divinities. A statue of the emperor Claudius from Rome, for example, depicts him in a form almost identical with that of Jupiter on the cameo discussed in chapter 1 (see Figure 5.2; compare Figure 1.2): he holds a scepter, the sign of Jupiter's divine rule, and is accompanied by an eagle, the traditional bird of Jupiter. Even his partial nudity is a marker of heroic or divine status; the real Claudius would never have appeared in public in such attire, nor is his physique likely to have been so splendid. Yet even so the implications are ambiguous: one person might interpret the image to mean that Claudius was the actual embodiment of Jupiter; someone else, that he was a representative of Jupiter; someone else, that he was merely like Jupiter. Adding to the ambiguity is the one key difference between the images of Claudius and Jupiter: where Jupiter holds a lightning bolt, Claudius holds a dish of the sort used to offer libations. As I noted in chapter 1, this is a conventional way of representing piety towards the gods in art.

So were emperors regarded as gods or humans? Did they themselves receive cult, or did they offer it to the gods? No simple answer to these questions is possible, since as we have seen the emperor's status flickered back and forth between divine and human. We may perhaps compare it with the sort of trick picture that appears at one moment as a vase and at another as two human profiles facing each other. The emperor was in a sense both divine and human, so that one's perspective in specific circumstances determined which aspect came into focus. It was for this reason that people employed such varied and ambiguous strategies to represent his religious role. They consecrated temples and priests for emperors just as they did for gods, yet they might offer sacrifice on their behalf rather than to them; they could depict Claudius as the ruler of the gods but simultaneously as a pious worshipper. Although it would be a mistake to try to resolve the ambiguity and reduce the variety of these strategies, three further observations may help to put them into a wider context.

Firstly, as I discussed in chapter 1, the divide between "divine" and "human" was not as sharp and profound in the Graeco-Roman tradition as it tends to be in monotheistic traditions. The concepts of the *daimôn*, the *hêrôs*, the *genius*, and the *numen*, for example, all served in different ways to bridge that gap. Similarly, there were myths of people who had been born the mortal children of gods, but who through their merits had

Figure 5.2   Statue of the emperor Claudius in the guise of Jupiter. Rome, Museo Vaticano 243. Reproduced by permission of Alinari Archives, Florence

achieved divinity: Herakles and Asklepios were two of the most famous. Even philosophers speculated on the immortality of the human soul and its kinship with the divine. In such a cultural context, the practice of treating such a uniquely important person as the emperor like a god would have been much less jarring than it would be in most modern societies.

Secondly, the ambiguity of the emperor's religious role resulted to some extent from the fact that he was envisioned as the key point of intersection between the divine and human spheres. This idea was given visual expression in the multiple representations of the emperor as a sacrificer, as in the statue of Claudius offering a libation (see Figure 5.2) or the relief of Marcus Aurelius presiding over a sacrifice (see Figure 1.1). Hence, just as members of the elite acted on behalf of their communities in their dealings with the gods, so too the emperor, at least symbolically, acted on behalf of the empire as a whole. Similarly, people prayed to the gods to bless the emperor, because it was through the emperor that they bestowed some of their most important blessings. As the author of a rhetorical handbook put it, "What prayers ought cities to make to the powers above, save always for the emperor? What greater blessing must one ask from the gods than the emperor's safety? Rains in season, abundance from the sea, unstinting harvests come happily to us because of the emperor's justice. In return, cities, nations, races, and tribes, all of us, garland him, sing of him, write of him" (Menander Rhetor 377.19–28, trans. D. A. Russell and N. G. Wilson). It was the emperor who ensured the peace, security, and prosperity of the empire; in this respect he was like a god for the people of the empire, since the ability to bestow benefits was a defining characteristic of the gods. In acting as a unique intermediary between the divine and mortal spheres, therefore, the emperor to some extent participated in both. The author of a speculative philosophical treatise described his position by saying that "the emperor is the last of the other gods, but the first of men; as long as he is on earth, he is removed from true divinity, but among men has something exceptional, which is like the divine" (*Hermetica*, fragment 24.3 in Nock and Festugière 1946–54).

Lastly, these ambiguous and varied expressions of the emperor's religious role actually increased his importance for the religious integration of the empire, since they allowed him to be accommodated within a tremendous range of different traditions. Even Judaeans and Christians, although rejecting any implication that the emperor was himself a god, granted his unique status in relation to the divine. The Judaeans, for example, sacrificed two lambs and a steer on his behalf every day in their temple in Jerusalem; similarly, Judaean communities elsewhere sometimes dedicated their assembly halls "on behalf of the emperor's well-being" and erected in them monuments in his honor. Christians likewise often prayed for the emperor. The author of *1 Clement*, for example, says in a prayer to God that "you, Master, have given [emperors] the power of sovereignty through your majestic and inexpressible might, so that we, acknowledging the glory and honor which you have given them, may be subject to them . . . ; grant to them, Lord, health, peace, harmony and stability" (*1 Clement* 61.1, trans. Holmes 1999). Thus it was that the emperor retained a unique religious role even in the Christian period, even after the trappings of imperial priests and temples had disappeared. It was the emperor who unified the empire, and this fact inevitably found religious expression.

5 Conclusion

Despite the close connections between religious devotion and local identity that I outlined in chapter 4, religion was as much a force for integration within the Roman Empire as it was an expression of its diversity. Widely shared assumptions about the divine world provided a basic framework that made possible a variety of interactions and assimilations. Many people engaged in local and even regional travel to join in the worship of gods outside their immediate environment, and some went even further afield, to visit famous shrines, take part in celebrated festivals, or increase their understanding of the divine. Even in their home territories people might encounter unfamiliar gods and traditions, introduced by immigrants or mobile groups such as soldiers, officials, and merchants. Some of these cults attracted relatively little interest, but others achieved widespread popularity. Unfamiliar deities could also in various ways be identified with previously known gods, a process that not only decreased the distance between different traditions, but also allowed for the adoption of common cult practices, especially those of Greek or Roman origin. Lastly, and above all, the figure of the emperor provided a religious focus shared by the entire empire. All of these were dynamic processes that over time tended to promote the religious integration of the empire. Yet we should not therefore assume that the empire necessarily displayed more religious unity at the end of the third century CE than it had at the beginning of the first. As we shall see in the following chapter, there were equally strong tendencies that produced diversity of a rather different sort.

FURTHER READING

On travel for religious purposes, see in general the survey of Dillon 1997, although it focuses on earlier Greek periods, and the papers in Elsner and Rutherford 2005;

Elsner 1992 discusses Pausanias as a pilgrim. Irby-Massie 1999 studies the religion of the Roman army in one province; Noy 2000 provides a detailed study of foreigners in the city of Rome, with comments on their cults. Nock 1933 includes a classic discussion of the diffusion of cults; Goodman 1994 is a critical analysis of proselytism, with a focus on the Judaean tradition; on the spread of the worship of Mithras, see briefly Clauss 2001: 21–41. On the role of the emperor, Klauck 2003: 250–330 provides a useful survey with further bibliography; Hopkins 1978 is a lively general discussion. Price 1984 is a groundbreaking and highly influential study; Friesen 1993 provides some important qualifications, in a careful analysis of provincial cult. Fishwick's multi-volume study (1987–2005) is the most detailed and thorough exposition of the evidence, with material on the east as well as the west; Gradel 2002 is an important recent contribution.

CHAPTER 6

Religious Options

ᔆᔆᔆᔆ

One of the key features of the Graeco-Roman tradition was its accessibility: everyone was able to perform the basic rituals of prayer and sacrifice and to experience the gods as an immediate presence in his or her life. Some people, however, were attracted by the possibility that there was something else, some special experience or knowledge that was not accessible to everyone, but available only to select individuals. A wide range of options existed to satisfy the interests of people like this: texts that purported to contain the wisdom of ancient sages and seers, wonder-workers and ritual specialists who claimed a privileged access to divine power, mystery cults that offered a more intense communion with a deity and special blessings in life and death. In this chapter I try to give some idea of these options by examining them from two slightly different angles. Firstly, I consider their sources of appeal, the external features that made them appear to some people more attractive than mainstream traditions. Secondly, I examine the particular advantages that they could offer, the benefits they claimed to provide for those who turned to them. As we shall see, in every respect these religious options were extremely varied.

1 Attractions

Broadly speaking, religious options were attractive because they appeared to offer something outside the usual range of possibilities. This could take a wide range of forms, but for the sake of convenience we can distinguish two broad categories: appeals to esoteric wisdom and claims to a special connection with the divine. Although there was often in practice considerable overlap between these two categories, the distinction can nevertheless help us analyze specific sources of appeal.

1.1 Esoteric wisdom

In the Roman world as in our own, different people had different tastes in matters of religion. Some found comfort in the familiar, and valued the practices and beliefs that were current in their communities and that they had known all their lives. Others, by contrast, were attracted to what seemed remote from ordinary life, esoteric traditions reputedly handed down from the distant past or imported from an exotic foreign culture. In the Roman world, again as in our own, the two qualities "ancient" and "foreign" often went together, since Greeks and Romans believed the cultures of the Near East to be much older than their own (in many cases quite rightly). Yet the Greek tradition had its own ancient religious authorities, and they also played an important role.

Some of these Greek authorities were legendary figures of remote antiquity. Orpheus, for example, was, according to Greek myth, the greatest singer of all time, whose music was so captivating that it could tame wild animals and even move trees and rocks. Given this reputation, it is not surprising that some poets began to circulate their own compositions under his name: the earliest evidence we have for this practice dates to the late sixth century BCE, but it apparently continued into late antiquity. The most important of these "Orphic" poems were theogonies, accounts of the origin of the cosmos and the gods similar to the *Theogony* of Hesiod but differing in many details. Over time, other types of writings were also attributed to Orpheus: ritual prescriptions, incantations and hymns, theological and cosmological works, and treatises on divination. In short, "Orpheus" eventually became a sort of all-purpose religious authority, whose name could be co-opted to lend a special aura to almost any kind of esoteric lore. Another important figure of legend was the Sibyl, or rather Sibyls, since people came to believe that there had been a number of them. The Sibyl was imagined as a female seer of the distant past whose oracles survived in written form. Authorities in Rome maintained an official collection of Sibylline books that they consulted in times of crisis, but a wide range of other Sibylline oracles circulated throughout the Mediterranean world well into late antiquity; the only examples now extant come from the circles of Judaeans and Christians who co-opted the figure of the Sibyl in order to provide "external" confirmation of their own traditions. But alongside these mythic figures, genuine historical figures also came to be honored as religious authorities. One of the most important was Pythagoras, a thinker of the sixth century BCE about whom so many diverse traditions developed that it is now virtually impossible to know anything definite about his real life and thought.

In all these cases we are dealing with pseudepigrapha, writings (Greek *graph-*) with a false (Greek *pseud-*) attribution. Pseudepigraphy is a widespread phenomenon in Graeco-Roman antiquity, especially in the context of the religious options under discussion here. The origin of pseudepigraphic texts no doubt varied considerably: some were perhaps produced by people who sincerely believed that they were carrying on a genuine tradition, others by people who simply wanted to validate their own beliefs by attaching them to an evocative name, and still others by people who were just out to make a quick profit by preying on the gullible. The use of the names attached to these texts also varied: some were closely associated with a particular type of material, as "Sibyl" was with oracles, whereas others could be assigned to almost anything, as was eventually the case with "Orpheus".

Pseudepigrapha played an important role in the spread of "oriental" wisdom, although it had living representatives as well. The satirist Juvenal, in a lengthy and vitriolic denunciation of women, attacks them among many other things for their fascination with what he regards as foreign religious quacks; he singles out a eunuch priest of the Great Mother, functionaries of the cult of Isis, a Judaean woman who teaches the Law and interprets dreams, diviners from Asia Minor, and "Chaldaean" astrologers (*Satires* 6.511–91). The obvious contempt with which Juvenal describes these figures is a good reminder that foreign religious traditions struck some people of Graeco-Roman culture as distasteful and even repulsive. For others, however, like the women whom Juvenal satirizes (and numerous men as well), they held a strong attraction. Many different eastern traditions had this cachet to a greater or lesser extent; here we will consider the three most important.

Egyptian tradition lent itself particularly well to this type of appeal, with its mysterious hieroglyphs, its exotic representations of the gods, its temple ceremonies hidden from public view, and its distinctive priestly caste trained in millennia-old traditions. There is ample evidence that some Egyptian priests were quite willing to capitalize on the Graeco-Roman fascination with things Egyptian. The Egyptian priest acting as free-lance wise man and wonder-worker is a stock character in literature: Zatchlas, who calls back the soul of a dead man in Apuleius' *The Golden Ass* (2.28); Pankrates, who surfs the Nile on crocodiles and turns his staff into a servant in Lucian's *Lover of Lies* (34–5; the story is the ultimate source for Disney's "Sorcerer's Apprentice"); Kalasiris, who acts as a fairy godfather for the young lovers of Heliodorus' novel *An Ethiopian Story*. But such figures were not simply figments of the literary imagination; there is evidence that Pankrates, for example, was a real person, even if not a real crocodile rider. Similarly, a self-described "sacred scribe of Egypt" named Arnouphis was said to have saved the emperor Marcus Aurelius' army by calling up a rainstorm at a crucial moment (Cassius Dio, *History* 71.8.4), and in the third century CE, Porphyry describes how a visiting Egyptian priest demonstrated his power by summoning up the philosopher Plotinus' attendant *daimôn* (*Life of Plotinus* 10).

Porphyry's priest performed this ritual in the temple of Isis, which he said was the only place in Rome pure enough for it to be effective. As we have already noticed, the cult of Isis was widely popular throughout the Mediterranean, and part of its appeal lay in its Egyptian trappings. Its temples had ostentatiously Egyptian decor, the functionaries of the cult adopted the shaved heads and linen robes of traditional Egyptian priests, and some of the cult practices, such as the elaborate daily ritual centering on the goddess's statue, had obvious Egyptian antecedents. Lastly, there was a wide range of texts written in Greek that purported to transmit ancient Egyptian wisdom. Many of these pseudepigrapha were associated with Hermes Trismegistos, "Thrice-Greatest Hermes," the Greek name for the Egyptian god Thoth (see also Text Box 6.1). The most famous "Hermetic" texts are dialogues on the nature of the cosmos and the role of humanity within it; these were later to have a great vogue among the philosophers of the Italian Renaissance. Like Orpheus, however, Hermes was credited with a great variety of writings, and other extant works deal with rituals and spells, astrology, alchemy, and medicine. Nor was Hermes the only name in Egyptian pseudepigrapha: the legendary king Nechepso and his priest Petosiris were also regarded as authorities, especially in astrology.

The appeal of Judaean tradition is equally well attested, although it took rather different forms. The basis of its appeal was in general much like that of the Egyptian tradition: its exotic customs, its fabulous antiquity, and its sacred scriptures written in a strange and mysterious language (even if many Judaeans in fact used a Greek translation). In addition, Judaean tradition had a distinctive "philosophical" appeal all its own. As we saw in chapter 1, philosophers began at an early date to criticize Greek traditions about the gods, especially the idea that they had human form and engaged in immoral actions, and gradually developed in their place a conception of the divine as beyond human understanding, perfect and good, remote from the everyday world and yet deeply concerned with human morality. The Judaean tradition seemed in many ways to conform precisely to this philosophical conception of the divine, and consequently must have seemed to some people much more "correct" than the Graeco-Roman mainstream. For whatever reason, it is clear that some people who were not ethnically Judaean were very interested in Judaean traditions. The Judaean historian Josephus claims that many Greeks adopted Judaean customs (*Against Apion* 2.123), and the Greek historian Cassius Dio seems to agree (*History* 37.17.1). The author of *Acts of the Apostles* several times refers to the worshippers in synagogues as including both Judaeans and "those who fear/reverence god" (13.16, 17.17), and similar terms have turned up in inscriptions. Most scholars identify these "God-fearers" as non-Judaeans who worshipped the Judaean god without fully converting, and many have suggested that it was from among them that the first gentile Christians came.

The central importance of scripture in Judaean tradition meant that it was well suited to the creation of pseudepigrapha. One particular genre that became popular in the Roman period was an account of revelations received by a notable figure of the Israelite past, usually called an "apocalypse" (from Greek *apokalypsis*, "uncovering"); these revelations, received either in visions or in the course of guided tours through the cosmos, concerned not only the secrets of the heavenly realm but also divine judgment and the end of the world (it is for this reason that the word "apocalypse" now has the connotation of "cataclysm"). A relatively early example is the biblical book of Daniel, and later works circulated under the names of Enoch, Abraham, Baruch, and Ezra. Most of these pseudepigrapha seem to have been written for people who already saw themselves as in some sense the heirs of the Judaean tradition. Other pseudepigrapha attributed to Judaean figures represent more widespread esoteric traditions. For example, an astrological treatise circulated under the name of Shem, one of the sons of Noah, and spells and ritual lore were often ascribed to Moses or Solomon (see Text Box 6.1 for an example of a spell attributed to Solomon). A particularly striking example is a text entitled "The Eighth Book of Moses," which provides directions for a complex ritual intended to cause the supreme god of the cosmos to appear before the person who performs it (*PGM* XIII).

Different yet again were the attractions of the Persian tradition. A large number of pseudepigrapha attributed to real or imagined Persian sages circulated in the Roman Empire. Zoroaster was the most prominent of these, and like Orpheus and Hermes Trismegistos was credited with a wide range of texts, dealing especially with astrology but also other arcana; the only fully extant "Zoroastrian" text presents a version of the so-called "gnostic" myth (discussed in the following section). Other alleged Persian sages were Ostanes, associated with treatises on alchemy and the occult uses of plants and gems; Hystaspes, the supposed author of an apocalypse; and Astrampsychos, credited with a popular do-it-yourself book of oracles. A more important expression of interest in things Persian was the cult of Mithras, the ancient Iranian deity Mithra, whose worship, as I noted in chapter 2, survived in Asia Minor into the Roman period. It was perhaps in that region that Mithras became the focus of the mystery cult that became so popular in the army. The cult of Mithras was highly unusual in having no public elements at all, no temples, sacrifices, or rituals open to non-initiates. It instead took the form of small groups of initiates, exclusively male, who met in underground chambers to share a communal meal and perform the ceremonies of the cult; initiates passed through a hierarchy of seven grades, one of which was actually called "Persian." The chief decoration of the meeting place was a depiction of Mithras killing a bull and dressed in stereotyped "Persian" clothing: long trousers, a full tunic with long sleeves, and the so-called "Phrygian" cap (see Figure 6.1). This was clearly the most important episode in an entire cycle of myths, of which others were sometimes depicted in small panels on the side of the main scene; unfortunately, the absence of any textual sources makes it impossible to reconstruct these in any detail.

The attractions of the exotic and esoteric are perhaps most apparent in what is usually described as ancient Greek "magic." The term itself derives from a Persian word that denoted an expert in divine lore, ritual, and divination; this word was transliterated into Greek as *magos* (plural *magoi*; Latin *magus, magi*), with its associated adjective *magikos* (Latin *magicus*). Although Greeks and Romans continued throughout antiquity to use the word *magos*/*magus* in the technical sense of "Persian wise man," they also from an early date used it as a derogatory term for anyone who claimed expertise in arcane ritual lore. Such free-lance ritual experts had always existed in the Graeco-Roman tradition, but in the imperial period they apparently began to heighten the exotic appeal of their services by incorporating or mimicking elements of foreign traditions. We have first-hand evidence for their techniques in the form of inscribed gems and amulets, curse tablets, and above all the papyrus texts from Egypt known as the "Greek Magical Papyri." These sources reveal the extensive use of Greek, Egyptian, and Judaean material, with smatterings of a few others. Somewhat surprisingly, there are very few references to Persian tradition; even the word *magos* and its derivatives rarely occur, suggesting that those terms were primarily used by people other than the practitioners themselves. Much of this material is extravagantly and self-consciously esoteric, as in the example quoted here (see Text Box 6.1). It begins with a heading that attributes the ritual to Solomon, followed by an oath to ensure secrecy and proper use. The ritual itself consists of both a spoken formula and a set of actions. The prescriptions for the latter are highly elaborate and abound in precise details (the unbaked bricks, the male date palm, the black cow). The formula, despite the alleged authorship of Solomon, invokes the authority of the Egyptian Hermes Trismegistos, and is full of the nonsense words and phrases, similar to the modern "hocus-pocus," that are conventionally known as *voces magicae*, "magic words." Some *voces magicae* can be identified as garbled forms of genuine Egyptian or Hebrew words; here, for example, the names "Osiris" and "Amun" are embedded in the initial invocation, and the section closes with a string of compounds of "Osiris."

Text Box 6.1

PGM IV.850–929 (selections), trans. W. C. Grese in Betz 1992: 55–6

Charm of Solomon that produces a trance (works both on boys and on adults): I swear to you by the holy gods and the heavenly gods not to share the procedure of Solomon with anyone and certainly not to use it for something questionable unless a matter of necessity forces you, lest perchance wrath be preserved for you.

Formula to be spoken: "Ouriôr amên im tar chôb klamphôb phrê phrôr ptar ousiri saiôb têlô kabê manatathôr asiôrikor bêeinôr amoun ôm mênichtha machtha chthara amachtha aou [etc.]. Hear me, that is, my holy voice, because I call upon your holy names, and reveal to me concerning the thing which I want, through the NN man or little boy, for otherwise I will not defend your holy and undefiled names. . . . Come to me through the NN man or little boy and tell me accurately since I speak your names which thrice-greatest Hermes wrote in Heliopolis with hieroglyphic letters: arbakôriph mêniam ôbaôb abniôb mêrim baiax chenôr phênim ôra orêsiou ousiri pnamousiri phrêousiri hôriousiri [etc.]"

After you have purified the designated man by keeping him from intercourse for three days, you yourself also being pure, enter together with him. After you have taken him up to an open place, seat him on unbaked bricks, dress him and give him an anubian head of wheat and a falconweed plant so that he will be protected. Gird yourself with a palm fiber of a male date palm, extend your hands up to heaven, toward the rays of the sun, and say the formula seven times. Next make an offering of male frankincense after pouring out wine, beer, honey, or milk of a black cow onto grapevine wood. Then say the formula seven times just into the ear of the NN man or little boy, and right away he will fall down. But you sit down on the bricks and make your inquiry, and he will describe everything with truth. You should crown him with a garland of indigenous wormwood, both him and you, for god delights in the plant [etc.].

To what extent did these manifestations of "oriental wisdom" in the Graeco-Roman world represent genuine eastern traditions? No simple answer is possible. The only "Persian" elements in the Persian pseudepigrapha were apparently the names of the alleged authors. Similarly, although the god Mithras is unquestionably Iranian in origin, most scholars now regard the mystery cult itself as almost entirely the product of Graeco-Roman culture. With the Judaean tradition, by contrast, the situation was very different. The sacred texts of the Judaeans had been translated into Greek and were thus accessible to anyone with a basic education; moreover, people could easily visit the Judaean synagogues that existed in many cities of the eastern Mediterranean. Even the incorporation of Judaean elements into "magical" lore had roots in genuine Judaean tradition. Josephus, for example, asserts that Solomon composed charms for healing people and exorcizing malicious demons, and claims that he himself witnessed a Judaean named Eleazar successfully perform exorcisms in the presence of the emperor Vespasian by using the techniques bequeathed by Solomon (*Judaean Antiquities* 8.45–9). As for Egyptian material, there were certainly many Egyptian priests learned in both Egyptian and Greek who could facilitate the transmission of genuine Egyptian traditions, and such transmission certainly at times took place; for example, the fact that some of the "magical papyri" are written in both Greek and Demotic Egyptian shows that there was movement across these cultural and linguistic lines. On the other hand, it is equally certain that Greeks and Romans were at times keen to increase the allure of their own traditions by presenting them as Egyptian. Hence, for example, scholars differ sharply about the Hermetic literature: some view it as almost purely Greek in origin, others as very largely Egyptian. Similarly with the cult of Isis: the goddess herself is Egyptian in origin, and so is her myth as recounted by Plutarch (*On Isis and Osiris* 12–19, 355d–358e); but the associated mysteries reflect Greek traditions. In cases like these, it is perhaps best to assume a real fusion of Graeco-Roman and eastern traditions.

1.2 Divine inspiration

While anyone could pray and make offerings, and even interact directly with the gods through oracles, dreams, and visions, some people claimed a special connection with the divine that gave them insights and abilities unavailable to ordinary people. Within the normative Graeco-Roman tradition, the socio-economic elite tended to view such charismatic religious leaders with suspicion, inasmuch as they constituted a potential threat to their own authority; I consider this topic in more detail in chapter 7. Yet they flourished all the same, if more often on the fringes of the mainstream Graeco-Roman tradition than near its center.

Before turning to specific examples, we must first consider the nature of the evidence. Rarely do we have any first-hand evidence for the way these figures presented themselves and their ideas. Instead, we typically have accounts only at second- or third-hand, sometimes dating many years after the fact, that reflect the views of their followers or enemies. This is important for a number of reasons. Most obviously, it makes it difficult if not impossible to ascertain the actual deeds and claims of these people; consequently, many of them are the subjects of ongoing scholarly controversy. Yet the legends and uncertainties are in themselves important evidence for the strong reactions that they could inspire. It is clear that many of them were highly controversial; even when most of our evidence for a particular figure is entirely positive or negative, we can usually find traces of the opposite view as well. Their followers often regarded them as in some way superior to ordinary mortals, and credited them with miraculous feats and inspired teachings, the accounts of which undoubtedly grew more elaborate over time. Their detractors, on the other hand, attacked them as fraudulent or disreputable or wicked, and interpreted stories about their power and wisdom as evidence for deceit or malign influences. In short, the significance of these figures often lies as much in the stories and controversies that grew up around them as in anything that they themselves may have actually done or said.

By far the most famous, as well as the most controversial, of these charismatic religious leaders is Jesus of Nazareth, a village in Galilee. Our knowledge of Jesus comes almost entirely from accounts of his sayings and deeds (known as "gospels" in English) that circulated among his devotees. Most scholars now agree that the earliest of these was composed at least 40 years after his death, and that it is impossible to determine with any certainty which elements in these accounts go back to the historical Jesus and which represent the later ideas of his followers. They depict Jesus as a wonder-worker who could heal the sick, cast out demons, and even raise the dead; as a moral teacher who emphasized compassion for the poor and outcast; as a prophet of a coming "Kingdom of God"; and ultimately as himself divine. We have relatively little information about the views of Jesus' detractors, but that he aroused strong opposition is clear enough; one of the few facts about his life attested by a relatively early non-Christian source is that "in the reign of Tiberius he was executed by the procurator Pontius Pilatus" (Tacitus, *Annals* 15.44.3).

Paul of Tarsus, a city in Cilicia, was originally an opponent of those who continued as Jesus' followers after his death, but after an intense religious experience, which he interpreted as a revelation of Jesus Christ, he presented himself as Christ's divinely appointed representative to non-Judaeans (Paul, *Letter to the Galatians* 1.11–17; cf. *Acts of the Apostles* 9.1–30). Paul is one of the relatively few charismatic religious leaders for whom we have first-hand evidence, in the form of letters he wrote to followers in Asia Minor, Macedonia, Greece, and Rome (although some "Pauline" letters are clearly pseudepigrapha). Since he composed these not as comprehensive expositions of his teaching but rather as responses to particular situations, they do not necessarily yield a coherent account of his ideas.

But we can at least be sure that central to them was the notion that faith in Christ would free people from the control of certain negative forces, usually identified as sin but sometimes also associated with external superhuman powers. The author of *Acts of the Apostles* depicts Paul also as a wonder-worker, striking a rival with blindness (13.6–12) and driving out demons (16.16–18). According to a plausible later tradition, Paul too was eventually executed by Roman authorities in the early 60s CE.

Apollonius of Tyana, a city just to the north of Tarsus, was a wandering Pythagorean philosopher active in the first century CE. Almost nothing of his own writings survives, apart from a collection of probably pseudepigraphic letters, and we depend for our information almost entirely on a highly romanticized account of his life written by Philostratus in the early third century CE. This presents Apollonius as an ascetic who rejects animal sacrifice and the eating of meat, as a moral teacher and religious reformer, and as a wonder-worker who can prophesy the future, drive away malevolent spirits, and raise the dead; having been arrested and tried before the emperor Domitian, he simply vanishes from the courtroom and reappears to his followers in another city. Apollonius' followers evidently regarded him as *theios*, "god-like," but his opponents called him a *magos* and a quack. It was partly in response to what he considered unjust accusations of this sort that Philostratus wrote his account.

The first treatise of the *Corpus Hermeticum* contains an anonymous first-person account of a religious teacher who was probably active in Egypt sometime in the second or third century CE. The author describes how he had a vision of a divine being named Poimandres, who revealed to him the true nature of the cosmos and the human condition; at the core of this revelation is the doctrine that the material world is corrupt and inferior, and that humanity contains within itself an element from a higher level of existence to which people should strive to return. Poimandres instructed the author to proclaim this message to his fellows, and he did so. He then describes how some of his audience, "who had surrendered themselves to the way of death, resumed their mocking and withdrew, while those who desired to be taught cast themselves at my feet. Having made them rise, I became guide to my race, teaching them the words – how to be saved and in what manner – and I sowed the words of wisdom among them, and they were nourished from the ambrosial water" (29; trans. Copenhaver 1992: 6). Although this narrative may be no more than a literary fiction, the evidence for other divinely inspired religious leaders suggests that it is at least an entirely plausible fiction.

These figures present significant differences as well as similarities, and the differences would be even more striking if we were to consider further cases. The extent to which it is possible to identify a distinct category of "holy men" or "divine men" in the Graeco-Roman world is the subject of considerable scholarly controversy, but is not an issue that needs to be resolved here. The important thing to keep in mind is that there were people whose religious authority derived not from holding an official priesthood or even from expertise in arcane lore, but from the belief that they in some way enjoyed privileged access to divine power and knowledge. As I noted in the introduction to this section, there was significant overlap between these claims to special connections with the divine and the appeals to esoteric traditions that I discussed above. Apollonius, for example, evidently presented himself as a follower of Pythagoras and was said to have visited "oriental sages" in Babylon, India, and Ethiopia; the author of *Poimandres* was in some way associated with Hermes Trismegistos; and both Jesus and Paul, of course, were Judaeans and exponents, if radically innovative ones, of Judaean tradition. We can nevertheless regard these divinely inspired religious leaders as having a distinct appeal of their own, and thus as providing a distinctive type of religious option.

2 Advantages

Appeals to esoteric wisdom and claims to divine inspiration alike created a sense that certain traditions and individuals provided a privileged access to divine power and knowledge that was unavailable elsewhere, and this sense of privilege was one of the things that, for some people at least, made these religious options more attractive than mainstream modes of interaction with the divine. But did these options offer anything beyond the promise of special access? The question is important, because for many years most scholars assumed that people turned to these religious options because the mainstream Graeco-Roman tradition no longer satisfied their spiritual needs. Although this may seem a reasonable hypothesis, it is very difficult to evaluate. For one thing, as many people in these days of mass marketing are aware, many "needs" are not innate, but develop in response to what is available: thirty years ago, for example, almost no one "needed" a personal computer. More importantly, there is relatively little evidence from the ancient world that would allow us to determine people's actual spiritual needs. There is, however, evidence for what these religious options were thought to provide, and it is on this that I focus in this section.

For the purposes of analysis we may divide them into three categories. Firstly, some options offered an alternative and apparently more effective means of addressing the same concerns that motivated much traditional religious activity; in this respect, their attraction presumably lay entirely in the promise of that special access to the divine that I have already discussed. Secondly, some provided what we might call an intensification of traditional religious experience: a feeling of a more profound encounter with the divine or an unusually intimate relationship with a deity that provided special blessings both in life and after death. Lastly, some proposed new models of the cosmos and a new understanding of the human role within it; in doing so, they also created the need for new types of salvation that previously seem to have been unknown. We will consider each of these in turn. But it is important to keep in mind throughout that the various religious options available in the Roman world did not fall neatly into one or another of these three categories. On the contrary, many of them offered, at least potentially, something in all three areas, even though for the sake of simplicity I focus on one or another.

2.1 Traditional benefits

Two examples will illustrate the extent to which exotic religious options could function simply as alternative means to obtain familiar benefits. First, in 49 CE a Roman noblewoman named Lollia Paulina, who had allegedly hoped to marry the emperor Claudius, was charged with "questioning Chaldaeans, *magi*, and the oracle of Clarian Apollo about the emperor's marriage" (Tacitus, *Annals* 12.22.1). Making inquiries about emperors was forbidden as a form of treason, but what is interesting for us is the way that Tacitus' account juxtaposes the exotic Chaldaeans and *magi* with the highly respectable Greek oracle of Apollo as equally serviceable forms of divination. The second example is the story mentioned above of the Egyptian priest Arnouphis saving the Roman army by calling up a rainstorm; according to the historian Cassius Dio, who describes Arnouphis as a *magos*, he did this by invoking Hermes "of the air," presumably a form of the Egyptian god Thoth (*History* 71.8.4). Popular opinion, however, apparently attributed the storm instead to the intervention of Jupiter, the traditional Roman patron and weather god (Fowden 1987). The fact that people could attribute the same blessing to both the exotic rituals of an Egyptian *magus* and a traditional cult like that of Jupiter suggests that they perceived these as alternative means to the same ends. In this section I focus on two traditional concerns that often appear in connection with religious options, and then briefly consider some similar but less respectable motivations.

A concern for health, which as we saw in chapter 3 was a major reason for people turning to the gods, was equally prominent in these religious options. For example, one of the Greek Magical Papyri, a spell-book compiled in the third century CE, contains prescriptions for treating a wide variety of ailments, including scorpion sting, rheumy eyes, headache, cough, hardening of the breast, swollen testicles, and fever (*PGM* VII.193– 214). Here is one of them, a prayer for healing the condition that the ancients called a "wandering womb": "'I conjure you, O Womb, by the one estab- lished over the Abyss, before heaven, earth, sea, light, or darkness came to be; who created the angels, being foremost, amichamchou and chouchaô chêrôei oueiachô odou proseioggês, and who sit above the cherubim . . . , that you return again to your seat. . . . Hallelujah! Amen!' Write this on a tin tablet and clothe it in seven colors" (*PGM* VII.260–71, trans. J. Scarborough in Betz 1992: 123–4). The exotic qualities of this spell are obvious: it adopts phrases from Judaean tradition, and includes for good measure a selection of "magic words." Yet a person with the condition that it aims to heal could just as easily have turned instead to a traditional healing deity such as Asklepios.

The power to heal was also often attributed to those with special connections to the divine. The *Gospel of Mark*, for example, recounts how Jesus healed a leper (1.40–5), a paralytic (2.1–12), a man with a withered arm (3.1–5), a woman with hemorrhages (5.25–34), a deaf and dumb man (7.31–7), and two blind men (8.22–6 and 10.46–52); similarly, his follower Peter was said to have healed a lame man and a paralytic (*Acts of the Apostles* 3.1–10 and 9.32–5). But stories about miraculous powers of healing were not limited to the Christian tradition. Philostratus records a tradition that Apollonius of Tyana healed a lame man, a blind man, and a paralytic (*Life of Apollonius of Tyana* 3.39); he also foretold a plague at Ephesus and was later able to identify its demonic source (4.4 and 10). The last story is a reminder that many people regarded malevolent spirits as a cause of illness, especially what we would call mental illness. For example, in a Greek romantic novel, when the heroine becomes lovesick but refuses to divulge the reason for her condition, her parents bring in diviners and priests who attempt through ritual means to placate the spirits causing her illness (Xenophon of Ephesus, *An Ephesian Tale* 1.5). That this particular fiction was based on actual practice is suggested by a remark of the Roman legal scholar Ulpian, who distinguishes legitimate doctors from those who use incantations, imprecations, and exorcisms: "for those are not kinds of medicine, even though there are people who swear that these men have helped them" (*Digest* 50.13.1.3). Both Apollonius and Jesus were said to have had the ability to cast out malevolent spirits, and the latter's name was thought to be effective for such purposes in and of itself.

Another major need common to both traditional practice and religious options was that for advice and insight into the future. The spell-book mentioned above (*PGM* VII) also includes instructions for "direct visions," "dream oracles," "lamp divination," and "saucer divination." An example of this sort of ritual has been quoted above (see Text Box 6.1). In this particular case, the ritual was supposed to send a boy or a man into a trance so that he could act as the mouthpiece of a god; the person performing the ritual could then make inquiries of him as he would of an oracle. In fact, the whole process provided a sort of do-it-yourself substitute for the oracles of Delphi or Claros, with the added attraction that it claimed to be even more effective.

To some extent, then, religious options simply offered an alternative and possibly more effective means of obtaining the same benefits that people sought through traditional cult. Some of them, however, held a particular attraction for people with goals that were socially unacceptable, who wanted, for example, to constrain or harm an opponent or rival, or to inspire sexual passion in another person. These desires could be addressed through the use of binding spells, which are attested both in the magical papyri and in curse tablets, small lead sheets inscribed with ritual formulae and placed underground, sometimes in a grave. A few examples will illustrate the type.

Then as now, spectator sports tended to arouse strong emotions in their audiences, and people used binding spells to give their favored team an edge. Here, for example, is the opening of a curse tablet from Berytus in Phoenicia, commissioned by a fan of chariot racing: "Oreobarzagra akrammachari phnoukentabaôth ôbarabau, you holy angels, ambush and restrain lulatau audônista them. The spell oiatitnounamintou maskelli maskellô phnoukentabaôth oreobarza now attack, bind, overturn, cut up, chop into pieces the horses and the charioteers of the Blue colors" (trans. Gager 1992: no. 5). Although this seems a particularly vicious and bloodthirsty wish, we must remember that the person responsible may not have intended it any more literally than a sports fan of today who wants his or her team to "crush" or "slaughter" its opponents. Another area of life that can rouse strong emotions is business competition, which is perhaps what lies behind this curse tablet from Carthage: "Arthu lailam semeseilam aeêiouô bachuch bakaxichuch mene baichuch abrasax bazabachuch mene baichuch abrasax, lord gods, restrain and hinder the Falernian baths, lest anyone should be able to approach that place; bind and bind up the Falernian baths from this day, lest any person should approach that place" (trans. Gager 1992: no. 82). The person responsible was possibly the owner of another bath house, seeking to undermine a rival establishment.

Lastly, sexual desire has always been a powerful motivating force, and there are many examples, both in the papyri and in curse tablets, of spells meant to "attract" the desired person. A lead tablet from a grave in Hadrumetum in North Africa records the prayer of a woman trying to win back a man who apparently broke up with her: "I invoke you, *daimonion* spirit who lies here, by the holy name Aôth abaôth, the god of Abraham, and Iaô, the god of Jacob, Iaô aôth abaôth, god of Israma, hear the honored, dreadful, and great name, go away to Urbanus, to whom Urbana gave birth, and bring him to Domitiana, to whom Candida gave birth, so that loving, frantic, and sleepless with love and desire for her, he may beg her to return to his house and become his wife" (trans. Gager 1992: no. 36). We find a similar spell in an Egyptian papyrus, although with Egyptian rather than Judaean coloring: "I adjure you, Euangelos, by Anubis and Hermes and all the rest down below; attract and bind Sarapias whom Helen bore, to this Herais, whom Thermoutharin bore, now, now; quickly, quickly" (*PGM* XXXII.1–9, trans. E. O'Neil in Betz 1992: 266).

Although popular ideas about "black magic" might make these spells seem natural, it is worth asking why people apparently preferred to employ this particular kind of ritual to help with these particular concerns. Part of the explanation no doubt lies in the hope that such coercive techniques might be more effective than simply praying to a deity. But part of it must also lie in their very secrecy. The usual forms of traditional cult tended to be highly public: people normally spoke their prayers out loud, and publicly dedicated and memorialized their offerings to the gods. Those who wanted to harm their rivals or compel another person to have sex with them may well have preferred not to make their wishes widely known. Nevertheless, we must remember that people could also seek to satisfy desires of this sort through more traditional means: lovers, for example, might appeal for the favor of Aphrodite or Venus, goddesses traditionally associated with sexual passion. Thus even religious options like these were in a significant respect simply alternatives to traditional cult, even if they had distinct practical advantages.

2.2 Intensification

Many religious options, however, were not merely alternatives to traditional practices and beliefs, but offered something more as well. The secret initiations known as mysteries, for example, could provide a more intense religious experience than was typical in the usual forms of cult. These rituals were Greek in origin, the great model being the ancient and renowned mysteries of Demeter and Kore at Eleusis. By the fifth century BCE, mysteries of a rather different sort were associated with the cult of Dionysos; unlike those of Eleusis, the mysteries of Dionysos were not tied to a particular shrine and a regular schedule but could take place anywhere and at any time, conducted by local priests or itinerant specialists, and usually performed on an individual basis. In the imperial period, there were also mysteries associated with various deities of eastern origin, especially the Great Mother, Isis, and Mithras. Although the various mysteries differed in some significant ways, the core of their appeal was in all cases the same: they offered a profound and emotionally powerful experience of the divine. Dio Chrysostom, for example, compares the contemplation of the physical cosmos to the experience of a initiate: "if one were to deliver a man . . . into a mystic recess of extraordinary beauty and size to be initiated, where he would see many mystic spectacles and hear many sounds of the same kind, with darkness and light appearing to him in alternation and a thousand other things taking place . . . , is it likely that such a man would experience nothing in his soul?" (*Orations* 12.33). Clearly, initiation into a mystery was a much more extraordinary experience than participation in the usual cult practices.

Mysteries also allowed initiates to establish a particularly intimate and privileged relationship with a deity and thereby obtain special blessings. Apuleius' novel *The Golden Ass*, although fictional, provides the richest and most detailed account of the sort of relationship that an initiate might have with the deity. At the novel's climax, the goddess Isis appears to the hero Lucius, who has inadvertently transformed himself into a donkey; she promises to restore him to human form, and says that he will henceforth be pledged to her. After his transformation, Lucius can hardly bear to be away from the goddess's image. After thanking as quickly as possible the family and friends who congratulate him on his restoration, "I betake myself once more to the supremely pleasing sight of the goddess; having rented a dwelling within the temple precinct, I establish a temporary home and attach myself, unofficially as yet, to the service of the goddess and the fellowship of the priests, as the constant and inseparable worshipper of her great godhead" (*The Golden Ass* 11.19). By the novel's end, Lucius has not only undergone a whole series of initiations but has also become an official in the goddess's cult. His religious life thus seems to become focused on Isis: his relationship with her is strongly emotional and deeply personal, he participates in her worship on a daily basis, and ultimately adopts a public sign of his identification with the cult by keeping his head shaved.

Lastly, a mystery initiation was thought to bestow unusual benefits on the initiate. Although the sources are not too specific, it seems that what most people expected was that they would thereafter receive the particular care of the deity. As Isis says to Lucius, "you will live in my safekeeping, blessed and glorious" (*The Golden Ass* 11.6); the blessings and glory that she brings Lucius included most notably a successful and lucrative career as an advocate in the law courts. Some mysteries also promised initiates a better lot after death. This was certainly true of the mysteries of Demeter at Eleusis, as several sources make clear; Cicero, for example, says that through those initiations "we have received a reason not only for living with joy but also for dying with a better hope" (*On Laws* 2.36). Similarly, Isis continues her speech to Lucius by saying that "when you have measured out your life's span and journey to the underworld, there also in that underground hemisphere I whom you see will shine amidst the gloom of Acheron and reign in the Stygian depths, gracious to you, and you, as you dwell in the Elysian fields, will constantly adore me" (*The Golden Ass* 11.6).

It has often been assumed on the basis of such evidence that mystery initiations provided a unique benefit, a type of "salvation" that was unobtainable in traditional cults. But we must be careful not to overestimate the significance of the evidence. For one thing, the study of the thousands of epitaphs that survive from the Roman world suggests that for most people the fate of the individual after death was not a major concern. Moreover, the promises regarding the afterlife in these cults are fairly limited in scope: Isis does not say to Lucius that he will escape death, but merely that he will be nicely situated in the underworld and will continue worshipping her there. To a large extent, such promises seem simply to have been an extension of the more important promise of heightened divine favor during life. Isis concludes her speech to Lucius not with her promises about the afterlife, but by informing him that "if by zealous obedience and dutiful service and rigorous abstinence you have gained the favor of my godhead, you will discover that to me alone is it also permitted to extend your life beyond the span allotted by your fate" (*The Golden Ass* 11.6): presumably this is meant as an even greater blessing than residence in the Elysian fields.

In most respects, then, the difference between mystery cults and other forms of worship was one of degree rather than of substance. Intense religious experiences could also be had outside mystery cults, as the evidence for dreams and visions of the gods discussed in chapter 3 suggests. Likewise, people could have deeply personal relationships with a deity, as the orator Aelius Aristides had with Asklepios: like Lucius with Isis, Aristides lived for a while in the god's precincts, experienced regular and close interactions with him, and credited him with his worldly success. Even the blessings that mysteries were thought to bestow were to a large extent only more intensive versions of the same divine assistance that people sought in all cults. Yet we should not for these reasons discount them as a significant and distinctive form of ancient religious practice. Mysteries were unique in their insistent focus on intense religious experiences and profound encounters with the divine, and as a result they acquired a tremendous cultural importance as the standard for other experiences of the same sort. The terms "mystery" and "initiation" became common metaphors for any revelation of the divine, widely used by philosophers, magicians, and Christians alike. In this respect they overlap with the phenomena that we will examine in the following section.

2.3 Salvation

To a large extent, despite the exotic allure of "oriental wisdom" and "divine men," many religious options still operated within the general framework of the mainstream Graeco-Roman tradition. A few, however, by modeling a new understanding of the cosmos and of humanity's place within it, offered real alternatives. In the mainstream tradition, as we saw in chapter 3, both gods and mortals were innate parts of the natural world, and what people mostly sought from the gods was assistance with the problems and concerns of day-to-day life. In radical contrast to this were views of the cosmos that sharply separated the divine from the material world of ordinary experience, and even disparaged the physical world as an inferior or corrupt sphere of existence. In this context, the chief task for humanity was to free itself from this lower realm and ascend into the sphere of the divine, which was in some sense its true home: in other words, to attain some form of salvation.

The origins of these new views of the world, so at odds with mainstream tradition, are much debated. To some extent the influence of the philosopher Plato must have played a role. Plato had proposed that the world of everyday experience, in which things change and decay, is merely a dim and weak reflection of true reality, the realm of unchanging Forms. The most famous expression of this proposition is his simile of the cave, in which he compared those whose knowledge is limited to the material world to people who can see only the shadows cast on the walls of a cave by models of the real things that exist outside (*Republic* 7, 514a–17c); the philosopher, accordingly, must train his mind to rise from the shadows of this world to the higher world of Forms. Other scholars have suggested that a new astronomical model of the physical universe was of crucial importance. In this model, the earth is the center of a series of concentric spheres; first are the spheres of the seven "planets," the celestial bodies that move, and then comes the sphere of the fixed stars and constellations. Above the lowest planetary sphere, that of the moon, the cosmos is perfect, unchanging, and eternal; below the lunar sphere, however, everything is subject to chance, change, and decay. Some scholars have also emphasized the social and political developments that came in the wake of Alexander the Great's conquests, in which the bounded and ordered communities of earlier antiquity were subsumed within disorienting and complex cosmopolitan empires; as a result, people no longer felt at home in this world and looked instead for their true home outside it.

Although all these suggestions have merit, none seems entirely satisfactory, and it is likely that a wide variety of factors was involved in the spread of these new models of the cosmos, which themselves took a wide variety of forms. Some people, following Plato, saw the material world merely as inferior, bad only in comparison with a superior level of existence; others, in contrast, viewed the world as a positive evil, either because matter itself was inherently evil or because it was subject to malign influences. Opinions about human salvation differed sharply as well. Some taught that people were able to free themselves if they tried, especially by cultivating true knowledge and disciplining their bodies; others believed that people were instead dependent on aid from above; still others thought that some people had by their very nature a share in the higher realm while others did not. Rarely did these different views exist in pure form, however; even within the same system people might emphasize now one and now another. I will here briefly consider just a few specific examples.

As I noted earlier, the cult of Mithras was in several respects quite unlike other cults; it seems to have been unusual as well in offering a complex theology to match its complex iconography and organization. The scarcity of written sources makes interpretation difficult and certainty impossible, but astronomical symbolism seems to have played a major part. Figures in the typical cult relief of Mithras present striking correspondences to a particular group of constellations (see Figure 6.1): the bull itself corresponds to Taurus, the dog to Canis Major, the snake to Hydra, and the scorpion to Scorpio. In many representations, there are other figures as well: a raven, corresponding to Corvus, and two torchbearers, corresponding to Gemini. Similarly, the seven grades of Mithraic initiation were correlated with the seven planets, and the underground chamber in which the initiates performed their rites was apparently meant as a symbolic model of the physical universe. That, at least, is what the third-century philosopher Porphyry says: "Similarly, the Persians call the place 'a cave' where they introduce an initiate to the mysteries, revealing to him the path by which souls descend and go back again. For Eubulus tells us that Zoroaster was the first to dedicate a natural cave in honor of Mithras, the creator and father of all. . . . This cave bore for him the image of the cosmos which Mithras had created, and the things which the cave contained, by their proportionate arrangement, provided him with symbols of the elements and climates of the cosmos" (*On the Cave of the Nymphs* 6, "Arethusa" translation). Some scholars have argued cogently that a central belief of the cult was that the human soul descended into the

Figure 6.1 Statue from central Italy depicting Mithras slaying the bull. Rome, Museo Nazionale 124668. Reproduced by permission of Alinari Archives, Florence

physical cosmos at the point of the summer solstice in Cancer, journeyed through the planetary spheres to the earth, and ultimately ascended back out of it at the winter solstice in Capricorn; the raised and lowered torches of the two torchbearers symbolized this descent and ascent of the soul. The precise role in all this of Mithras and his killing of the bull is unclear, although a graffito from a "cave" in Rome is suggestive: "you have saved us by the shedding of blood."

There is no evidence to indicate whether or not worshippers of Mithras viewed the earth, the site of the soul's sojourn, in negative terms. In other religious systems, however, this was definitely the case. Some later followers of Plato took his distinction between matter and form to an extreme. For example, the second-century philosopher Numenius of Apamea, a city in Syria, apparently taught that matter is not something indifferent or inter-mediate between good and evil, but is instead "completely noxious" and the cause of evil; the world, which is compounded from matter and form, is thus a blend of good and evil (fragment 52 in des Places 1973). Even those Platonists who did not take such a negative view of the material world still saw it as a place from which people must free themselves. According to Porphyry, "we are like those who, exiled willingly or unwillingly among a race of foreigners, are not only banished from what is properly theirs, but have also in this strange land become filled with passions and habits and customs alien to them"; to return to our true home, we must abandon everything that is material and mortal and raise ourselves towards the higher world by an upward movement of the soul, thereby reversing the movement of its original descent (*On Abstinence* 1.30.2–5).

The metaphor that human existence in the material world is a form of exile was used by a number of religious options. Another common metaphor is that of enslavement, which was a favorite of the Christian teacher Paul of Tarsus in the mid-first century CE; Paul interpreted the death of Jesus as a sacrifice whereby God freed people from enslavement to sin and death. "When you were slaves of sin, you were free from the control of righteousness; and what was the gain? Nothing but what now makes you ashamed, for the end of that is death. But now, freed from the commands of sin, and bound to the service of God, your gains are such as make for holiness, and the end is eternal life" (*Letter to the Romans* 6.20–3, trans. New English Bible). The sacrifice of Jesus was necessary because people are so enslaved to sin that they are unable to help themselves: "We know that the law is spiritual, but I am not: I am unspiritual, the purchased slave of sin. I do not even acknowledge my own actions as mine, for what I do is not what I want to do, but what I detest . . . ; and if what I do is against my will, clearly it is no longer I who am the agent, but sin that has its lodging in me" (*Romans* 7.14–20, trans. New English Bible). But God has "rescued us from the domain of darkness and brought us away into the kingdom of his dear Son, in whom our release is secured and our sins forgiven" (*Letter to the Colossians* 1.13–14, trans. New English Bible).

For Paul, God enabled humanity to escape from sin, by which he seems to have meant something internal to the individual, even if at times he speaks of it almost as an external force. Other Christians believed that it was the material world from which humanity needed rescuing. The author of a pseudepigraphic "secret book" attributed to Jesus' disciple John presents a highly elaborate mythic account of the cosmos that, among other things, turns Judaean tradition on its head. It begins with an ineffable godhead, which generates a series of emanations that together constitute the Entirety (Greek *Plêrôma*). The last of these, Wisdom, produces an emanation of her own, Ialdabaôth, who is unaware of the Entirety and creates the material cosmos: this is the God of *Genesis*, reinterpreted as an inferior or even malevolent being. Without his knowledge, some of the power of the Entirety enters into the first man, Adam, and through his third son Seth passes into a portion of the human race. Eventually, a savior is sent from the Entirety to bring the descendants of Seth "knowledge" (Greek *gnôsis*) of their true origin and thereby assist them to return to the realm where they truly belong. This "gnostic" myth, as it is usually called, is known from a number of texts, originally composed in Greek but now available only in Coptic translations. Although there are numerous variations, they all emphasize that a part of humanity must come to "know" that it belongs not to this world but to a higher plane of existence, to which this "knowledge" will enable it to return.

The author of the Hermetic treatise *Poimandres* presents a similar if less elaborate account of the cosmos, and draws from it similar conclusions about human nature and human salvation. According to him, "mankind is twofold – in the body mortal but immortal in the essential man. Even though he is immortal and has authority over all things, mankind is affected by mortality because he is subject to fate; thus, although man is above the cosmic framework, he became a slave within it" (15, trans. Copenhaver 1992: 3). The language of enslavement here is reminiscent of Paul, although "fate" takes the place of "sin." In other respects the language is more like that of gnostic texts: "life and light are god and father, from whom the man came to be; so if you learn that you are from light and life, and that you happen to come from them, you shall advance to life once again" (21, trans. Copenhaver 1992: 5). In the end, "stripped of the effects of the cosmic framework, the human enters the region of the ogdoad; he has his own proper power, and along with the blessed he hymns the father. . . . They rise up to the father in order and surrender themselves to the powers, and, having become powers, they enter into god. This is the final good for those who have received knowledge: to be made god" (26, trans. Copenhaver 1992: 6).

The variety in these texts and traditions is obvious. What unites them is a view of the cosmos that differs fundamentally from the one traditional in Graeco-Roman culture, and that creates the need for some form of radical salvation. To this extent, religious options like these functioned as real alternatives to the mainstream.

3 Conclusion

Throughout this chapter I have used the term "religious options" as a catch-all phrase for a range of extremely diverse phenomena. The only thing that unites them is that they all existed more or less on the margins of the mainstream religious tradition of the empire described in the preceding chapters; in particular, they all invoked sources of religious authority that lay outside the chief social and political structures. Yet we should not for this reason assume that these religious options were always in competition with the mainstream tradition. To be sure, a few of them, notably those that developed out of the Judaean tradition, involved ideas and practices so radically opposed to the mainstream that they forced people to choose one or the other exclusively. Yet options of this sort formed a definite minority. For the most part, the phenomena discussed in this chapter did not compete with the regular forms of religious behavior that I have already sketched, but instead provided specific sorts of supplements. This is true even of those that were sufficiently flexible and complex enough to dominate the religious lives of their adherents. Lucius, for example, appears at the end of *The Golden Ass* to focus all his attention on Isis and her cult, yet there is no reason to suppose that in doing so he excluded himself from acknowledging or even participating in other forms of religious activity.

We must also be careful not to exaggerate the importance of these religious options. This is easy to do, for a variety of reasons. For one thing, many of them intersect in some way with the early stages of Christianity, and the later historical importance of Christianity can thus make them seem to loom larger than they may actually have done at the time. Another partly connected reason is that many of these phenomena are attested in extensive surviving texts, and so in some respects are better attested than other phenomena that were probably more widespread. Yet it is likely that for most people in Roman times these were simply options, and nothing more: they might engage with them for particular purposes, but in their day-to-day lives probably had more to do with the mainstream structures outlined in the previous chapters. For those who did become too closely identified with these religious options, moreover, there was the danger of attracting the unfavorable notice of neighbors or more importantly of imperial officials. This is the topic of the next chapter.

FURTHER READING

West 1983 provides a thorough although highly technical account of Orphic literature; Parke 1988 surveys the Sibylline tradition; Kahn 2001 is the best brief introduction to the Pythagorean tradition. On Egyptian priests, see Frankfurter 1998: 217–37; Fowden 1986 is an excellent discussion of the Hermetic tradition and its context; Copenhaver 1992 provides an English translation of the chief Hermetic writings, with extensive notes. On the attractions of the Judaean tradition see the concise account in Schürer 1973–87: 3.150–76; translations and brief discussions of Judaean pseudepigrapha are available in Charlesworth 1983. Beck 1991 discusses Persian pseudepigrapha; Clauss 2001 is a succinct overview of the evidence for the cult of Mithras, while the collected papers of Gordon 1996 and Beck 2004 provide the best discussions of its theology. For an overview of ancient magic, see Graf 1997; English translations of the Greek Magical Papyri are available in Betz 1992, and a selection of curse tablets in Gager 1992. On charismatic religious leaders, see Anderson 1994 and Francis 1995. Burkert 1987 is a critical overview of mystery cults. On new models of the cosmos, see Dodds 1965 and Martin 1987; Layton 1987 provides a clear introduction to gnostic texts, with translations of many key texts.

CHAPTER 7

Roman Religious Policy

╒╤╒╤╒╤╒╤

The title of this chapter would perhaps be better framed as a question than as a statement, since its focus will be the extent to which the rulers of the Roman Empire actually had a religious policy at all. If we compare Roman imperialism with that of later Christian and Islamic powers, we can answer this question easily and in the negative, since the expansion of Roman rule certainly did not involve pressures on subjugated peoples to convert to the religion of their conquerors. This was not because Roman rulers had a positive respect for diversity and a commitment to religious freedom, but simply because there was no "religion" to which people could convert. As I have argued, the Graeco-Roman tradition was not a cohesive system of integrated practices and beliefs, but instead involved overlapping sets of cult practices, myths, iconographic conventions, and philosophical propositions. The norm was thus one of multiple traditions, not of one monolithic system to which everyone was expected to conform. Moreover, the pervasive tendencies towards particularization and generalization provided a framework within which new traditions could be incorporated almost indefinitely and with a minimum of conflict.

Nevertheless, Roman rule did have a dramatic impact on the religious lives of people in the empire. We have already considered the most notable effects in chapter 5: on the one hand, the spread of Graeco-Roman ideas, practices, and conventions usually labeled Romanization and Hellenization, and on the other the focus on the emperor as a unifying element in worship. As I have mentioned, there is considerable debate over the extent to which these developments came about through direct Roman intervention or resulted from indirect pressures and incentives. My own view is that the latter played a more important part, since evidence for active intervention by Roman authorities in matters of religion is fairly rare. It was certainly not the case, for example, as is often assumed, that Roman officials required people to worship the emperor. Although governors and other officials issued decrees mandating the celebration of imperial accessions and victories, local authorities were the ones who implemented them; in many cases it was the local elites themselves who took the initiative in establishing honors for the emperors. But neither local authorities nor Roman officials monitored and enforced individual participation in these ceremonies, any more than in other public cults.

In addition to the positive if indirect promotion of Graeco-Roman traditions and religious honors for the emperor, Roman rule also had a negative impact, in that certain traditions and behaviors were restricted, repressed, and criminalized. It is on this negative impact that I focus in this chapter. In the first section I provide some general background by tracing widespread ideas about what constituted improper religious behavior. In the second I discuss the specific obligation of Roman officials to maintain peace and good order, and explore its relevance to religious issues. In the last section I briefly survey three particular areas in which we may identify something like an official policy, and consider in more detail the nature of Roman religious policy.

1 Atheism and Superstition

Two sets of terms were available to describe improper religious practices and behaviors. One set emphasized the failure to engage in accepted forms of worship or show proper respect for the divine. In Latin, a person who did this was called *impius*, "impious," or a *sacrilegus*, the technical term for a person who stole property consecrated to a god. The corresponding Greek terms are *asebês*, "impious," and *atheos*, which means literally "without god." The latter word can be somewhat misleading, since it is convenient to translate it by its English derivative "atheist." But the connotations of the two words differ somewhat. We must keep in mind that the emphasis in the Graeco-Roman tradition was more on ritual practices than statements of belief. In this context, *atheos* meant not only a person who formally denied the existence of the gods, but also, and perhaps more frequently, anyone who rejected or neglected the traditional modes of honoring them.

Chief among these was the practice of animal sacrifice, which served as the most important and widespread symbol of piety. People who steadfastly refused to perform sacrifices or even acknowledge them might well arouse the hostility of their neighbors. To be sure, as I noted in chapter 1, there was a long philosophical tradition of criticizing animal sacrifice, associated especially with the name of Pythagoras and the practice of vegetarianism. The philosopher Porphyry, for example, wrote a lengthy treatise on vegetarianism in which he advanced a detailed argument that animal sacrifice was not in accordance with divine will. He was nevertheless careful to point out that he did not advocate the abolition of normal observances: bloodless sacrifices are also traditional, he says, and allow the philosopher to satisfy both his conscience and the requirements of religious propriety (*On Abstinence* 2.33). Porphyry had some need to be cautious, since an earlier philosopher by the name of Demonax was apparently publicly attacked in Athens because "he had never been seen to sacrifice and had not, out of all the city, been initiated in the Eleusinian mysteries" (Lucian, *Demonax* 11). Demonax, it seems, was able to charm the assembly and escape condemnation, and indeed, many people apparently made some allowance for the eccentricities of philosophers. With others, however, matters could be quite different, as we shall see below in connection with the Christians.

While *atheos* and similar terms were used of people who showed insufficient respect for the gods, another set of words was applied to people whose interactions with the gods were regarded as deviant. The key Latin word in this group is the noun *superstitio*, from which the modern English "superstition" obviously derives; the equivalent Greek word is *deisidaimonia*, which means literally "fear of the divine." *Superstitio* seems etymologically to have meant something like "standing over," although its original significance is uncertain; under Greek influence, it came in the historical period to have much the same connotations as *deisidaimonia*. Yet for both words the precise meaning is somewhat hard to pin down, and with good reason: superstition was defined more by what it was not than by what it was. Whatever religious behavior people regarded as improper, unacceptable, or incorrect, that they called superstition. For the Graeco-Roman elite, the contrast between religion and superstition could be correlated with a number of similar oppositions: between rich and poor, urban and rural, civilized and barbarian, men and women, adults and children, educated and uneducated. In each pair, what the former did was religion, and whatever the latter did that was different could be dismissed as superstition. *Superstitio* and *deisidaimonia* were thus more evaluative terms than words with clear-cut meanings. Nevertheless, we can associate them with some recurring concerns, as a couple of examples will reveal.

The Roman philosopher Seneca, for example, wrote a now-lost treatise *Against Superstitions*, from which Augustine quotes some interesting passages. In one of these, Seneca expresses his disgust at the self-mutilation practiced by some of the devotees of the Phrygian Great Mother (see Text Box 7.1). A similar work that survives intact is Plutarch's treatise on *deisidaimonia*. Plutarch's basic strategy is to juxtapose superstition and atheism. As I mentioned in chapter 3, he regards *deisidaimonia* as an even

---

Text Box 7.1

Seneca, *Against Superstitions* (as quoted by Augustine,
The City of God 6.10)

One man cuts off his male organs, another slashes his arms. If this is the way they win the gods' favor, what do they do when they fear their anger? The gods ought not to be worshipped at all, if this is the worship they want. So great is the frenzy of disturbed and displaced minds, that the gods are pleased by savageries unknown even to the most terrible of men, whose cruelty has become the stuff of legend. Tyrants have sometimes lacerated people's limbs; they have never ordered people to lacerate their limbs themselves. Some men have been castrated for the pleasure of royal lust, but no one has with his own hands unmanned himself on the orders of a master. These men hack at themselves in temples, they make an offering of their wounds and gore. If anyone had the opportunity to observe what they do and what they undergo, he would discover things so shameful for respectable men, so unworthy of free men, so irregular for sane men, that no one would doubt that they are mad, if only they shared their madness with fewer others; as things stand, the defense of sanity is the number of the insane.

---

worse error than atheism, since atheists simply reject the gods, whereas the superstitious believe that the gods are tyrannical and the source of ills. Atheists, for example, blame their misfortunes on bad luck, but the superstitious person "regards the divine as responsible for everything"; consequently, when anything bad happens he believes that he is "not unlucky but hateful to the gods," and so "is deservedly punished by the gods, paying the penalty and suffering for his own actions" (*On Superstition* 7, 168a–b). Such an attitude, Plutarch insists, is not only degrading for worshippers but insulting to the gods. "You see what the superstitious think about the gods, supposing them to be capricious, unreliable, fickle, vengeful, savage, and petty; as a result, the superstitious person necessarily hates and fears the gods" (11, 170d–e). Even though he sees superstition and atheism as opposite errors, he argues that the former ultimately leads to the latter by making the whole notion of religion contemptible. "The ridiculous actions and passions of superstition, the phrases and gestures, the charms and spells, the running around and drumming, the impure purifications and filthy sanctifications, the barbarous and shocking penances and mortifications before shrines: these are the things that allow some people to say that belief in no gods at all is better than belief in gods who accept and take delight in this sort of thing, gods who are so arrogant, so captious and petty" (12, 171a–b).

Both Seneca and Plutarch singled out foreign religious practices as examples of superstition, but apparently not merely because they were foreign; Plutarch, after all, also wrote a reverential treatise on Isis and Osiris. Instead, they seem to have had two chief sets of concerns. In terms of style, so to speak, they objected to what they regarded as frenzy and a lack of emotional restraint. The Graeco-Roman elite always placed great emphasis on self-control, something simply incompatible with the extravagant emotionality of certain religious traditions. Closely connected with this almost aesthetic distaste was a more ideological concern, an objection to the conception of the human–divine relationship that these practices seemed to imply. In the mainstream Graeco-Roman tradition, this relationship was imagined as essentially reciprocal: although the gods were much more powerful than humans, they were in a sense members of the same community and behaved according to accepted rules of behavior, bestowing benefits upon those who gave them their due. In this respect, traditional worship reinforced the dominant social structures, in which the elite and the masses were similarly bound together by mutual obligations that emphasized their community while articulating their differences in status. Religious practices that involved displays of humility and self-mortification implicitly treated the gods as tyrannical and their worshippers as servile, and hence were viewed by people like Seneca and Plutarch as completely out of keeping with Graeco-Roman social norms.

Although Seneca and Plutarch were philosophers, not Roman officials, the sentiments that they expressed in these passages were evidently widespread among the elite classes from which Roman officials came. The attitudes of specific individuals no doubt varied widely, but we may expect that by and large they shared a basic set of assumptions. Nevertheless, hostility towards atheism and superstition did not result in any systematic efforts to repress them. The reason for this is that the aims of Roman rule were largely limited to the collection of taxes and the maintenance of peace and social stability, including the administration of justice and the resolution of disputes. As a result, it was simply not the job of Roman officials to correct any perceived peculiarities of religious practice or belief among the people over whom they had authority. They thus rarely intervened in religious matters unless public peace and order seemed to be at stake. It was perhaps for this reason that members of the elite often seem to have regarded superstition as a more serious problem than atheism, as Plutarch did. Plutarch of course provides a philosophical justification for his position, namely, that it is better to deny the gods than to slander them. Yet there may have been an underlying ideological concern as well: superstition could more easily result in social disruption than atheism. People who were credulous, excitable, and prone to fear the gods might easily be swayed by self-proclaimed religious authorities, and this, in turn, could pose a threat to the socio-political hierarchy. As we shall see in the following section, Roman officials frequently took action to eliminate any serious challenges to the established social order.

2 Religious Authority

In the mainstream Graeco-Roman tradition, religious authority, together with other forms of social and political authority, was supposed to be in the hands of the economic elite. As we saw in chapter 4, this was one of the underlying principles in the organization of civic religion: the elite used their wealth and influence to benefit the city, and in exchange received social prestige and authority over the city's relations with its gods. Claims to religious authority made on a basis other than socio-economic status were thus potentially subversive of the entire social and political system on which the Roman Empire was founded, and could elicit a sharp response from Roman authorities.

As we saw in chapter 2, a number of regional traditions within the empire did not conform to the Graeco-Roman model of civic religion, and some of them involved quite different structures of religious authority. In the eastern parts of the empire, for example, from Asia Minor through Egypt, there were large temple complexes independent of any associated city, whose priests wielded considerable power and often formed distinct castes. In the Celtic tradition, the Druids seem to have played a broadly similar role. The Roman response to these alternative forms of religious organization varied. In some cases, as in Asia Minor, they apparently encouraged the transformation or incorporation of traditional temple states into more familiar Graeco-Roman civic cults; elsewhere, as in Egypt and, at least initially, in Judaea, Roman authorities upheld the traditional roles of the priests, while subjecting them to increasing regulation and control. In yet other cases, they took the more drastic step of eradicating traditional structures of religious authority altogether, as they did with the Druids. This last response was the least common; most of the time, Roman officials apparently preferred to exert more indirect pressures in order to reshape traditional societies in accordance with their expectations.

More problematic than these variant regional traditions, however, were claims to religious authority by individuals. As I noted in chapter 6, the socio-economic elite tended to view self-proclaimed religious leaders with great suspicion, insofar as they provided a potential alternative to their own authority and could easily become a rallying point for the disaffected. When such a figure was involved in a serious disturbance of the peace,

Roman authorities had no hesitation in bringing to bear all the force at their disposal. The most famous example is the execution of Jesus of Nazareth. From the Roman point of view the execution was completely appropriate: Jesus had entered Jerusalem with a number of followers and caused a serious disturbance in the temple, thereby stirring up considerable excitement among a notoriously excitable people. A person like this could, if unchecked, cause a great deal of trouble. Other popular religious leaders in Judaea met with similar fates. In the mid-40s CE, a man named Theudas, who claimed to be a prophet, led a number of followers to the Jordan river, which he promised would part at his command; the Roman governor sent out a squadron of cavalry, who beheaded Theudas and killed or captured his followers (Josephus, *Judaean Antiquities* 20.97–9; cf. *Acts of the Apostles* 5.36). Some ten years later, another self-proclaimed prophet, an Egyptian, gathered a large group on a hill outside Jerusalem, allegedly planning to lead them into the city and take it over; the Roman military again broke up the assembly, although the Egyptian himself slipped away (Josephus, *The Judaean War* 2.261–3; cf. *Acts of the Apostles* 21.38). Such disturbances were not limited to Judaea. In Thrace, for example, the priest of a local god identified with Dionysos won a band of followers by "performing many deeds under divine inspiration." He led them in revolt against the Roman-backed king and seized power himself; again, the Romans sent in troops (Cassius Dio, *History* 54.34.5–7). In the late 60s CE a seeress named Veleda helped fuel a revolt in northeastern Gaul by prophesying the destruction of Roman troops; the natives showed her great honor, and it was not until several years later that the Romans finally captured her (Tacitus, *Histories* 4.61 and 65).

It was not only charismatic individuals whom Roman authorities regarded as potentially subversive. Esoteric texts could also arouse suspicion, especially books of alleged prophecies. Some of these were explicitly anti-Roman in their sentiments, such as the following passage from one of the extant *Sibylline Oracles*:

> One day, proud Rome, there will come upon you from above an equal heavenly affliction, and you will first bend the neck and be razed to the ground, and fire will consume you, altogether laid low on your floors, and wealth will perish and wolves and foxes will dwell in your foundations. Then you will be utterly desolate, as if you had never been. (*Sibylline Oracles* 8.37–42, trans. J. J. Collins in Charlesworth 1983: 1.418–19)

And a bit later in the same text:

> No longer will Syrian, Greek, or foreigner, or any other nation, place their neck under your yoke of slavery. You will be utterly ravaged and destroyed

for what you did. Groaning in panic, you will give until you have repaid all, and you will be a triumph-spectacle to the world and a reproach to all. (*Sibylline Oracles* 8.126–30, trans. J. J. Collins in Charlesworth 1983: 1.421)

Similarly, a prophecy attributed to the legendary Persian sage Hystaspes foretold that "the power and name of Rome would be removed from the earth" and that "power would revert back to Asia: again the east will rule and the west will serve" (quoted by Lactantius, *Divine Institutes* 7.15.19 and 11). But it would be wrong to suppose that all prophetic texts were actively hostile to Roman rule; the majority were probably not, although they might still include predictions of coming disasters. Yet all such texts had the potential to stir up popular sentiment. Cassius Dio, for example, relates that in 19 CE "a supposedly Sibylline oracle, completely unsuited to that point in the city's history but nevertheless applied to current conditions, caused considerable agitation; for it said that 'when thrice three hundred years have run their course, civil strife shall destroy the Romans'" (*History* 57.18.5).

In light of all this, it is not surprising that Roman authorities repeatedly attempted both to control the circulation of such texts and to restrict the activities of those who set themselves up as free-lance diviners or religious authorities. Already in 12 BCE the emperor Augustus collected more than 2,000 prophetic texts in Greek and Latin and had them burned (Suetonius, *Augustus* 31.1). Towards the end of his reign, "seers were forbidden to make predictions in private or to make predictions about death even if others were present" (Cassius Dio, *History* 56.25.5). A few years later, early in the reign of Tiberius, a young Roman nobleman named Libo Drusus was accused of plotting to win imperial power for himself and of consulting various astrologers, *magi*, and dream-interpreters about his prospects; in the wake of his trial the Senate issued a decree condemning all free-lance diviners of this sort (Tacitus, *Annals* 2.27–32). In the mid-second century CE, the Christian writer Justin complained that "death has been decreed against those who read the books of Hystaspes, the Sibyl, or the prophets" (*First Apology* 44.12). A legal handbook dating to the end of the third century CE contains a whole series of prescriptions: "Prophets who pretend that they are divinely inspired are to be driven from the city so that the conduct of the people should not be corrupted through human credulity. . . . Those who introduce new sects or irrational religious observances, by which people's minds are upset, are to be exiled, if upper class, or executed, if lower class. . . . Whoever consults astrologers, seers, diviners, or prophets about the emperor's health or crucial matters of state is to be executed, along with the person who gave the response" (*The Opinions of Paulus* 5.21).

As I have argued, underlying all these measures was a general concern with threats to public order, in particular the possibility that individuals from outside the socio-economic elite who set themselves up as religious authorities could undermine the status quo. But attitudes towards the actual practices and traditions on which these individuals based their claims were curiously ambivalent. On the one hand, there was as we have seen a tendency to dismiss them as mere superstition. On the other hand, many members of the imperial elite took very seriously the idea that it was possible to gain special insight into the will of the gods and the shape of future events; as I discussed in chapter 1, divination was an integral part of the Graeco-Roman religious tradition. From this perspective, allowing people easy access to free-lance diviners and prophets was dangerous not because it encouraged superstition, but because it could place important information in the wrong hands; this motivation is apparent, for example, in Augustus' law against the private consultation of diviners and the passage from *The Opinions of Paulus* that forbids consultations about the emperor and important public issues. But whether they took them seriously or not, Roman leaders viewed all these people as potential threats to the established social and political hierarchy, and so were ready to take action against them whenever they considered it necessary.

3 Three Particular Cases

As I have argued, Roman officials had no mandate to intervene in religious affairs as such, but did so only when these posed a threat to public peace and order. This is an important point to remember when considering the question of Roman religious policy. Another important point is that Roman rule was largely reactive. That is to say, Roman officials responded to problems that others brought to their attention more often than they made efforts to identify and resolve problems on their own. For both reasons the whole notion of a Roman religious policy is somewhat misleading, since it suggests a comprehensive and detailed plan for action in the area of religion.

Nevertheless, the word "policy" remains useful in discussing the impact of Roman rule on religious life in the empire. We can apply it to two different situations. Firstly, we can identify patterns in the responses of Roman officials that over time acquired a degree of coherence. As we have seen, Roman officials shared with the rest of the imperial elite some basic assumptions about improper religious behavior, expressed in the ideas of atheism and superstition, and moreover had a specific concern with any claims to religious authority that might undermine the status quo. These shared assumptions and concerns assured a basic similarity in the way that different officials responded to similar problems. Moreover, when a Roman official was faced with a problem, such as a public disturbance, a legal dispute, or an allegation of disruptive behavior, he took into account not only his general sense of what was appropriate, but also any useful precedents in the responses of earlier authorities to similar situations. The most important precedents were the rulings of emperors, but there were others as well: senatorial decrees, legal decisions, actions taken by other officials. Since these were not compiled into official codes, individual officials might have only a haphazard knowledge of them. But when similar problems arose again and again over a period of time, people became increasingly aware of earlier responses and hence tended more and more to follow established precedent. For all these reasons, we can identify what we might call ad hoc "policies" at work in the reactions of Roman officials to various religious issues.

Secondly, Roman rule was not always reactive. The power of emperors was effectively unlimited, and they could in theory order whatever they liked. Although they did not often initiate a drastic change or establish a universal program, at times they did, and we may reasonably describe the result as a new policy. As we will see below, policies of individual emperors had a tremendous impact on the status of Christianity from the mid-third to the early fourth centuries CE, and they may have had an equally dramatic impact on Judaean tradition.

In this section I discuss in more detail three particular areas in which we can identify religious policies in one or both of the two senses that I have outlined. In the case of magic, precedent played the most important role, whereas with Judaean tradition and even more with Christianity we can distinguish the impact of both precedent and the policies of individual emperors.

3.1 Magic

In the late 150s CE, the writer and philosopher Apuleius was tried before the Roman governor of North Africa on a charge of magic. The speech that he delivered in his defense has survived, although no doubt in a form reworked for publication, and is a valuable source of evidence for the popular perception of magic in the Roman Empire. As I argued in chapter 6, the word *magus* could be used of anyone who claimed particular expertise in arcane ritual lore; Apuleius himself notes that, although it was strictly speaking the Persian word for "priest," it had come in everyday speech to mean someone "who through shared speech with the immortal gods has ability in all things that he wishes, by means of a certain amazing power of incantations" (*Apology* 26.6).

For present purposes, the most important thing that we learn from this speech is the very fact that in the Roman Empire the practice of magic was illegal. Yet we must be clear about what this actually means. To begin with, Roman authorities were not constantly on the look-out for anyone engaged in magic, but instead simply reacted to cases that the local inhabitants brought before them. In other words, when social tensions resulted in accusations of magic, Roman officials were willing to accept them as formal legal charges. What sorts of social tensions could result in accusations of magic? We may distinguish two, although they were in fact closely interwoven. One was the suspicion that people often have for those who do not quite fit with the rest of the community. In this case, Apuleius was a newcomer, a cosmopolitan and sophisticated intellectual in a fairly small provincial city, someone with an interest in arcane traditions that, while attractive to some people, no doubt seemed suspect to others. A second source of tension was the tendency, found in many cultures, to blame any misfortune or unexpected event on the hidden influence of people with special access to unusual power and knowledge. In this case, the people who brought the charge against Apuleius were in-laws of a local woman whom he had married, a very wealthy widow named Pudentilla who had supposedly vowed never to wed again. Her decision to marry a young and handsome stranger must have been both a personal shock and a threat to their financial interests. All these concerns came together in the charge that Apuleius was a *magus* and had used his arcane powers to compel Pudentilla to marry him.

But why were Roman authorities willing to give legal weight to charges of this sort? For one thing, there were in Roman law long-established precedents for penalizing any attempt to harm others by occult means. The very first codification of Roman law, the Twelve Tables compiled in the mid-fifth century BCE, contained clauses condemning those who "chant malicious chants" against people or who meddle with the fertility of their neighbors' fields. A law of the first century BCE made it a criminal offense to possess or deal in dangerous drugs with the intent to kill someone; this law was eventually extended to cover maleficent rituals as well, what we might call "black magic." There were thus clear precedents to punish people thought to have caused harm to others by ritual means. As we saw in chapter 6, there is ample evidence that people did make considerable use of curse tablets and binding spells to attack rivals and to win sexual favors. Apuleius' marriage to Pudentilla was no doubt presented by his accusers as the result of exactly some such spell as this.

Yet if the case of Apuleius is any indication, there was more involved in trials for magic than a simple concern with causing harm to others. Apuleius' accusers seem to have made their allegation about his marriage less as a charge in itself than as evidence for the more general charge that he was a *magus*. In support of this general charge they made a number of other allegations as well: that he had tried to purchase certain types of fish, that he had enchanted a slave boy and caused him to collapse, that he had hidden some secret object among the household gods of his stepson, that he had performed nocturnal ceremonies with a friend, and that he had hired a woodcarver to fashion a ghoulish image to which he paid cult. Apuleius denies very few of these allegations outright, and argues instead that his accusers have misinterpreted his actions, which in fact result from his philosophical and religious interests. The trial thus seems in an important sense to have turned on the issue of acceptable religious behavior. The great interest that some people had in religious arcana must have appeared to others as beyond the pale; if in addition they perceived it as in any way a direct threat, they could attack it as magic, and petition the Roman authorities to punish the person involved. For their part, the concern Roman authorities had with social disturbances must have led them at least to hear such cases. If, as Apuleius apparently did, the accused could persuade the presiding official that his behavior fell within the limits of the normal, he could hope to be found innocent; if he failed to do so, however, the official would have little hesitation in condemning him. In this respect, trials for magic were at their heart a context in which Roman authorities and the people of the empire could work together to determine the limits of acceptable religious interests and activities.

3.2 Judaean tradition

As we saw in chapter 2, the Judaean tradition, while sharing some basic characteristics with other religious traditions in the Near East, had by the Roman period developed highly distinctive features: to uphold their tradition, Judaeans were expected to acknowledge their god as the only true god and to observe the moral, cultic, and social prescriptions enshrined in their sacred writings. As a result, Judaeans constituted a somewhat anomalous group within the empire, and their relations with their neighbors and overlords were quite complex. As I noted in chapter 6, some people looked upon Judaean tradition with fascination or even admiration, partly because it was perceived as an ancient and exotic "oriental" tradition, partly because it apparently conformed to certain philosophical assertions about the nature of the divine. At the same time, there were aspects of Judaean tradition that tended to generate friction between Judaeans and non-Judaeans. To some people in the mainstream Graeco-Roman tradition, certain practices prescribed by Judaean law seemed absurd or repulsive. Their dietary practices, especially their abstention from pork, were widely derided, and their observance of the Sabbath was considered bizarre or even an excuse for laziness. Worst of all was the practice of circumcision, which Greeks and Romans regarded as a barbaric form of genital mutilation. For all these reasons, Judaean tradition was open to attack as a superstition.

A much more serious problem, however, was the perception of Judaean isolationism and hostility towards outsiders. The views of the Roman historian Tacitus, although particularly virulent in their expression, do not in substance seem to have been exceptional: "Moses . . . introduced novel religious observances, contrary to those of the rest of humanity; everything that is sacred among us is impious for them, whereas what is impure for us is permitted among them." Although with one another they are honest and compassionate, they display "the hatred of an enemy for all others": they eat apart, do not intermarry, and practice circumcision to mark themselves off from other men (*Histories* 5.4–5). The issue of separatism was especially important for Judaean communities in Graeco-Roman cities. As we saw in chapter 4, shared religious rites played a crucial role in creating and reinforcing a sense of community. Observant Judaeans necessarily took no part in the public ceremonies of the cities in which they lived, although there were no doubt debates over what constituted "taking part": I noted in chapter 4 the rabbinic injunction against even doing business with shops that were decorated for a public festival, although many Judaeans were probably less strict in their interpretation. Yet whatever the extent of their non-participation, it was not surprisingly interpreted as a rejection of the larger community. Hence the Alexandrian scholar Apion pointedly asked about the Judaeans of his city, "why, if they are citizens, do they not worship the same gods as the Alexandrians?" (Josephus, *Against Apion* 2.65).

The Roman response to these tensions varied. Partly because the Roman elite had respect for ancestral traditions, even ancestral traditions that they considered bizarre, and partly because of effective diplomatic maneuvering on the part of Judaean leaders, Roman authorities by and large upheld the petitions of Judaeans to observe their ancestral practices without interference. The Judaean historian Josephus, writing in the late first century CE, preserves a number of official documents that illustrate this. For example, when Judaeans in the province of Asia complained to the emperor Augustus that local civic magistrates were confiscating the money they collected to send to Jerusalem and otherwise hindering the observance of their traditions, Augustus responded with a decree that they should "follow their own customs according to their ancestral law" and that, specifically, they be allowed to send money to Jerusalem and not be compelled to appear in court on the Sabbath; moreover, he directed that anyone caught stealing their sacred funds or scriptures should be treated as a *sacrilegus* (Josephus, *Judaean Antiquities* 16.162–5).

Although some scholars have argued that these documents are evidence for a comprehensive Roman law regarding the status of Judaism, they more probably represent ad hoc responses to specific appeals for support against hostile neighbors. The leaders of local Judaean communities preserved these documents precisely because they feared they might have to make similar appeals in the future, and would then need to cite them as precedents. The rights of the Judaeans to observe their traditions was thus not inscribed in law, but depended on the continued support of Roman authorities. If the latter came to view Judaeans as trouble-makers, they might well withdraw this support. The emperor Claudius, for example, helped to resolve a bitter and violent dispute between Judaeans and Greeks in Alexandria by decreeing that the former should preserve all their previously established rights. Yet he closed his edict by emphasizing his chief concern: "I direct both parties to take the greatest precautions that no disturbance take place after the posting of my edict" (Josephus, *Judaean Antiquities* 19.285). In a follow-up letter he informed the Judaeans that if they persisted in causing trouble he would not hesitate to take action against them; Claudius in fact seems to have either restricted or even expelled the Judaean community in Rome as a result of disturbances there.

Roman policy towards Judaeans, although by no means uniform, was thus generally supportive. The late 60s CE, however, brought a drastic shift. Judaea and the surrounding territories had for several decades been the site of periodic disturbances. After the death of King Herod in 4 BCE, there were outbreaks of violence serious enough to require large-scale military intervention. There was further agitation ten years later, when Judaea passed under direct Roman rule, and periodically thereafter; I mentioned in the preceding section some of the self-proclaimed prophets who provoked Roman military intervention during this period. The reasons for this unrest are complex. For one thing, the Roman governors of Judaea were not especially competent in dealing with Judaean sensibilities, and some were overtly hostile. On the other side, some Judaean extremists regarded the mere fact of Roman rule as a challenge to the rule of god. In addition, there was considerable social unrest among the poorer inhabitants of the region. Although it is difficult to sort out the mix of factors, the combination of social grievances and religious tensions led ultimately to a large-scale uprising, the Judaean War of 66–73 CE. This presented a serious challenge to the Roman rulers, and its suppression was a massive military undertaking that resulted in the sack of Jerusalem and the destruction of the temple. Two further major revolts followed: one by the Judaean population of Egypt and adjacent areas in 115–17 CE, and another in Judaea itself in 132–5 CE under the popular leader Bar Kochba; both were ultimately suppressed by the Roman rulers, but only with considerable effort.

The end result of this sequence of clashes was the transformation of the Judaean tradition and its role within the empire. With the destruction of the temple, the Romans effectively put an end to the Judaean sacrificial cult, and they seem to have taken steps to ensure that it was not revived. Later, in the wake of the Bar Kochba revolt, they re-founded Jerusalem as the new Roman colony of Aelia Capitolina, complete with a temple of Jupiter on the site of the Judaean temple; they even changed the name of the province from Judaea to Syria Palaestina. The Roman rulers thus effectively destroyed the centralizing institutions of temple, priesthood, and national cult that had previously served as a focus for the unity of Judaeans everywhere, so that Judaeans from then on had fewer of the distinguishing characteristics of a separate nation. Nevertheless, Judaean communities continued to exist in many cities of the eastern Mediterranean, and even expanded to the western parts of the empire; especially in areas of dense Judaean settlement like Galilee, a new class of teachers, the rabbis, began to formalize oral traditions that laid the basis for what became the normative Judaism of the medieval and modern periods. In this later period, from the mid-second century CE onward, there is relatively little evidence for tension, a situation that changed only when Christianity became the dominant religion of the empire.

3.3 Christianity

The Roman policy towards Christianity, it might be supposed, is well known: it consisted of intolerance and persecution. Hollywood movies provide the standard images of soldiers bursting into Christian meetings and dragging everyone to prison, supercilious officials forcing Christians to worship the emperor, defenseless Christians facing wild beasts in the arena. But these images, although accurate in certain respects, also involve a number of misconceptions whose origins extend far beyond the days of Hollywood moguls back to those of the early church. In the course of the fourth century CE, Christianity was rapidly transformed from a persecuted religion to a favored and even dominant one; with worldly success came a sort of nostalgia for the days of persecution, which served both to justify the Christian triumph and to provide models of virtue and fortitude for those who lived in laxer times. There was consequently a tendency to exaggerate the rigor of the persecutions; many accounts of martyrdoms in particular were extensively reworked or invented from whole cloth. At the same time, earlier anti-Christian material was destroyed or allowed to disappear; as a result, we have extremely few documents dealing with the persecution from the viewpoint of Roman officials. Contemporary evidence for the Roman persecution of Christians thus consists of scanty and unreliable sources, and there is consequently much debate concerning its nature. Although some scholars believe that there was from an early date a comprehensive law banning the observance of Christianity, the majority now agree that there were two main phases in the treatment of Christians.

The situation during the first phase is best known from one of the few surviving official documents concerning the treatment of Christians: an exchange of letters between the emperor Trajan and the younger Pliny in the early second century CE, when the latter was serving as governor of Bithynia (Pliny, *Letters* 10.96–7). Pliny reports that several people have been brought before him on the charge of being Christians; he is uncertain of the correct procedure in these cases, never having been present at trials involving Christians, and so is writing to Trajan to make sure that the practices he has adopted are suitable. His procedure has been to ask the accused whether they are indeed Christians. If they deny it, he has them invoke the gods, offer wine and incense before a statue of Trajan, and revile Christ, things that he knows true Christians would not do. If they affirm it and persist in affirming it despite his warnings, he has them executed or, if they are citizens, sent to Rome for trial. But now he is faced with an anonymous pamphlet that accuses many people of being Christians; he is also uncertain what to do with people who claim that they have ceased being Christians and are willing to worship the gods. Trajan responds briefly to say that he approves of Pliny's conduct, "for it is impossible to establish something for all occasions, which would have a fixed format." Christians are not to be sought out, he says, but if they are brought to trial by an accuser and convicted, they must be punished. Anyone who denies being a Christian and proves it by worshipping the gods is to be excused, whatever their past conduct, and anonymous accusations are not to be tolerated.

The situation revealed by these letters seems to have been the normal one down to the mid-third century CE. On the one hand, it was widely accepted that being a Christian was in itself a punishable offense, although anyone willing to conform to normative religious behavior was let off. On the other hand, Roman officials did not themselves engage in any active persecution of Christians, but instead merely responded to charges brought by others; in this regard, the treatment of Christianity was very similar to that of magic. All of this means that the persecution of Christians, down to the mid-third century at least, was local, ad hoc, and reactive. There was no comprehensive law establishing general procedures, as Trajan himself implies; rather, individual officials responded to particular situations as they saw fit, taking into account both general precedents and specific circumstances. But how and why was the precedent established that being a Christian was a punishable offense?

The general reasons are clear enough: Christians rejected virtually all the traditional markers of piety, and consequently made themselves outcasts from their society. Like Judaeans, they refused to sacrifice or make offerings to other deities; but whereas Judaeans had at least offered sacrifices to their own god, Christians did not even do that. As we have seen, in the Graeco-Roman world this was tantamount to atheism. Again like Judaeans, they took no part in the communal rituals of the cities in which they lived; they thereby both resisted integration into the local community and rejected the standard modes of honoring the emperor. Unlike Judaeans, however, they did not even have the excuse of ancestral traditions to justify their behavior. They instead acted almost like political conspirators, meeting in secret and worshipping a man who had been executed by a Roman governor. It is not surprising that many people considered them impious, disloyal, and subversive, and were willing to believe the worst of them. In the second century CE, for example, rumors spread that Christians engaged in disgusting practices such as incest and cannibalism; although these rumors may have been sparked by a misunderstanding of Christian practices such as the Eucharist, they derived their vitality from the underlying perception that Christians were beyond the pale of civilized society. Although Christian intellectuals responded to these slanders, they recognized that the main issues were more fundamental. Tertullian, in a rhetorical address to the opponents of Christianity, sums up the situation this way: "you say, 'you do not worship the gods, and you do not offer sacrifices on behalf of the emperors.' . . . Thus we are charged with both sacrilege and treason. This is the primary issue, or rather the entire issue" (*Apology* 10.1).

But if the general reasons for hostility towards Christians are clear enough, the specific details of the official response are somewhat obscure. An episode that took place in Rome in the mid-60s CE was no doubt crucial. According to the Roman historian Tacitus, the emperor Nero, in order to dispel a rumor that he was responsible for a fire that had devastated the city, "put the blame and inflicted the most elaborate punishments on a group loathed for their shocking offenses, popularly known as the Christians. . . . First, those who confessed were arrested; then on their evidence a great crowd was convicted, not so much on the charge of arson as for hatred of the human race" (*Annals* 15.44). This episode provided a very clear precedent that being a Christian was in itself enough to justify condemnation to death. Thereafter, if anyone came before a Roman governor with a charge that someone was a Christian, the governor would have been fully justified in following this precedent and condemning that person, provided that he or she did nothing to disprove the allegation. Roman officials nevertheless had considerable leeway in how they responded to particular situations. When popular hostility towards Christians resulted in riots and public disorder, they tended to react harshly; in other circumstances, they followed their personal inclinations in taking a stricter or a looser stance with regards to charges of Christianity. It is no doubt for this reason that actions against Christians were apparently sporadic: a trial here, a pogrom there, but no constant and universal system of oppression.

In the year 249 CE, however, the situation changed dramatically. In that year the emperor Decius issued a decree that every inhabitant of the empire was to perform a sacrifice and obtain official certification that he or she had done so. Whether or not Decius intended this specifically as an attack on Christians, it had the result of initiating the first empire-wide persecution, since Christians could of course not comply with the decree without compromising their beliefs. Decius was killed in battle less than two years later, and his decree seems to have died with him. Within a few years, however, the emperor Valerian instituted a more systematic persecution: in 257 he required Christian clergy to "acknowledge" Roman ceremonies and forbade any Christian assemblies, and the following year he decreed immediate punishment for all Christian clergy and severe reprisals for all Christians of high social status who did not renounce their faith. The motivations behind this sharp change of policy are not entirely clear. Decius' measure seems to some extent the culmination of earlier concerns with religious propriety, insofar as it enforced at least token conformity to the norms of traditional piety. Valerian, by contrast, whose actions were aimed more against the internal organization of the church than against the practices of individual Christians, may have become alarmed at its increasingly formal and universal structure, which was gradually transforming the Christian community into an entire alternative society with its own values and loyalties. At any rate, Valerian's capture by enemies in the year 260 put an end to his persecution, since his son and successor Gallienus immediately rescinded his measures. Gallienus' decrees guaranteeing the return of church property and freedom from harassment provided the first official recognition of the Christian church.

The effective tolerance of Christianity established by Gallienus lasted for over 40 years, a period that probably saw a considerable increase in the size and strength of the church. It ended in 303 CE with the most comprehensive persecution yet, under the emperor Diocletian and his successors. An initial edict ordered the destruction of Christian meeting places and sacred texts, the confiscation of church property, and restrictions on the social and legal privileges of Christians; later edicts required first the clergy and then all Christians to offer traditional sacrifices on pain of death. Yet this persecution was to be the last. In the year 312 the emperor Constantine defeated his chief rival Maxentius with what he regarded as the support of the Christian god, and from then on was an active promoter and patron of the church. His sons and successors followed his lead, with the result that the church rapidly became wealthy, powerful, and influential. By the end of the century the tables had effectively been turned, when Christian emperors issued a series of decrees that ultimately outlawed any public celebration of the rites that for so many centuries had been the traditional markers of piety.

4 Conclusion

The limited aims of Roman rule meant that Roman officials had no formal mandate to monitor and regulate the religious beliefs and activities of the people over whom they ruled. Yet we should not mistake this general laissez-faire attitude for an active policy of religious toleration and respect for diversity. On the contrary, the imperial elite shared a number of definite if not clearly articulated assumptions about what constituted proper and improper religious behavior. Whenever the latter was associated with social disturbances or potential threats to the status quo, imperial officials were both willing and able to take action. Moreover, an accumulation of precedents concerning similar problems could result in what amounted to an informal policy. It is within this framework that we should understand the illegality of magic and the complex response of Roman authorities to Judaeans. It also provides the context for the persecution of Christians, at least down to the mid-third century CE. But as the history of Christianity in this period well illustrates, the intervention of individual emperors could result in dramatic shifts in policy. There is little question that the emperor Constantine's decision to champion Christianity is one of the turning points in world history. Nevertheless, we can understand that decision and its effects only against the broader background of religious change in the Roman Empire.

FURTHER READING

On religious tolerance in the Graeco-Roman world, see Garnsey 1984. Beard, North, and Price 1998: 1.211–44 provide a valuable general survey of the ways that the Roman elite defined and controlled unacceptable religious behavior, and Potter 1994 has a stimulating discussion of prophecy and issues of authority. On the legal status of magic, Phillips 1991, Gordon 1999: 243–66, and Rives 2003 cover the key issues. Schäfer 1997 provides a good survey of popular attitudes towards and conflicts with Judaeans; on Roman policy, Rajak 1984 is crucial. On attitudes towards Christians, see Wilken 1984. The fundamental studies of the first phase of Christian persecution remain de Ste. Croix 1963 and Barnes 1968, although both are quite technical; for a more general discussion, see Lane Fox 1986: 419–92 and 592–608.

Epilogue: Religious Change in the Roman Empire

⌐⌐⌐⌐

In this book I have tried to trace what I regard as the fundamental features and underlying dynamics that characterized religion in the Roman Empire. In order to present these as clearly as possible, I have for the most part downplayed the temporal dimension, providing only sporadic indications of the changes and developments that took place in this period. In this epilogue I want to provide a more systematic if very brief survey of the more important developments, and also to suggest how these fit into the broader context of religious change.

The most obviously "imperial" aspect of religion in the Roman Empire was of course the worship of the emperor. In chapter 5 I stressed the variety of strategies that existed for incorporating the emperor into religious life. Here I would add that this variety also had a significant temporal dimension: the strategies changed and shifted over time, with some increasing in importance while others faded away. This was due in part to the fact that the very position of "emperor" was constantly evolving. Although it is conventional, as well as convenient, to describe Augustus as the first emperor, his position was very much a personal one. As the bundle of powers and honors devised for him passed from one successor to another, however, it acquired a more distinct institutional identity, so that the rulers of the second century CE were emperors in a much more defined way than Augustus ever was. By the time of Diocletian and Constantine, a sharp symbolic divide had developed between the emperor and his subjects. The religious dimension of the emperor's position played a key part in this process. For example, whereas the deification of deceased emperors occurred only occasionally throughout the first century CE, in the early second century it became increasingly common, so that it was easy to see the current emperor as one in a long line of deities. Thus by the end of that century the emperor Septimius Severus was known as "son of

Divus Marcus Aurelius, brother of Divus Commodus, grandson of Divus Antoninus Pius, great-grandson of Divus Hadrianus, great-great-grandson of Divus Traianus, great-great-great-grandson of Divus Nerva"; although the genealogy is largely fictitious, the effect is obvious enough. Yet along with expansion came contraction: after the death of Severus the whole system of posthumous deification began to decline in significance, to be replaced by new strategies for giving religious expression to the unique status of the emperor. Yet one change that has often been assumed did not in fact take place: at no point did worship of the emperor effectively replace the cults of traditional deities. As we have seen, the latter continued to flourish, and indeed provided the larger ritual framework within which the emperor was accommodated.

Another element in the religious landscape of the Roman Empire has also at times received more emphasis than it ought. Some earlier scholars regarded the spread of what they called "oriental religions" or "mystery cults," primarily the worship of Cybele, Isis, and Mithras, as the crucial development of this period, arguing that through them the influence of "oriental" conceptions brought about a fundamental transformation in people's understanding of the divine. More recent scholars have raised cogent objections against this theory, demonstrating among other things that much of what was thought to be distinctively "oriental" in these cults is actually Graeco-Roman; as I noted in chapter 6, for example, the whole phenomenon of mysteries and initiations is Greek in origin. I would add the further objection that the spread of these particular cults is simply part of the much wider phenomenon that I described in chapter 5 as the movement of gods: the worship of deities in regions far from where they originated. This phenomenon was not unique to the Roman imperial period, but can be observed whenever political circumstances facilitated contact and exchange between different cultural regions. Immigrant populations had always taken their gods with them, as the Judaeans had done during the "Babylonian Captivity," and cities had established public cults of foreign deities for specific political or cultural reasons. Thus, as I noted in chapter 2, Athens instituted the cult of the Thracian goddess Bendis in the late fifth century BCE, Carthage introduced that of Demeter and Kore from the Greek cities of Sicily in the early fourth century, and Rome that of Cybele from Anatolia in the late third century. The Roman Empire, which brought together an immense territory under a common ruler, simply made this sort of movement more possible, so that to a large extent we are dealing with a quantitative rather than a qualitative change.

If there was any qualitative change, it had to more do with the form that the worship of foreign deities took than with their mere introduction into new areas. Traditional patterns were certainly maintained: immigrants continued to worship their ancestral deities and cities continued to establish new public cults. Yet the worship of some deities spread beyond the people for whom they were ancestral without being incorporated into any public cults; what we find instead are voluntary associations of worshippers. This was especially true of Jupiter Dolichenus and Mithras, whose worship was largely confined to closed cult associations, but also to some extent of Isis and other deities. It has sometimes been proposed that during the imperial period private cult associations of this sort gradually came to replace public cults as the focus of people's religious lives. Although there does seem to have been an increase in the number and variety of such associations, this was again more a change in degree, since cult groups of one sort or another seem always to have existed in the Graeco-Roman tradition. Moreover, it is difficult to demonstrate any real decline in the importance of public cults; if anything, we can perhaps in the third century trace a kind of streamlining, whereby greater attention was focused on fewer cults. Certainly civic life itself remained strong in almost all parts of the Roman Empire into the fourth century CE.

As we have seen, however, the very existence of civic life was itself an innovation in some regions. Even in the absence of a sharply defined policy, Roman rule had a tremendous impact on religious life in the empire. In chapter 5 I discussed the spread of Graeco-Roman religious conventions as part of the broader phenomena that are usually called Romanization and Hellenization. These processes, although sometimes gradual, were ongoing throughout the entire imperial period and in many cases resulted ultimately in the significant transformation of local cultures. For example, in the course of the second and third centuries CE, the Nabataeans of Arabia adopted many Graeco-Roman conventions in the cult of their national deity Dusares: they began to represent him in human form as well as by the traditional aniconic symbols, and in the mid-third century the city of Bostra, in what is now southern Syria, even established Greek games in his honor. Yet we should note that changes of this sort, brought about by local adaptation to an expanding culture, were not a new phenomenon in the territory of the Roman Empire; they had taken place earlier as well, under Greek or Punic or Celtic influence. The difference was again one of degree: the Roman Empire meant that a huge area came under the influence of a single dominant tradition, so that much the same cultural influences were at work in Britain as in Arabia.

In virtually all parts of the empire for which we have evidence, the local elites seem to have gradually adapted their religious traditions to Graeco-Roman norms as they became more and more closely integrated with the mainstream culture of the empire. We must not suppose, however, that these developments always proceeded smoothly: although some people may have regarded them with approval or even indifference, for others they perhaps constituted a violation of traditional religious practices. The vicissitudes of the Judaean tradition provide a very clear sense of the conflicts that could result. Once again, the dynamics in operation during the imperial period can be traced back to earlier times. In the early second century BCE, a crisis developed among the elite of Judaea over the extent to which the adoption of Greek cultural practices constituted an abandonment of their own traditions. This crisis finally led to the establishment of a new ruling dynasty who presented themselves as the defenders of tradition. Yet the underlying issues remained, and under Roman rule acquired new urgency. The eventual outcome, as we have already seen, was the destruction of the Judaean temple, the effective abolition of traditional cult, and the apparently rapid marginalization of the priesthood. In place of the latter there arose a new class of teachers, the rabbis; while not abandoning hope for the restoration of the temple and its cult, they reoriented the Judaean tradition to focus on personal and household activities and the study of the sacred writings. For the Judaean tradition, then, the ultimate result of Graeco-Roman cultural influence was a new insistence on its own distinctiveness.

The Judaean tradition was highly unusual, of course, because of the stress it placed on the exclusive relationship between the people and their god and on their god's uniqueness. Yet the idea of monotheism was no longer restricted to the Judaean tradition. Some philosophical schools had for a long time insisted that there was only one ultimate deity, and during the imperial period this idea seems to have become steadily more widespread, although in a wide variety of forms. Particularly within the Platonic tradition, there developed the notion of a celestial hierarchy, in which the traditional gods were regarded as the offspring or agents of the supreme deity. Others took a more syncretistic approach, as I discussed in chapter 5, identifying different gods with each other and, in some cases, as simply various aspects of a single universal deity. These tendencies towards monotheism were not merely theoretical. For example, in the later third century CE the cult of the sun as a supreme god seems to have acquired considerable importance. In the year 274 the emperor Aurelian established in Rome an official cult of Deus Sol Invictus, "the Divine Unconquered Sun," complete with its own priesthood and quadrennial Greek games, and Constantine's devotion to the sun is thought by some to have helped prepare the way for his conversion to Christianity. While the cult of Sol seems to have had a significant political dimension, with the idea of "one god, one emperor," other cults with monotheistic tendencies were apparently more popular in origin. The most intriguing of these is that of a god called Zeus Hypsistos or more often Theos Hypsistos, "God the Highest," or simply Hypsistos. Judaeans had long employed this term for their god, but in the second and third centuries CE it was apparently also used by some non-Judaeans as a title for the supreme deity, whose worshippers rejected animal sacrifice and refused to depict their god in human form. This cult is widely attested in Asia Minor and elsewhere in the eastern Mediterranean, and seems to have evolved under significant Judaean influence.

The influence of the Judaean tradition in the cult of Hypsistos is also an example of another religious trend in the imperial period, the growing interest in the sort of esoteric traditions that I discussed in chapter 6. We can trace this development in a number of areas. For example, although there was a long tradition of Orphic and Pythagorean pseudepigrapha, the number and variety of such texts seem to have increased during the imperial period; they began also to be attributed to other figures, such as the Egyptian Hermes Trismegistos. In the first century BCE, the techniques employed by the free-lance ritual experts popularly known as *magi* started to become much more elaborate, so that in the place of fairly simple charms passed down orally we find written handbooks with complex and self-consciously esoteric rituals of the sort discussed in chapter 6. The same period saw the beginnings of widespread interest in astrology, which continued to expand steadily throughout the imperial period. More important still is the appearance of what I described in chapter 6 as new models of the cosmos, which emphasized the separation of humans from the divine and thereby created the need for more radical forms of salvation. We can identify variations on this theme in a wide range of contexts: the cult of Mithras, Platonic philosophy, gnostic and Hermetic writings, and perhaps most significantly some forms of Christianity. These new views of the cosmos did not necessarily displace traditional views and the established modes of interacting with the divine; the latter continued with little sign of decline. Yet there seems nevertheless to have been a significant increase in religious options.

The most famous of these options, and ultimately the most important, was of course Christianity. It is difficult to reach much certainty about the original teachings and activities of Jesus of Nazareth, as I noted in chapter 6, but there can be little doubt that he was a Judaean teacher and reformer. What would eventually be called Christianity thus began as a movement or a group of related movements within the Judaean tradition. Very quickly, however, by the middle of the first century CE, the movement had expanded to include non-Judaeans as well; it also expanded geographically, beyond its original home in Galilee and Judaea, to include groups of adherents in Syria, Asia Minor, Greece, and Rome. It was about this time that the members of this movement came to be called

Christians, a name apparently first used by outsiders but soon adopted internally as well. When and how these Christians began to see themselves as distinct from Judaeans is far from clear. Many scholars see the destruction of the Jerusalem temple in 70 CE as a crucial turning point, although most would now agree that the process was gradual, varied, and complex.

The second century CE saw some major developments, in addition to a continued geographic spread. One was the crystallization of a formal structure of leadership, consisting of deacons (from Greek *diakonoi*, "servants"), priests (*presbyteroi*, "elders"), and bishops (*episkopoi*, "overseers"). Another was the deepening engagement with the Graeco-Roman cultural tradition, above all with philosophy; some Christian intellectuals began to argue that Christianity accomplished more effectively and more fully the goals towards which Greek philosophers had long been striving. This engagement with Graeco-Roman culture was motivated in part by the need to counteract the popular hostility and official disfavor from which Christians suffered. A third development was an increasing concern with diversity of belief and practice among those who called themselves Christians, and a growing feeling that all Christians should be in agreement on all matters of importance. This led to the refinement of mechanisms for deciding on common policy, such as regional councils of bishops and exchanges of letters between the bishops of different regions, as well as attacks on certain forms of Christianity as "heresies."

By the third century CE, there existed a fairly cohesive and far-flung institution that we call the Christian church, with distinctive rituals, a more or less sharply defined membership, and a complex priestly hierarchy. The organized persecutions of the mid-third century resulted to a large extent in a strengthening of its internal organization, and the subsequent period of toleration seems to have encouraged its growth as well as its popular acceptance. By the early fourth century CE, it is not surprising that Constantine, quite apart from any considerations of personal devotion, would have regarded the church as an extremely attractive political ally.

As I noted at the end of the last chapter, the most profound religious changes of the imperial period took place during the fourth century CE. In less than a century, Christianity was transformed from the religion of a persecuted minority to the dominant religion of the empire, its leaders wielding tremendous social and political power; at the same time, religious practices and beliefs that had been central to Graeco-Roman culture for centuries were marginalized and in some cases even criminalized. The practice of animal sacrifice, once one of the strongest and most widely recognized markers of piety, was now regarded as a repulsive rite honoring false gods and pandering to the blood-lust of demons. Divination, which had long played a central role in virtually all the religious traditions of the empire, was now either dismissed as superstition or condemned as magic, a marginalized position that in western culture it has continued to occupy down to the present.

But as dramatic as these changes in religious practice were, the more important changes took place on what we might describe as a structural level. The looseness and variety of traditional religion, which allowed for the effective integration of the various regional traditions within the empire, was replaced by the exclusivity of Christianity. Whereas the Graeco-Roman tradition could accommodate new traditions, deities, and customs almost indefinitely, Christianity could not: non-Christians must convert, or remain in error. Similarly, the diversity of practice and belief that had characterized traditional religion was replaced by an insistence on homogeneity: all Christians were expected to adhere to the same teachings. To be sure, diversity continued to exist, but it was now deeply problematic, and in the fourth and fifth centuries resulted in bitter religious controversies with far-reaching political consequences. The nature of religious authority also underwent a fundamental transformation, since the comprehensive and universal organization of the Christian church was quite unlike anything that had existed before. There was now a separate priestly class whose participation was required for the most important religious rituals and who thus acted as necessary intermediaries with the divine. As a result, the relation between religion and empire also changed. The haphazard mechanisms that I sketched in chapter 5 were replaced by a universal institution that paralleled the secular organization of the empire.

Perhaps the most important change of all, however, was that the loosely related set of approaches to the divine that I discussed in chapter 1 was replaced by a much more coherent and comprehensive system, that is, something that we can more readily identify as "a religion." Christianity combined both cult and philosophy into a single whole, a fact that some Christian thinkers were keen to emphasize. Lactantius, for example, in a lengthy defense of Christianity that he wrote in the early fourth century CE, attacked traditional religion precisely because "philosophy and the cult of the gods have been dissociated and kept far apart; inasmuch as some are teachers of wisdom, through whom there can of course be no approach to the gods, and others are leaders of cult, through whom wisdom is not taught, it is clear that the former is not true wisdom and the latter not true cult. Consequently, neither can philosophy attain the truth nor the cult of the gods render an account of itself, which it lacks." However, "where wisdom is conjoined with cult in an inseparable bond, each must necessarily be true, because we ought both in worship to be wise, that is to know what and how we should worship, and in wisdom to worship, that is to fulfill in actual deed what we know" (*Divine Institutes* 4.3.4–6). To use the Roman scholar Varro's scheme of the three theologies that I outlined in chapter 1, Christianity took the place of both the physical theology of the philosophers and the civic theology of statesmen; the mythical theology disappeared, although its cultural space was filled by a rich literature recounting the histories of apostles, martyrs, and saints.

In all these respects, Christianity differed significantly from traditional forms of religion in the Roman Empire. The decision of Constantine and his successors to become patrons and advocates of the Christian church thus had profoundly momentous consequences, whose effects have shaped the world in which we live today. To understand this development, to assess both the extent to which Christianity differed from earlier traditions and the ways in which it reflected the general trends of the time, we must try to understand religion in the Roman Empire on its own terms, as far as we are able, and not simply as the background for the "rise and triumph" of Christianity. As I have tried to indicate, this is not always easy to do. The presuppositions and assumptions that shaped people's understanding of the divine world in the Roman Empire were often radically different from those that inform the three great traditions of Judaism, Christianity, and Islam, the traditions that have since antiquity dominated the history and culture of Europe, North Africa, and the Middle East. But without such an understanding, we cannot hope to understand this crucial historical development.

But there is another reason why the attempt to understand religion in the Roman Empire is valuable, a reason connected specifically with the difficulty of the attempt. The concept of "religion" now current is not an immutable one, representing an unchanging element of human culture in all times and places. Like many of the other conceptual categories that shape our understanding of the world, it is instead the product of specific historical developments; as such, it has changed and evolved over time, and will no doubt continue to do so in the future. Seeing that some of the most urgent social and political issues in the world today are grounded in ideas about religion, we need urgently to expand our understanding of religion beyond what we take for granted, and to gain some insight, however slight, into other ways of experiencing the world. The attempt to recreate the long-vanished religious world of the Roman Empire, requiring as it does both careful attention to detail and a self-conscious awareness of our own assumptions, provides a valuable exercise along those lines. An understanding of the past is thus important simply for its own sake, because those who are ignorant of the past are inevitably prisoners of the present.

FURTHER READING

Cumont 1911 is a classic statement of the argument that "oriental cults" transformed Graeco-Roman religion, of which Turcan 1996 is essentially an updated version; for a critique, see Burkert 1987. On monotheism, see Versnel 1990 and Athanassiadi and Frede 1999. On the implications of the transition to Christianity, see Lane Fox 1986, Fowden 1993, and Rives 2005.

Glossary of Major Deities

Aesculapius: Latin form of the Greek name "Asklepios"; see below.

Ammon: Greek form of the Egyptian name "Amun"; see below.

Amun: Major Egyptian god, identified by the Greeks with Zeus.

Anubis: Egyptian god, depicted with the head of a jackal; a divine guardian of the dead, associated with Isis and Osiris.

Aphrodite: Greek goddess of sexual desire, identified with Italic Venus and various Syrian goddesses, such as Astarte and Baalat of Byblos; the Syrian Aphrodite is often distinguished by the Greek epithet "Ourania," "Heavenly."

Apollo: Greek god, worshipped under the same name by the Romans; associated with prophecy, music, and healing. His temples at Delphi in Greece and Claros in Asia Minor were the sites of important oracles. He was identified with a range of local gods throughout the empire, including warrior gods in parts of Asia Minor and the healing god Grannus in Celtic areas.

Ares: Greek god of war, identified with Italic Mars and with local warrior gods throughout the eastern part of the empire.

Artemis: Greek goddess, associated with the moon, with hunting and wildlife, and with childbirth and the young. Identified with Italic Diana and with various goddesses in Asia Minor; the latter influenced the distinctive form under which she was worshipped at Ephesus.

Asklepios: Greek god of healing, called "Aesculapius" or "Asclepius" in Latin; his sanctuaries drew many visitors seeking cures for medical problems.

Astarte: Greek and Latin form of the Semitic name "Ashtart"; an important goddess of Syria, worshipped especially in Sidon and Tyre, and identified with Greek Aphrodite.

Atargatis: Greek form of the Semitic name "Atar-Ata"; the "Syrian Goddess" worshipped at Hierapolis in Syria whose cult spread through the eastern Roman Empire.

Athena: Greek goddess of skill and strategy, crafts and craftiness. Worshipped especially at Athens, and identified with Italic Minerva.

Baal: Semitic title, meaning "Master" or "Lord," applied to various high gods in Syria.

Baal Hammon: Chief god of Punic North Africa, identified with Italic Saturn.

Bakkhos: In Latin, "Bacchus"; an alternative name for Dionysos; see below.

Bellona: Roman war goddess, identified with the Anatolian goddess Ma.

Caelestis: Latin title, meaning "Heavenly," given to the chief goddess of North Africa; a continuation of the Punic goddess Tanit, she was identified with Italic Juno.

Capitoline Triad: The three chief deities of Rome, Jupiter Optimus Maximus, Juno, and Minerva, whose main temple was on the Capitoline Hill in Rome.

Ceres: Italic goddess of agricultural fertility, identified from an early date with Greek Demeter.

Cybele: Mother goddess from Asia Minor whose cult was originally located at Pessinus, but spread throughout the Greek and Roman world; known in Latin as Mater Deum Magna Idaea, the "Great Idaean Mother of the Gods."

daimôn: Generic Greek term for a divine being, especially one intermediate between gods and mortals.

Demeter: Greek goddess of grain and agricultural fertility, the mother of Kore; her worship included mysteries, most famously at Eleusis near Athens. Identified with Italic Ceres.

Diana: Italic goddess associated with the moon and the wilderness; identified at an early date with Greek Artemis.

Dionysos: Greek god associated with wine and drama, also known as Bakkhos; his worship often included mysteries. Identified with the Roman god Liber Pater.

divus: Latin word meaning "god," an alternative to the more common word *deus*; used especially as a title for emperors who were officially deified after their deaths, e.g., Divus Iulius, Divus Augustus, etc.

Dusares: The Greek and Latin form of the Semitic name "Dushara," the chief god of the Nabataean Arabs.

Endovellicus: Iberian god worshipped in the province of Lusitania, apparently associated with the underworld.

Epona: Celtic goddess whose name is etymologically related to the Celtic word for "horse," perhaps also associated with fertility.

genius: Latin word etymologically related to the verb *gignere*, "to beget." Conceived originally as a divine alter-ego or guardian spirit of an individual; over time, every locality and corporate body was thought to possess a *genius*.

Great Mother: Title used especially for the mother goddesses of Asia Minor; see "Cybele."

Helios: Greek word meaning "sun"; worshipped as a god.

Hera: Greek goddess of marriage, the wife of Zeus; identified with the Italic Juno and sometimes with Syrian goddesses such as Atargatis.

Herakles: Greek hero and god, whose worship was adopted at a very early date in Rome under the Latinized name "Hercules"; identified with a range of gods, notably the Phoenician Melqart and various local gods in western Europe.

Hermes: Greek god associated with travel and prosperity, identified with the Italic Mercury and the Egyptian Thoth; as the latter, he is specifically called Hermes Trismegistos, "Thrice-Greatest Hermes."

Heros: The Greek word *hêrôs* designated a mortal who continued to exert power after death; as a title, it was often applied to the Thracian Rider God.

Hestia: Greek goddess of the hearth.

Horus: Egyptian god, the son of Isis and Osiris; often depicted with the head of a hawk.

Hygia: Latin form of the Greek word *hygieia*, "health," personified as a goddess and often worshipped with Aesculapius.

Isis: Egyptian goddess, wife of Osiris, whose cult became widespread throughout the Graeco-Roman world and sometimes featured mysteries; she had a wide range of associations.

Juno: Italic goddess associated especially with women and identified from an early date with Greek Hera; worshipped especially as part of the Capitoline Triad.

Jupiter: Italic god associated with sovereignty and the heavens; identified from an early date with Greek Zeus. As Jupiter Optimus Maximus, "Best and Greatest," he was the chief deity of Rome, the central figure in the Capitoline Triad. He was sometimes identified with other supreme gods, especially those of Syria, and in those contexts given specific epithets associating him with specific sites, e.g., Dolichenus and Heliopolitanus.

Kore: Greek word meaning "maiden"; the usual name in cult for Persephone, daughter of Demeter; called Proserpina in Latin. Worshipped with her mother in mystery cults, but also imagined as the queen of the underworld.

Kronos: Greek god, the father of Zeus, who in myth castrates his father Ouranos and devours his children; identified with Italic Saturn.

Lares: Roman gods, usually attested in the plural form, although the singular "Lar" is also found; guardian spirits, associated especially with the household and crossroads.

Liber Pater: Italic god of fertility and wine, associated from an early date with Greek Dionysos.

Ma: Anatolian war goddess, identified with Roman Bellona.

Malagbel: one of the chief gods of Palmyra; also spelled Malachbel.

Mars: Italic god, associated with warfare and the protection of farmland; identified with Greek Ares and with a range of Celtic and Germanic gods.

Matres: Latin word meaning "mothers"; title given to the mother goddesses worshipped in Germanic and Celtic regions.

Melqart: Phoenician god, the chief deity of Tyre; identified with the Graeco-Roman Herakles/Hercules.

Men: Anatolian moon god.

Mercury: Italic god, associated especially with trade and travel; identified from an early date with Greek Hermes and later with a number of local Celtic gods.

Minerva: Italic goddess of crafts, identified from an early date with Greek Athena; worshipped especially as part of the Capitoline Triad.

Mithras: Latin form of the Persian name "Mithra"; identified with the sun, he was the focus of a widespread mystery cult in the Roman Empire.

Neptune: Italic god of water, identified from an early date with Greek Poseidon.

Osiris: Egyptian god, husband of Isis and ruler of the underworld.

Penates: Roman divinities associated with the household; the name occurs only in the plural.

Pluto: Greek god of the underworld, worshipped with his consort Kore; popular in Africa, where the name was probably used for an indigenous god of agriculture.

Poseidon: Greek god of the sea, earthquakes, and horses; identified with Italic Neptune and with local warrior gods in Asia Minor.

Proserpina: the Latin form of the name "Persephone"; see "Kore" above.

Sarapis: Graeco-Egyptian god, often identified with Zeus and sometimes worshipped with Isis.

Saturn: Italic god known especially for his festival of the Saturnalia; identified with Greek Kronos and in North Africa with the Punic Baal Hammon.

Sequana: Celtic goddess, the personification of the river Seine; her shrine at the source of the river was the site of a healing cult.

Silvanus: Italic god of the countryside, widely popular especially in Italy and the Danubian provinces.

Sol: The Latin word for "sun," worshipped as a god; often called Sol Invictus, "the Unconquered Sun."

Sulis: Celtic goddess associated with the springs at Bath; identified with Italic Minerva.

Syrian Goddess: see above, "Atargatis."

Tanit: Chief goddess of Punic Carthage, identified with Italic Juno.

Thoth: Egyptian god of wisdom and writing, identified with Greek Hermes.

Venus: Italic goddess of charm and seduction, identified from an early date with Greek Aphrodite.

Vesta: Roman goddess of the hearth.

Zeus: Greek god of sovereignty and the sky, whose cult at Olympia was the context for the Olympic games; as Zeus Herkeios and Ktesios, he played a key role in household cult. Identified with a range of gods in Asia Minor and Syria, and with Italic Jupiter; Zeus Kapitolios is the Greek name for the Roman god Jupiter Optimus Maximus.

Glossary of Authors and Texts

In the following, I provide some very basic information about the writers and texts I have cited in this book; where helpful, I have included the Greek or Latin title in parentheses. I also indicate some of the available English translations, using the following abbreviations for standard series: L = Loeb Classical Library; O = Oxford World's Classics; P = Penguin Classics.

Acts of the Apostles: Account of early followers of Jesus, especially Paul, written by the author of the *Gospel of Luke* (late first or early second century CE); incorporated into the Christian New Testament. Many translations.

Aelius Aristides: Greek orator and writer from Asia Minor (b. 117 CE, d. after 181); his *Sacred Tales* (*Orations* 47–52) are an autobiographical account of his relationship with the god Asklepios. *Orations*: C. A. Behr (Leiden: Brill 1981).

Alcinous: Named as the author in the manuscripts of the Greek *Handbook of Platonism* (*Didaskalikos*), but otherwise unknown; the work is thought to date to the second century CE. *The Handbook of Platonism*: J. Dillon (Oxford: Oxford University Press 1993).

Apollonius of Tyana: Greek philosopher and holy man (active in the latter half of the first century CE); the letters attributed to him are of uncertain authenticity. *Letters*: R. J. Penella (Leiden: Brill 1979).

Apuleius: Latin orator, philosopher, and writer from North Africa (b. c.125 CE, d. after early 160s). *The Golden Ass* (*Metamorphoses*): A. J. Hanson (L 1989), P. G. Walsh (O 1994), E. J. Kenney (P 1998); *Apology, On the God of Socrates* (*De deo Socratis*), *Bouquet* (*Florida*): S. J. Harrison, ed., *Apuleius: Rhetorical Works* (Oxford: Oxford University Press 2001); *On Plato and his Doctrine* (*De Platone et eius dogmate*): no English translation.

Aristotle: Greek philosopher, active in Athens (b. 384 BCE, d. 322); his *Exhortation* (*Protreptikos*) is known only from quotations in later writers. *Politics*: many translations; *Constitution of the Athenians* (with *Politics*): S. Everson, ed. (Cambridge: Cambridge University Press 1996).

Artemidorus: Greek writer on dreams from Asia Minor (active mid/late second century CE). *The Interpretation of Dreams*: R. J. White (Park Ridge, NJ: Noyes Press 1975).

Athenagoras: Greek Christian writer; his *Embassy for Christians* (*Legatio*) can be dated to c.177 CE. Extant works: J. H. Crehan (New York: Newman Press 1955), W. R. Schoedel (Oxford: Oxford University Press 1972).

The Augustan History (*Historia Augusta*): A series of Latin biographies of Roman emperors from Hadrian to Carinus (117–284 CE); although attributed in the manuscripts to six different authors of the late third and early fourth centuries, it is now thought to be the work of one writer in the very late fourth century. Complete: D. Magie (L 1922–32); *Hadrian* through *Elagabalus*: A. R. Birley (P 1976).

Augustine: Latin Christian writer from North Africa (b. 354 CE, d. 430); much of his voluminous output survives, including *The City of God* (written 413–26 CE). *The City of God*: G. E. McCracken and others (L 1957–72), H. Bettenson (P 1972), R. W. Dyson (Cambridge: Cambridge University Press 1998). *Confessions*: H. Chadwick (O 1991).

Caesar (C. Julius Caesar): Roman statesman, general, and writer (b. 100 BCE, d. 44); he wrote his *Gallic War* in the 50s BCE. *The Gallic War*: H. J. Edwards (L 1917); C. Hammond (O 1996).

Cassius Dio: Greek historian (b. c.164 CE, d. after 229). His history of Rome from the beginnings to his own day survives only in part, although later excerpts and summaries cover the missing portions. Extant works: E. Cary (L 1914–27).

Cicero (M. Tullius Cicero): Roman statesman, orator, and writer (b. 106 BCE, d. 43); his dialogue *Hortensius* is known only from references in later writers, but many other works survive complete. *On Laws*: C. W. Keyes (L 1928); *On the Nature of the Gods* (*De natura deorum*): H. Rackham (L 1933), H. C. P. MacGregor (P 1972), P. G. Walsh (O 1998); *On Divination*: W. A. Falconer (L 1923); *Letters to Atticus*: D. R. Shackleton Bailey (L 1999).

1 Clement: Traditional title of Greek letter from the Christian community of Rome to that of Corinth, written probably in the 90s CE. In Holmes 1999 and B. D. Ehrman, *Apostolic Fathers* (L 2003).

Didache: Anonymous Greek Christian tractate of the late first or early/mid-second century CE. In Holmes 1999 and B. D. Ehrman, *Apostolic Fathers* (L 2003).

Digest: A compendium of excerpts from Latin legal authorities, especially those of the early third century CE, compiled under the emperor Justinian in the 530s CE. Complete: Alan Watson, ed. (Philadelphia: University of Pennsylvania Press 1985).

Dio Chrysostom: Greek orator and philosopher from Asia Minor (b. c.40–50 CE, d. after 110). Extant works: J. W. Cohoon and H. L. Crosby (L 1932–51).

Diodorus Siculus: Greek historian, working in Rome from c.56 to c.30 BCE. *Library*: C. H. Oldfather and others (L 1933–67).

Epictetus: Greek philosopher of the Stoic school, taught in Rome and Greece (b. c.55 CE, d. 135); although he wrote nothing himself, his pupil Arrian published the notes he had taken of his teachings, of which the *Handbook* (*Encheiridion*) is a summary of the chief points. Complete works: W. A. Oldfather (L 1925–8); *Handbook*: N. White (Indianapolis: Hackett 1983).

Epistle to Diognetus: Anonymous Greek Christian tract, dating probably between 150 and 225 CE. In Holmes 1999 and B. D. Ehrman, *Apostolic Fathers* (L 2003).

Euhemerus: Greek statesman and writer, active in the late fourth and early third centuries BCE; his *Sacred Writing* is known only from references and paraphrases by later writers. No English translation.

Gospel of Mark: Anonymous account of the career and teachings of Jesus, written probably between 65 and 80 CE; incorporated into the Christian New Testament. Many translations.

Greek Magical Papyri: Modern collection of ancient papyri, written in Greek and Demotic Egyptian and dating mostly to the third through fifth centuries CE. Complete collection: Betz 1992.

Heliodorus: Greek novelist, active in the mid-third or possibly mid-fourth century CE. *An Ethiopian Story*: J. R. Morgan in Reardon 1989.

Hermetica: Writings attributed to Hermes Trismegistos. A Byzantine collection of 18 Greek dialogues and treatises is known as the *Corpus Hermeticum*, of which the first is entitled *Poimandres*; there also survives a Latin dialogue entitled *Asclepius* and some extensive Greek excerpts in late authors. The most complete edition, with French translation, is Nock and Festugière 1946–54; English translation of the *Corpus Hermeticum* and *Asclepius* in Copenhaver 1992.

Herodotus: Greek historian active in the mid-fifth century BCE. *History*: A. de Selincourt, rev. J. Marincola (P 1996).

Hesiod: Greek poet, active in Greece perhaps c.700 BCE. *Theogony* and *Works and Days*: M. L. West (O 1988), S. Lombardo (Indianapolis: Hackett 1993).

Homer: According to tradition, the author of the Greek epic poems the *Iliad* and the *Odyssey* (mid- to late eighth century BCE). Many translations.

Homeric Hymn to Demeter: Anonymous Greek poem, dating probably to the seventh century BCE and written in "Homeric" style. Complete Homeric hymns: M. Crudden (Oxford: Oxford University Press 2001), J. Cashford (P 2003), M. L. West (L 2003); *Hymn to Demeter*: H. P. Foley (Princeton: Princeton University Press 1994).

Horace (Q. Horatius Flaccus): Roman poet (b. 65 BCE, d. 8 BCE); the first three books of his *Odes* appeared in 23 BCE. Many translations.

Josephus (Flavius Josephus): Judaean historian writing in Greek (b. 37/8 CE, d. after the mid-90s CE). His *Judaean* (or *Jewish*) *War*, an account of the war between Rome and the Judaeans, appeared in the late 70s CE; his *Judaean* (or *Jewish*) *Antiquities*, an account of the Judaean people from the creation of the world to his own day, appeared in the mid-90s CE; *Against Apion*, a defense of Judaean tradition against its detractors, appeared shortly afterwards. Complete works: H. St. J. Thackeray and others (L 1927–65), S. Mason, ed. (Leiden: Brill 2001–).

Justin (Justin Martyr): Greek Christian teacher and writer, active in Rome (b. c.100 CE, d. c.165). His defense of Christianity, traditionally known as the *First Apology*, was written in the mid-150s CE. *First and Second Apologies*: L. W. Barnard (New York: Paulist Press 1997).

Juvenal: Latin satirical poet, active in Rome in the 110s and 120s CE. *Satires*: N. Rudd (O 1991), S. M. Braund (L 2004).

Lactantius: Latin Christian teacher and writer (b. c.240 CE, d. c.320); his *Divine Institutes* was written in 303–13 CE as a comprehensive defense of Christianity. *Divine Institutes*: A. Bowen and P. Garnsey (Liverpool: Liverpool University Press 2003).

Livy: Roman historian (b. 59 BCE, d. 17 CE). His history of Rome, from its foundation down to 9 BCE, survives only in part. Complete works: B. O. Foster and others (L 1919–59); Books 21–30: A. de Selincourt (P 1965); 31–40: J. C. Yardley (O 2000).

Lucan (M. Annaeus Lucanus): Roman epic poet (b. 39 CE, d. 65). *Civil War*: J. D. Duff (L 1928), S. H. Braund (O 1992).

Lucian: Greek satirist and essayist from northern Syria (b. c.120 CE, d. after 180). Complete works: A. M. Harmon and others (L 1913–67); *On the Syrian Goddess*: Lightfoot 2003.

Manilius: Latin poet whose *Astronomica*, an exposition of astrology, was apparently written in the second decade CE. *Astronomica*: G. P. Goold (L 1977).

Maximus of Tyre: Greek orator and popular philosopher (active mid-second century CE). No English translation.

Menander Rhetor: Greek writer on rhetoric, active probably in the late third century CE. Extant works: D. A. Russell and N. G. Wilson (Oxford: Oxford University Press 1981).

Mishnah: Hebrew collection of the legal opinions of Judaean teachers, compiled in Palestine c.200 CE and comprising 63 tractates. Complete: H. Danby (Oxford: Oxford University Press 1933), J. Neusner (New Haven: Yale University Press 1987).

Numenius: Greek philosopher from Syria (second century CE). The standard edition, with French translation, is des Places 1973; no English translation.

The Opinions of Paulus (Sententiae Pauli): Pseudonymous summary of Roman law, composed c.300 CE. No English translation.

Orpheus: Mythical Greek poet to whom many later writings were attributed, most now known only from quotations and references in later writers; the exception is a collection of 87 hymns. Hymns: A. N. Athanassakis (Atlanta: Scholars Press 1977); for the cosmogonies, see the reconstructions in West 1983.

Ovid: Roman poet (b. 43 BCE, d. 17 CE); he completed only the first six books of his *Fasti*, a poetic commentary on the Roman calendar. *Fasti*: J. G. Fraser, rev. G. P. Goold (L 1989), B. R. Nagle (Bloomington: Indiana University Press 1995), A. J. Boyle and R. D. Woodard (P 2000).

Paul: A Judaean who after the death of Jesus became active in bringing others to regard him as the savior (active c.35 to c.60 CE). A number of his Greek letters to Christian communities are preserved in the New Testament: seven are generally considered authentic (*Romans*, 1 and 2 *Corinthians*, *Galatians*, *Philippians*, 1 *Thessalonians*, *Philemon*); others, including *Colossians*, are doubtful or pseudepigraphic. Many translations.

Pausanias: Greek travel writer (active probably in the mid-second century CE). *Description of Greece*: W. H. S. Jones (L 1918–35), P. Levi (P 1979).

Philo: Judaean philosopher writing in Greek, active in Alexandria in the first half of the first century CE. Complete works: F. H. Colson, G. H. Whitaker, and others (L 1929–53).

Philostratus: Greek writer, active in the first half of the third century CE. *Life of Apollonius of Tyana*: C. P. Jones (L 2005).

Plato: Greek philosopher, active in Athens (b. c.429 BCE, d. 347). Complete works: H. N. Fowler and others (L 1914–27), J. M. Cooper, ed. (Indianapolis: Hackett 1997).

Pliny the Elder: Roman official and writer (b. 23/4 CE, d. 79 CE). *Natural History*: H. Rackham and others (L 1938–63).

Pliny the Younger: Roman orator and writer, nephew and adopted son of the elder Pliny (b. c.61 CE, d. c.112). Extant works: B. Radice (L 1969).

Plutarch: Greek philosopher and writer (b. before 50 CE, d. after 120); best known for his parallel lives of famous Greeks and Romans, he also wrote numerous essays on a wide range of subjects, conventionally known as the *Moralia*; all the texts cited here, except for the life of Sertorius, are in the *Moralia. Lives*: B. Perrin (L 1914–26); *Moralia*: F. C. Babbitt and others (L 1927–69).

Porphyry: Greek philosopher (b. 234 CE, d. c.305); only a small part of his wide and varied output survives intact, although other works (such as his *Philosophy from Oracles*) are known from quotations in later writers. His *Life of Plotinus* is available in translations of Plotinus: A. H. Armstrong (L 1969), S. MacKenna, ed. J. Dillon (P 1991); *On Abstinence*: G. Clark (London: Duckworth 2000); *On the Cave of the Nymphs*: trans. by Seminar Classics 609, State University of New York at Buffalo (Arethusa Monographs 1, 1969), R. Lamberton (Barryton: Station Hill Press 1983).

Pythagoras: Greek philosopher and religious thinker, active in the later sixth century BCE. Pythagoras himself wrote nothing, but many later works were attributed to him; see Kahn 2001 for an overview.

Sallustius: Wrote probably during the emperor Julian's revival of the Graeco-Roman religious tradition (361–3 CE). *On the Gods and the Universe*: A. D. Nock (Cambridge: Cambridge University Press 1926).

Seneca (L. Annaeus Seneca, the Younger): Roman philosopher, statesman, and writer (b. between 4 BCE and 1 CE, d. 65 CE). *Epistles*: R. M. Gummere (L 1917–25); *On Benevolent Deeds (De beneficiis)*: J. W. Basore (L 1935).

Sibylline Oracles: A collection of varied prophetic texts, many of which reflect Judaean or Christian contexts. Complete: J. J. Collins in Charlesworth 1983: 1.317–472.

Strabo: Greek historian and geographer (b. c.64 BCE, d. after 21 CE). His extensive *Geography*, his only extant work, dates probably to the early first century CE. *Geography*: H. L. Jones (L 1917–32).

Suetonius: Roman scholar and biographer (b. c.70 CE, d. after the mid-120s). His *Lives of the Caesars*, biographies of the Roman emperors from Julius Caesar to Domitian, is his only fully extant work. Complete: J. C. Rolfe (L 1914), R. Graves (P 1957), C. Edwards (O 2000).

Tacitus: Roman statesman, orator, and historian (b. c.56 CE, d. after 118). Both his *Annals*, a history of Rome from 14 CE to 68 CE, and his *Histories*, 69 to 96 CE, survive only in part. Extant works: various translators (L 1914–37); *Annals*: M. Grant (P 1966), A. J. Woodman (Indianapolis: Hackett 2004); *Histories*: K. Wellesley (P 1964), W. H. Fyfe, rev. D. S. Levene (O 1997).

Terence: Roman comic playwright; his six plays, which were based on Greek originals, were produced in the 160s BCE. Complete works: B. Radice (P 1965), J. Barsby (L 2001).

Tertullian: Latin Christian writer, active in Carthage (b. c.160 CE, d. c.240). *Apology*: T. R. Glover (L 1931); *On Idolatry* (*De idololatria*): J. H. Waszink and J. C. M. van Winden (Leiden: Brill 1987).

Ulpian: Roman official and legal authority (d. 223 CE); his voluminous writings on Roman law date mostly to the 210s, but survive only as excerpts in the *Digest.*

Valerius Maximus: Roman writer active in the reign of Tiberius (14–37 CE). *Memorable Deeds and Sayings*: D. R. Shackleton Bailey (L 2000); H. J. Winkler (Indianapolis: Hackett 2004).

Varro: Roman writer and scholar (b. 116 BCE, d. 27 BCE); his study of Roman religious traditions (*Antiquitates rerum divinarum*) is known only from quotations by later writers, especially Augustine in *The City of God.* No full English translation.

Vergil (also spelled **Virgil**): Roman poet (b. 70 BCE, d. 19 BCE); the *Aeneid*, his great epic of the founding of Rome, was left unfinished at his death. Many translations.

Verrius Flaccus: Roman scholar, active under Augustus (31 BCE–14 CE). His annotated version of the Roman calendar is partly preserved in an inscription (*Fasti Praenestini*). No English translation.

***Wisdom of Solomon*:** Pseudepigraphic treatise, written in Greek probably by a Judaean of Alexandria in the first century BCE; included in the Christian Apocrypha. Many translations.

Xenophanes: Greek philosopher and religious thinker (probably c.570–c.475 BCE). His writings are known only from quotations in later writers. The most important passages are translated in Kirk, Raven, and Schofield 1983.

Xenophon of Ephesus: Greek novelist writing probably in the period 100–50 CE. *An Ephesian Tale*: G. Anderson in Reardon 1989.

References

COLLECTIONS OF INSCRIPTIONS AND PAPYRI

IEph = Engelmann, H. et al. (eds.) 1979–81: *Die Inschriften von Ephesos.* Bonn: Habelt.

IGBulg = Mikhailov, G. (ed.) 1958–70: *Inscriptiones Graecae in Bulgaria Repertae.* Sofia: Academia Litterarum Bulgarica.

IGR = Cagnat, R., Toutain, J., Jouguet, P., and Lafaye, G. (eds.) 1901–27: *Inscriptiones Graecae ad Res Romanas Pertinentes.* Paris: E. Leroux.

ILAfr = Cagnat, R., Merlin, A., and Chatelain, H. (eds.) 1923: *Inscriptions latines d'Afrique.* Paris: E. Leroux.

ILS = Dessau, H. (ed.) 1892–1916: *Inscriptiones Latinae Selectae.* Berlin: Weidmann.

MAMA = Calder, W. M. et al. (eds.) 1928– : *Monumenta Asiae Minoris Antiqua.* Manchester: Manchester University Press.

PGM = Preisendanz, K. (ed.) 1973–4: *Papyri Graecae Magicae: Die griechischen Zauberpapyri.* 2nd edn., rev. A. Henrichs. Stuttgart: B. G. Teubner.

POxy = Grenfell, B. P. et al. (eds.) 1898– : *The Oxyrhynchus Papyri.* London: Egypt Exploration Society.

RIB = Collingwood, R. G. and Wright, R. P. (eds.) 1965–95: *The Roman Inscriptions of Britain.* Oxford: Clarendon Press.

SIG[3] = Dittenberger, W. (ed.) 1915–24: *Sylloge Inscriptionum Graecarum.* 3rd edn. Leipzig: S. Hirzel.

BOOKS AND ARTICLES

Anderson, Graham 1994: *Sage, Saint and Sophist: Holy Men and their Associates in the Early Roman Empire.* London: Routledge.

Ando, Clifford (ed.) 2003: *Roman Religion.* Edinburgh: University of Edinburgh Press.

Athanassiadi, Polymnia and Frede, Michael (eds.) 1999: *Pagan Monotheism in Late Antiquity.* Oxford: Clarendon Press.

Attridge, H. W. 1978: The Philosophical Critique of Religion under the Early Empire. In Wolfgang Haase (ed.), *Aufstieg und Niedergang der römischen Welt*, vol. II. 16.1. Berlin: Walter de Gruyter. 45–78.

Barnes, T. D. 1968: Legislation against the Christians. *Journal of Roman Studies* 58: 32–50.

Beard, Mary and North, John (eds.) 1990: *Pagan Priests*. Ithaca, NY: Cornell University Press.

Beard, Mary, North, John, and Price, Simon 1998: *Religions of Rome. Vol. 1: A History. Vol. 2: A Sourcebook*. Cambridge: Cambridge University Press.

Beck, Roger 1991: Thus Spake Not Zarathustra: Zoroastrian Pseudepigrapha of the Graeco-Roman World. In M. Boyce and F. Grenet, *A History of Zoroastrianism, Vol. 3: Zoroastrianism under Macedonian and Roman Rule*. Leiden: Brill. 491–565.

—— 2004: *Beck on Mithraism: Collected Works with New Essays*. Aldershot: Ashgate.

Behr, Charles A. 1968: *Aelius Aristides and the Sacred Tales*. Amsterdam: A. M. Hakkert.

Bendlin, Andreas 2000: Looking Beyond the Civic Compromise: Religious Pluralism in Late Republican Rome. In Edward Bispham and Christopher Smith (eds.), *Religion in Archaic and Republican Rome and Italy: Evidence and Experience*. Edinburgh: Edinburgh University Press. 115–35.

Bernand, Étienne 1969: *Les inscriptions grecques et latines de Philae, Tome II: Haut et Bas Empire*. Paris: Centre national de la recherche scientifique.

Betz, Hans Dieter (ed.) 1992: *The Greek Magical Papyri in Translation*. 2nd edn. Chicago: University of Chicago Press.

Bowman, A. K. 1986: *Egypt after the Pharaohs: 332 BC–AD 642, from Alexander to the Arab Conquest*. Berkeley: University of California Press.

Boyce, G. K. 1937: *Corpus of the Lararia of Pompeii*. Rome: American Academy in Rome.

Bruit Zaidman, Louise and Schmitt Pantel, Pauline 1992: *Religion in the Ancient Greek City*. Trans. Paul Cartledge. Cambridge: Cambridge University Press.

Burkert, Walter 1985: *Greek Religion*. Trans. John Raffan. Cambridge, MA: Harvard University Press.

—— 1987: *Ancient Mystery Cults*. Cambridge, MA: Harvard University Press.

Buxton, Richard 2004: *The Complete World of Greek Mythology*. London: Thames and Hudson.

Charlesworth, James H. (ed.) 1983: *The Old Testament Pseudepigrapha*. Garden City, NY: Doubleday.

Clauss, Manfred 2001: *The Roman Cult of Mithras: The God and his Mysteries*. Trans. Richard Gordon. New York: Routledge.

Cohen, Shaye J. D. 1987: *From the Maccabees to the Mishnah*. Philadelphia: Westminster Press.

—— 1999: *The Beginnings of Jewishness: Boundaries, Varieties, Uncertainties*. Berkeley: University of California Press.

Coleman, Kathleen 1990: Fatal Charades: Roman Executions Staged as Mythological Enactments. *Journal of Roman Studies* 80: 44–73.

Copenhaver, Brian P. 1992: *Hermetica: The Greek* Corpus Hermeticum *and the Latin* Asclepius *in a New English Translation with Notes and Introduction.* Cambridge: Cambridge University Press.

Crawford, Michael H. (ed.) 1996: *Roman Statutes.* London: Institute of Classical Studies.

Cumont, Franz 1911: *The Oriental Religions in Roman Paganism.* Trans. Grant Showerman. Chicago: Open Court.

Cunliffe, Barry 1997: *The Ancient Celts.* Oxford: Oxford University Press.

de Ste. Croix, G. E. M. 1963: Why Were the Early Christians Persecuted? *Past & Present* 26: 6–38.

Derks, Ton 1998: *Gods, Temples and Ritual Practices: The Transformation of Religious Ideas and Values in Roman Gaul.* Amsterdam: Amsterdam University Press.

des Places, Édouard (ed.) 1973: *Numénius: Fragments.* Paris: Les Belles Lettres.

Dignas, Beate 2002: *Economy of the Sacred in Hellenistic and Roman Asia Minor.* Oxford: Oxford University Press.

Dillon, Matthew 1997: *Pilgrims and Pilgrimage in Ancient Greece.* London: Routledge.

Dodds, E. R. 1965: *Pagan and Christian in an Age of Anxiety.* Cambridge: Cambridge University Press.

Dorcey, Peter F. 1992: *The Cult of Silvanus: A Study in Roman Folk Religion.* Leiden: Brill.

Dunand, Françoise and Zivie-Coche, Christiane 2004: *Gods and Men in Egypt, 3000 BCE to 395 CE.* Trans. David Lorton. Ithaca, NY: Cornell University Press.

Edelstein, Emma J. and Edelstein, Ludwig 1945: *Asclepius: Collection and Interpretation of the Testimonies.* Baltimore: Johns Hopkins University Press.

Elsner, Jaś 1992: Pausanias: A Greek Pilgrim in the Roman World. *Past & Present* 135: 3–29.

—— 1996: Image and Ritual: Reflections on the Religious Appreciation of Classical Art. *Classical Quarterly* 46: 513–31.

—— and Rutherford, Ian (eds.) 2005: *Pilgrimage in Graeco-Roman and Early Christian Antiquity: Seeing the Gods.* Oxford: Oxford University Press.

Fears, J. R. 1981: The Cult of Virtues and Roman Imperial Ideology. In Wolfgang Haase (ed.), *Aufstieg und Niedergang der römischen Welt*, vol. II. 17.2. Berlin: Walter de Gruyter. 827–948.

Feeney, Denis 1998: *Literature and Religion at Rome.* Cambridge: Cambridge University Press.

Festugière, André-Jean 1954: *Personal Religion among the Greeks.* Berkeley: University of California Press.

Fishwick, Duncan 1987–2005: *The Imperial Cult in the Latin West.* Leiden: Brill.

Fowden, Garth 1986: *The Egyptian Hermes: A Historical Approach to the Late Pagan Mind.* Cambridge: Cambridge University Press.

—— 1987: Pagan Versions of the Rain Miracle of AD 172. *Historia* 36: 83–95.

—— 1993: *Empire to Commonwealth: Consequences of Monotheism in Late Antiquity.* Princeton: Princeton University Press.

Francis, James R. 1995: *Subversive Virtue: Asceticism and Authority in the Second-Century Pagan World.* University Park: Pennsylvania State University Press.

Frankfurter, David 1998: *Religion in Roman Egypt: Assimilation and Resistance.* Princeton: Princeton University Press.

Friesen, Steven J. 1993: *Twice Neokoros: Ephesus, Asia and the Cult of the Flavian Imperial Family.* Leiden: Brill.

Furley, William D. and Bremer, Jan M. (eds.) 2001: *Greek Hymns.* Tübingen: Mohr Siebeck.

Gager, John G. 1992: *Curse Tablets and Binding Spells from the Ancient World.* New York: Oxford University Press.

Garnsey, Peter 1984: Religious Toleration in Classical Antiquity. In W. J. Shiels (ed.), *Persecution and Toleration.* Oxford: Blackwell. 1–27.

Goodman, Martin 1994: *Mission and Conversion: Proselytizing in the Religious History of the Roman Empire.* Oxford: Clarendon Press.

—— 1997: *The Roman World, 44 BC–AD 180.* London: Routledge.

Gordon, Richard 1979: The Real and the Imaginary: Production and Religion in the Graeco-Roman World. *Art History* 20: 5–34.

—— 1990: The Veil of Power: Emperors, Sacrificers and Benefactors. In Mary Beard and John North (eds.), *Pagan Priests.* Ithaca, NY: Cornell University Press. 201–31.

—— 1996: *Image and Value in the Graeco-Roman World: Studies in Mithraism and Religious Art.* Brookfield, VT: Variorum.

—— 1999: Imagining Greek and Roman Magic. In Bengt Ankarloo and Stuart Clark (eds.), *Witchcraft and Magic in Europe: Ancient Greece and Rome.* Philadelphia: University of Pennsylvania Press. 159–275.

Gradel, Ittai 2002: *Emperor Worship and Roman Religion.* Oxford: Clarendon Press.

Graf, Fritz 1997: *Magic in the Ancient World.* Trans. Franklin Philip. Cambridge, MA: Harvard University Press.

Grant, Frederick C. (ed.) 1953: *Hellenistic Religions: The Age of Syncretism.* Indianapolis: Bobbs-Merrill.

Green, Miranda 1986: *The Gods of the Celts.* Gloucester: Alan Sutton.

Hadot, Pierre 2002: *What is Ancient Philosophy?* Trans. Michael Chase. Cambridge, MA: Harvard University Press.

Harland, Philip A. 2003: *Associations, Synagogues, and Congregations: Claiming a Place in Ancient Mediterranean Society.* Minneapolis: Fortress Press.

Henig, Martin 1984: *Religion in Roman Britain.* London: B. T. Batsford Ltd.

Holmes, Michael W. (ed.) 1999: *The Apostolic Fathers.* Ed. and trans. J. B. Lightfoot and J. R. Harmer. Grand Rapids, MI: Baker Books.

Hopkins, Keith 1978: Divine Emperors or the Symbolic Unity of the Roman Empire. In *Conquerors and Slaves.* Cambridge: Cambridge University Press. 197–242.

Horden, Peregrine and Purcell, Nicholas 2000: *The Corrupting Sea: A Study of Mediterranean History.* Oxford: Blackwell.

Hunt, A. S. and Edgar, C. C. (eds.) 1932: *Select Papyri 1: Private Affairs.* Cambridge, MA: Harvard University Press.

Huskinson, Janet (ed.) 2000: *Experiencing Rome: Culture, Identity and Power in the Roman Empire*. London: Routledge, in association with the Open University.

Irby-Massie, Georgia L. 1999: *Military Religion in Roman Britain*. Leiden: Brill.

Kahn, Charles H. 2001: *Pythagoras and the Pythagoreans: A Brief History*. Indianapolis: Hackett.

King, Charles 2003: The Organization of Roman Religious Beliefs. *Classical Antiquity* 22: 275–312.

Kirk, G. S., Raven, J. E., and Schofield, M. 1983: *The Presocratic Philosophers*. 2nd edn. Cambridge: Cambridge University Press.

Klauck, Hans-Josef 2003: *The Religious Context of Early Christianity: A Guide to Graeco-Roman Religions*. Trans. Brian McNeil. Minneapolis: Fortress Press.

Kloppenborg, John S. and Wilson, Stephen G. (eds.) 1996: *Voluntary Associations in the Graeco-Roman World*. London: Routledge.

Koester, Helmut 1995: *Introduction to the New Testament, Vol. 1: History, Culture and Religion of the Hellenistic Age*. 2nd edn. Berlin: Walter de Gruyter.

Kraemer, Ross S. 1992: *Her Share of the Blessings: Women's Religions among Pagans, Jews, and Christians in the Greco-Roman World*. New York: Oxford University Press.

—— (ed.) 2004: *Women's Religions in the Greco-Roman World: A Sourcebook*. Oxford: Oxford University Press.

Lane Fox, Robin 1986: *Pagans and Christians*. New York: Alfred A. Knopf.

Layton, Bentley 1987: *The Gnostic Scriptures*. Garden City, NY: Doubleday.

Lengyel, A. and Radon, G. T. B. (eds.) 1980: *The Archaeology of Roman Pannonia*. Lexington: University Press of Kentucky.

Lewis, Naphtali 1983: *Life in Egypt under Roman Rule*. Oxford: Clarendon Press.

Liebeschuetz, J. H. W. G. 1979: *Continuity and Change in Roman Religion*. Oxford: Clarendon Press.

Lightfoot, J. L. 2003: *Lucian: On the Syrian Goddess*. Oxford: Oxford University Press.

MacKendrick, Paul 1980: *The North African Stones Speak*. Chapel Hill: University of North Carolina Press.

MacMullen, Ramsay 1981: *Paganism in the Roman Empire*. New Haven, CN: Yale University Press.

—— and Lane, Eugene N. (eds.) 1992: *Paganism and Christianity, 100–425 CE: A Sourcebook*. Minneapolis: Fortress Press.

Martin, Luther 1987: *Hellenistic Religions: An Introduction*. New York: Oxford University Press.

Meijer, P. A. 1981: Philosophers, Intellectuals and Religion in Hellas. In H. S. Versnel (ed.), *Faith, Hope and Worship: Aspects of Religious Mentality in the Ancient World*. Leiden: Brill. 216–63.

Merkelbach, R. 1985: Eine Inschrift des Weltverbandes der dionysischen Technitai (*CIG* 6829). *Zeitschrift für Papyrologie und Epigraphik* 58: 136–8.

—— and Schwertheim, E. 1983: Die Inschriften des Sammlung Necmi Tolunay in Bandirma (Teil II): Das Orakel des Ammon für Kyzikos. *Epigraphica Anatolica* 2: 147–54.

Meyer, Marvin W. (ed.) 1987: *The Ancient Mysteries: A Sourcebook*. San Francisco: HarperSanFrancisco.

Millar, Fergus 1993: *The Roman Near East, 31 BC–AD 337*. Cambridge, MA: Harvard University Press.

Mitchell, Stephen 1993: *Anatolia: Land, Men, and Gods in Asia Minor*. Oxford: Clarendon Press.

Mócsy, A. 1974: *Pannonia and Upper Moesia*. London: Routledge.

Mylonas, George E. 1961: *Eleusis and the Eleusinian Mysteries*. Princeton: Princeton University Press.

Nock, A. D. 1933: *Conversion: The Old and the New in Religion from Alexander the Great to Augustine of Hippo*. Oxford: Oxford University Press.

—— 1972: *Essays on Religion and the Ancient World*. Ed. Zeph Stewart. Oxford: Clarendon Press.

—— and Festugière, A.-J. (eds.) 1946–54: *Hermès Trismégiste*: Corpus Hermeticum. Paris: Les Belles Lettres.

North, J. A. 1976: Conservatism and Change in Roman Religion. *Papers of the British School at Rome* 44: 1–12.

—— 1979: Religious Toleration in Republican Rome. *Proceedings of the Cambridge Philological Society* 25: 251–8.

Noy, David 2000: *Foreigners at Rome*. London: Duckworth, with the Classical Press of Wales.

Orr, David G. 1978: Roman Domestic Religion: The Evidence of the Household Shrines. In Wolfgang Haase (ed.), *Aufstieg und Niedergang der römischen Welt*, vol. II. 16.2. Berlin: Walter de Gruyter. 1557–91.

Oster, Richard E. 1990: Ephesus as a Religious Center. In Wolfgang Haase (ed.), *Aufstieg und Niedergang der römischen Welt*, vol. II. 18.3. Berlin: Walter de Gruyter. 1661–726.

Parke, H. W. 1967: *Greek Oracles*. London: Hutchinson.

—— 1988: *Sibyls and Sibylline Prophecy in Classical Antiquity*. Ed. B. C. McGing. London: Routledge.

Petzl, G. 1994: *Die Beichtinschriften Westkleinasiens. Epigraphica Anatolica* 22.

Phillips, C. Robert, III 1986: The Sociology of Religious Knowledge in the Roman Empire to AD 284. In Wolfgang Haase (ed.), *Aufstieg und Niedergang der römischen Welt*, vol. II. 16.3. Berlin: Walter de Gruyter. 2677–773.

—— 1991: *Nullum Crimen sine Lege*: Socioreligious Sanctions on Magic. In C. A. Faraone and D. Obbink (eds.), *Magika Hiera: Ancient Greek Magic and Religion*. New York: Oxford University Press. 260–76.

Piggott, Stuart 1968: *The Druids*. Harmondsworth: Penguin Books.

Potter, David 1994: *Prophets and Emperors: Human and Divine Authority from Augustus to Theodosius*. Cambridge, MA: Harvard University Press.

—— (ed.) Forthcoming: *The Blackwell Companion to the Roman Empire*. Oxford: Blackwell.

Price, Simon 1984: *Rituals and Power: The Roman Imperial Cult in Asia Minor*. Cambridge: Cambridge University Press.

—— 1999: *Religions of the Ancient Greeks*. Cambridge: Cambridge University Press.

Rajak, Tessa 1984: Was There a Roman Charter for the Jews? *Journal of Roman Studies* 74: 107–23.

Reardon, B. P. (ed.) 1989: *Collected Ancient Greek Novels*. Berkeley: University of California Press.

Rives, James B. 1995: *Religion and Authority in Roman Carthage from Augustus to Constantine*. Oxford: Clarendon Press.

—— 2003: Magic in Roman Law: The Reconstruction of a Crime. *Classical Antiquity* 22: 313–39.

—— 2005: Christian Expansion and Christian Ideology. In W. V. Harris (ed.), *The Spread of Christianity in the First Four Centuries: Essays in Explanation*. Leiden: Brill. 15–41.

Rogers, Guy M. 1991: *The Sacred Identity of Ephesos: Foundation Myths of a Roman City*. London: Routledge.

Roller, Lynn E. 1999: *In Search of God the Mother: The Cult of Anatolian Cybele*. Berkeley: University of California Press.

Schäfer, Peter 1997: *Judeophobia: Attitudes Toward the Jews in the Ancient World*. Cambridge, MA: Harvard University Press.

Scheid, John 2003: *An Introduction to Roman Religion*. Trans. Janet Lloyd. Bloomington: University of Indiana Press.

Schürer, Emil 1973–87: *The History of the Jewish People in the Age of Jesus Christ*. Rev. and ed. Geza Vermes, Fergus Millar, Matthew Black, and Martin Goodman. Edinburgh: T&T Clark.

Schwartz, Seth 2001: *Imperialism and Jewish Society, 200 BCE to 640 CE*. Princeton: Princeton University Press.

Scullard, H. H. 1981: *Festivals and Ceremonies of the Roman Republic*. Ithaca, NY: Cornell University Press.

Smith, Jonathan Z. 1998: Religion, Religions, Religious. In Mark C. Taylor (ed.), *Critical Terms for Religious Studies*. Chicago: University of Chicago Press. 269–84.

Smith, Wilfrid Cantwell 1963: *The Meaning and End of Religion*. New York: Macmillan.

Sourvinou-Inwood, Christiane 2000a: What is *Polis* Religion? In R. Buxton (ed.), *Oxford Readings in Greek Religion*. Oxford: Oxford University Press. 13–37.

—— 2000b: Further Aspects of *Polis* Religion. In R. Buxton (ed.), *Oxford Readings in Greek Religion*. Oxford: Oxford University Press. 38–55.

Stafford, Emma 2000: *Worshipping Virtues: Personification and the Divine in Ancient Greece*. London: Duckworth and the Classical Press of Wales.

Teixidor, Javier 1977: *The Pagan God: Popular Religion in the Greco-Roman Near East*. Princeton: Princeton University Press.

Tudor, David 1969–76: *Corpus Monumentorum Religionis Equitum Danuviorum. I: The Monuments; II: The Analysis and Interpretation of the Monuments*. Leiden: Brill.

Turcan, Robert 1996: *The Cults of the Roman Empire*. Trans. Antonia Neville. Oxford: Blackwell.

van Straten, F. T. 1981: Gifts for the Gods. In H. S. Versnel (ed.), *Faith, Hope and Worship: Aspects of Religious Mentality in the Ancient World*. Leiden: Brill. 65–151.

Vanderlip, Vera F. 1972: *The Four Greek Hymns of Isidorus and the Cult of Isis*. Toronto: A. M. Hakkert.

Versnel, H. S. 1981: Religious Mentality in Ancient Prayer. In H. S. Versnel (ed.), *Faith, Hope and Worship: Aspects of Religious Mentality in the Ancient World.* Leiden: Brill. 1–64.

—— 1990: *Ter Unus: Isis, Dionysos, Hermes. Three Studies in Henotheism.* Leiden: Brill.

—— 1991: Beyond Cursing: The Appeal to Justice in Judicial Prayers. In C. A. Faraone and D. Obbink (eds.), *Magika Hiera: Ancient Greek Magic and Religion.* New York: Oxford University Press. 60–106.

Wardman, Alan 1982: *Religion and Statecraft among the Romans.* London: Granada.

Wells, Colin 1992: *The Roman Empire.* 2nd edn. Cambridge, MA: Harvard University Press.

West, M. L. 1983: *The Orphic Poems.* Oxford: Clarendon Press.

Wilken, Robert L. 1984: *The Christians as the Romans Saw Them.* New Haven, CN: Yale University Press.

Woolf, Greg 2003: *Polis*-Religion and its Alternatives in the Roman Provinces. In Clifford Ando (ed.), *Roman Religion.* Edinburgh: University of Edinburgh Press. 39–54.

Index